Trade Policy and the U.S. Automobile Industry

Eric J. Toder
with
Nicholas Scott Cardell
Ellen Burton

A Charles River Associates Research Report

The Praeger Special Studies program, through a selective worldwide distribution network, makes available to the academic, government, and business communities significant and timely research in U.S. and international economic, social, and political issues.

Trade Policy and the U.S. Automobile Industry

Praeger Publishers New York   London

Library of Congress Cataloging in Publication Data

Toder, Eric J
   Trade policy and the U.S. automobile industry.

   "A Charles River Associates research report."
   Includes bibliographical references.
   1. Automobile industry and trade—United States.
2. United States—Commercial policy. I. Cardell, Nicholas Scott, joint author. II. Burton, Ellen, joint author. III. Charles River Associates.
IV. Title.
HD9710.U52T6   381'.45'62920973   77-16273
ISBN 0-03-040956-X

PRAEGER SPECIAL STUDIES
200 Park Avenue, New York, N.Y., 10017, U.S.A.

Published in the United States of America in 1978
by Praeger Publishers,
A Division of Holt, Rinehart and Winston, CBS, Inc.

89   038   987654321

© 1978 by Praeger Publishers

All rights reserved

Printed in the United States of America

FOREWORD
Zvi Griliches

This volume is an excellent example of applied econometrics at work. A substantive problem is posed: the effect of raising or lowering tariffs on imported automobiles. Demand functions are specified and estimated; supply conditions are explored and quantified; labor displacement evidence is examined; and an assessment of social costs and benefits is made.

This book is the first large-scale study of the automobile industry in recent years. While it focuses on issues relating to the impact of foreign trade policies on the domestic industry, its empirical research in the area of automobile demand, automobile model choice, production costs, international comparative advantage, and demand for labor in the industry goes significantly further than the analyses in earlier studies of the automobile industry. It is an example of the high professional level of contract research in the United States when done by companies such as Charles River Associates.

In the area of automobile demand, the book's main contribution is in its analysis of factors influencing the choice between domestic and imported automobile models. Previous research on automobile demand has been concerned primarily with estimating equations for new car sales or new car stock, with little attention paid to the composition of sales. Earlier econometric work on automobile model choice included studies by Cowling and Cubbin and Triplett and Cowling on choice among brands. Their methodology is adapted by the authors of this volume to the study of choice between domestic and imported automobiles, utilizing a newly developed data base on the changing characteristics of domestic and imported automobiles over time. Other investigators have already utilized this data base and applied similar methods to study the choice of automobiles by size class.

One of the most striking aspects of this study, which puts it at the frontier of econometric research, is the hedonic market share model, developed largely by Scott Cardell. It abandons the assumption of the independence of binary choice in the presence of other alternatives and thereby provides a solution to the "red bus-blue bus" problem that has plagued recent attempts to extend such models into contexts where choices are truly multiple. Earlier approaches, such as the multinomial logit model, assume implicitly that the introduction of a new good will reduce all the probabilities of choosing previously existing goods by the same proportion. If there are similarities between the new good and some of the existing goods, such models overpredict the probability that the new good will be chosen. The CRA hedonic market share model generalizes such approaches by allowing for differences in consumer tastes and preferences for characteristics of the commodity. This gives the more realistic prediction that a new model will take its market share more from similar than from dissimilar goods. Accounting

for such variation in tastes makes this model more realistic and gives it a much wider range of application, but it also makes it significantly more difficult to compute. This study develops new algorithms and estimation techniques that push the computational and estimation technology of choice models far beyond their recent boundaries. While only a small part of this work is described in this volume, it does provide an introduction to and an example of the potential applicability of hedonic market share models.

The work on automobile production costs, based in part on the previous research by Bain, McGee, and White, provides the first published estimates of the cost penalty of producing automobiles below optimal scale levels. Using an input-output model and data on factor and material prices, the authors develop new estimates of automobile production costs in the United States, Japan, and West Germany. Previous work in this area by Kravis et al. looked only at comparative automobile prices in different regions, without distinguishing among imported and domestically produced automobiles. The authors, using a different approach, studied the determinants of automobile supply prices in the major producing nations. Finally, the authors' work on the demand for labor in the automobile industry and the associated social cost accounting represents an application to the automobile industry of previous, more general research on factor demand and cost-benefit modeling.

The authors and their colleagues at Charles River Associates are to be commended for having produced a timely and fine piece of work and the United States Department of Labor for having supported it. Much still remains to be done in this area. In particular, an integration of the data on used and new car markets is long overdue. Though the volume before us does not answer all possible questions, it does present much new information and makes a solid contribution to our understanding of how the important automobile industry operates.

PREFACE

This book is based on research performed at Charles River Associates (CRA) under contract to the U.S. Department of Labor, Bureau of International Labor Affairs. The purpose of the original study was to assess the benefits and costs of potential trade policy changes affecting the U.S. automobile industry. The major part of the work was completed in October, 1975, although funding for revisions and extensions continued through August 1976. The principal author was a full-time employee at CRA at the time the research was conducted.

Because of the time frame of the research, all of the formal, quantitative models presented in this book use data available as of autumn 1975. For this reason, data on sales, production, prices, and imports of automobiles and on wages, labor productivity, and employment subsequent to the end of 1974 are not incorporated in any of the statistical analyses, although some more recent data are reported in tables. While discussion of the implications of the results has benefited from the opportunity to observe developments of the past two years, the conclusions are based largely on evaluation of 1974 and pre-1974 data. The authors hope that subsequent investigators find the methodology developed and applied in this book useful in analyzing more recent data.

As principal investigator on the original study, Eric Toder directed the research effort from its inception and wrote most of the final manuscript. Scott Cardell developed the CRA hedonic market share model used in Chapter 3 to simulate the effect of changes in imported car prices on shares by automobile type of new car sales. The model developed by Cardell represents the major methodological contribution of this book. Ellen Burton directed most of the research related to the automobile labor market, and wrote the initial draft of Chapter 7.

The contents of the book reflect the views of the authors alone, who are solely responsible for the conclusions and for any errors in data or analysis.

The authors wish to thank many people both within and outside of CRA, who assisted in the preparation of this book. James Burrows, vice president of CRA, provided overall management supervision during preparation of the original report and reviewed early drafts of the study. Zvi Griliches supplied expert advice throughout the preparation of the report, especially on the design of the hedonic market share model, and reviewed the final manuscript. As contract monitor on the original study, Harry Grubert of the U.S. Department of Labor followed the progress of the report throughout its preparation and reviewed and critiqued preliminary drafts. The suggestions of all three improved the quality of the final product.

Other people who supplied useful comments and suggestions at various stages of the research include Hayden Boyd, Gilbert DeBartolo, William Dewald, Donald DeWees, Mike Luckey, John McGowan, and Lawrence White.

In preparation of the report, use was made of prior research on the automobile industry by other consultants and firms. In that regard, special thanks are due to Merrill Ebner, who provided the results of his work on automobile production and patiently responded to numerous questions. Chapter 5 of the book is largely based on Ebner's contribution. The Public Research Institute of the Center for Naval Analyses (CNA) made available to the authors the results of their research on the earnings experience of displaced workers. Louis Jacobson of CNA was generous with his time in explaining the findings. Finally, Jack Baranson supplied the authors with data he compiled on labor productivity in the automobile industry in different countries.

Many of CRA's able research assistants contributed to the statistical work reported in this book. Sandy Lazo assembled most of the data reported in Chapter 2 and developed the data base for the cost comparisons reported in Chapter 6. Alan Matthews developed the data base used for the hedonic price indexes and the time series import share regressions in Chapter 3. Other research assistants who contributed to the study include Ken Chomitz, Marilyn Edling, Yvonne Haywood, Diane Hederich, Roberta Preskill, and Mark Weissberg.

Robert Snyder, Harriet Ullman, and Marsha Traugot edited successive drafts of the manuscript and provided needed good cheer and encouragement in periods of deadline pressure. Marilyn Daniels provided excellent secretarial support. Ronald Fairbrother and John Press supplied data-processing assistance.

Finally, the authors wish to thank Gerald Kraft for his encouragement and support to this project.

CONTENTS

	Page
FOREWORD	v
PREFACE	vii
LIST OF TABLES	xii
LIST OF FIGURES	xvi

Chapter

1 INTRODUCTION	1
2 TRADE BARRIERS AND PRODUCTION, CONSUMPTION, AND WORLD TRADE IN MAJOR AUTOMOBILE MARKETS, 1950–75	6
Location of Production and Consumption	8
Trade Barriers	15
U.S.-Canada Automobile Trade	21
Automobile Imports in the United States: A Brief History	29
Notes	34
3 RELATIVE PRICES AND THE DEMAND FOR DOMESTIC AND FOREIGN AUTOMOBILES	35
Effects of Tariffs on Foreign-Car Demand	35
Welfare Implications of Price Elasticities	37
Estimating Import Demand: Previous Research and Alternative Approaches	43
Econometric Estimates of Import Share Demand from Time Series Data	46
Econometric Estimates of Import Share Demand from Cross-Section Data	65
Econometric Estimates of Import Share Demand from CRA Hedonic Market Share Model	71
Summary of Findings	82

Chapter	Page
Appendix 3.A	83
Appendix 3.B	93
Appendix 3.C	96
Appendix 3.D	100
Notes	116
4 THE IMPACT OF AUTOMOBILE IMPORTS ON DOMESTIC AUTOMOBILE PRICES	118
5 THE SHAPE OF AUTOMOBILE COST FUNCTIONS	129
Methodology and Results	131
Some Problems and Qualifications	139
Conclusions and Implications	142
Notes	142
6 INTERNATIONAL COMPARISON OF PRODUCTION COSTS	144
Approach to Cost Comparison Computation	146
Sources of Data and Data Problems	148
Results and Implications	150
Appendix 6.A	159
Appendix 6.B	165
Appendix 6.C	166
Notes	168
7 THE EFFECT OF OUTPUT CHANGES ON DEMAND FOR LABOR IN THE U.S. AUTOMOBILE INDUSTRY	169
The Automobile Labor Market: Institutional Background	170
Theoretical Framework: Time Series Estimation	181
Estimation of Factor Demand from Cross-Section Data	189
Geographic Distribution of Employment Changes	191
Summary of Findings	192
Appendix 7.A	193
Appendix 7.B	194
Appendix 7.C	195
Notes	197
8 WELFARE EFFECTS OF TRADE POLICY CHANGES AFFECTING THE U.S. AUTOMOBILE MARKET	198
Product Market Welfare Loss: Methodology	201

Chapter	Page
Product Market Welfare Loss: Estimates	207
Effects of a Tariff in an Imperfectly Competitive Domestic Industry	212
Comparison of Product Market Welfare Costs to Labor Adjustment Costs	219
Notes	229
9 CONCLUSIONS	230
INDEX	236
ABOUT THE AUTHORS	245
ABOUT CHARLES RIVER ASSOCIATES	247

LIST OF TABLES

Table		Page
2.1	World Production of Motor Vehicles	8
2.2	Automobile Production by Major Producing Nations	9
2.3	New-Car Registrations in Leading Consuming Nations	10
2.4	Passenger Car Production, Consumption, Imports, and Exports in Leading Producing Nations, 1974	11
2.5	Automobile Trade Flows Between Major Producing Nations, 1973	13
2.6	Exports of New Passenger Cars by Major Producing Nations	14
2.7	1972 Passenger Car Output by Nondomestic Companies	16
2.8	Current and Pre-Kennedy-Round Tariffs, Selected Countries	18
2.9	History of Tariffs on Passenger Cars, Selected Major Producers	19
2.10	U.S.-Canada Trade in Finished Automobiles	24
2.11	U.S.-Canada Trade in Original Equipment Motor Vehicle Parts in Terms of Transfer Values	25
2.12	U.S.-Canada Trade in Motor Vehicle Parts as Reported by U.S. Department of Commerce	26
2.13	U.S.-Canada Trade Balance in Motor Vehicles and Parts in Transfer Values	27
2.14	U.S.-Canada Trade Balance in Motor Vehicles and Parts as Reported by U.S. Department of Commerce	28
2.15	Foreign-Car Sales and Small-Car Shares as Fraction of U.S. Market	31
3.1	Domestic and Imported Car Price Indexes	50
3.2	Comparison of Imported-to-Domestic Car Relative Price and Total Cost Indexes	52
3.3	Time Series Regression Results: Alternative Specifications, 1961–74	55
3.4	Time Series Regression Results: Alternative Specifications, 1961–73	58
3.5	Implied Short-Run and Long-Run Relative Price Elasticities from Time Series Regressions, 1961–74	62
3.6	Implied Short-Run and Long-Run Relative Price Elasticities from Time Series Regressions, 1961–73	63
3.7	Import Shares by States, 1974, Compared to Freight Charges	67
3.8	Cross-Section Regression Results, 1974	69
3.9	Cross-Section Regression Results, 1973	70

Table		Page
3.10	Import Shares by Region	71
3.11	Distribution of Estimated Marginal Values of Automobile Characteristics	75
3.12	Comparison of Predicted Shares to Actual Shares by Automobile Type, April–August 1974	78
3.13	Effect of Proportionate Changes in Import Prices on Market Shares from CRA Hedonic Market Share Model	79
3.14	Relative Price Elasticities for Simulated Changes in Import Prices	80
3.15	Comparison of CRA Hedonic Market Share Estimates to *Market Facts* Estimates of Effect of Price Increases for Imported Automobiles	81
3A.1	Description of Variables	85
3A.2	Computation of Foreign-to-Domestic Relative Price Index	90
3B.1	Computation of Total Gas Cost Indexes	94
3B.2	Computation of Relative Total Cost Index from Price and Gas Cost Indexes	95
3C.1	Additional Variables Added to Time Series Regression	99
4.1	Price Formation Equations: Effect of Import Share Changes on Domestic Auto Prices	120
4.2	Price Formation Equations: Relationship Between Import and Domestic Prices	123
4.3	Computation of Automobile Production Cost Index	126
5.1	Unit Costs of Automobile Production at Optimal Scale, 1974 Estimates	132
5.2	Minimum Efficient Scale for Automobile Production	133
5.3	Percentage Distribution of Manufacturing Costs	134
5.4	Percentage Breakdown Between Fixed and Variable Costs for Different Inputs	134
5.5	Derivation of Cost Curve for Minis (1974 Estimate)	136
5.6	Manufacturing Cost at Below Optimal Scale for Four Types of Automobiles	137
5.7	Manufacturing Cost at Below Optimal Scale for Four Types of Automobiles	138
5.8	Manufacturing Cost at Below Optimal Scale for Four Types of Automobiles	138
6.1	Summary of Automobile Industry Unit Cost Comparisons	151
6.2	Summary of Relative Unit Labor Cost Computations, 1974	151
6.3	International Transport Costs: Selected Imported Cars	153

Table		Page
6.4	Estimated Relative Supply Cost Index to United States of "Typical Imports" at Minimum Efficient Scale, 1973	154
6.5	Estimates of Relative Supply Costs to United States from U.S. and Domestic Production of Popular Imports at Different Annual Sales Levels in United States	155
6.6	Estimates of Relative Supply Costs to United States from U.S. and Domestic Production of Popular Imports at Different Annual Sales Levels in United States	156
6C.1	Comparison of Fitted Automobile Prices, 1969	167
7.1	Characteristics of Motor Vehicle and Equipment Labor Force in 1970	172
7.2	Comparative Real Average Weekly Earnings and Growth of Earnings in Motor Vehicle Industry	175
7.3	Distribution of Production Workers, SIC 371	177
7.4	Employment Characteristics of Motor Vehicle Workers Relative to Local Labor Forces	178
7.5	Estimated Structural Equations and Implied Long-Run Output Elasticities	185
7.6	Capacity Utilization Series for Automotive Products	187
7.7	Distributed Lag Relationship Derived Demand for Employment (Y_1)	189
7.8	Cross-Section Estimation SIC 371	190
7.9	Shutdowns of Auto Assembly Facilities	191
7C.1	Distributed Lag Relationships for Average Hours per Worker and Capacity Utilization	196
8.1	Computation of Product Market Welfare Loss from 10 Percent Import Price Increase, 1974	209
8.2	Summary of Product Market Welfare Loss Estimates from 10 Percent Import Increase, 1974	210
8.3	Annual Product Market Welfare Loss in Final Equilibrium from 10 Percent Import Price Increase with Alternative Substitution Elasticities, 1974	211
8.4	Annual Losses at 1974 Average Prices to Consumers of U.S. Automobiles from Price Increase of 10 Percent ($287.40) of Imported Automobiles: Hypothetical Case of Domestic Industry Profit Maximization	218
8.5	Comparison of Annual Losses to Consumers of Domestic and Imported Automobiles from 10 Percent Import Price Increase: Hypothetical Case of Domestic Industry	

Table		Page
	Profit Maximization	218
8.6	Estimated Earnings Loss per Displaced Automobile Worker	223
8.7	Estimated Earnings Loss per Displaced Worker Due to Unemployment: Assuming No Displaced Workers Return to Auto Industry	223
8.8	Estimated Earnings Loss per Displaced Worker Due to Unemployment: Assuming 50 Percent of Reemployed Workers Return to Automobile Industry	224
8.9	Losses Due to High Unemployment and Small Labor Market Size: Steel Industry	225
8.10	Estimated Losses per Displaced Worker Due to Unemployment: Alternate Scenarios Assuming 50 Percent of Reemployed Workers Return to Automobile Industry	225
8.11	Increased Output from Increased Employment Caused by 10 Percent Import Price Increase: Estimated Value for Earnings Loss per Worker of $15,000	226
8.12	Comparison of Upper Limit Employment Benefit and Product Market Welfare Costs from 10 Percent Increase in Price of Automobile Imports	227

LIST OF FIGURES

Figure		Page
2.1	Foreign-Car Sales and Small-Car Shares as Fraction of U.S. Sales, 1955–75	32
3.1	Welfare Loss from Tariff on Imported Cars: Pure Competition in Domestic Production	39
3.2	Adjusted Import and Domestic Prices, 1960–74	51
3.3	Comparison of Relative Price Index and Relative Total Cost Index	54
5.1	Qualitative Comparison of Our Cost Curve Estimates with "True" Long-Run Cost Curve	141
8.1	Product Market Loss from Tariff on Imported Automobiles	202
8.2	Effects on Domestic Industry of Change in Import Tariff Assuming Domestic Industry Profit Maximization	214
8.3	Partial Welfare Effects of Import Price Change with Industry Profit Maximization in Domestic Market	215

Trade Policy and the U.S. Automobile Industry

CHAPTER

1

INTRODUCTION

Imported cars have gained an increasing share of new car sales in the United States in recent years. During the 1974-75 recession, while output and employment in the United States automobile industry declined drastically, sales of new imports continued to grow. These developments have revived public and congressional interest in the use of trade barriers, especially tariffs and quotas, as a device to ease problems resulting from high unemployment in the U.S. automobile industry.*

Economists generally oppose government-imposed trade barriers, such as tariffs and quotas, because they interfere with the efficient allocation of productive activities among countries. In a world of free trade, each nation would

---

*In 1975, the United Automobile Workers (UAW) suggested "harmonization" of U.S. duties with duties imposed by the Common Market. UAW's position at that time amounted, in effect, to advocacy of a U.S. tariff increase, at least until Europeans would agree to lower their rates. The UAW was even more worried about legislation then under consideration requiring U.S. manufacturers to meet fuel efficiency standards. The legislation ultimately passed; the Energy Policy and Conservation Act of 1975 (EPCA), included one provision strongly favored by the UAW: Beginning in 1979, the "captive imports"—that is, models manufactured by U.S. companies in foreign countries—would be excluded from the computation of the average fuel-efficiency of passenger cars produced by U.S. companies.

The UAW also believed that U.S. jobs in the automobile industry were being lost because of imports of autos at less than fair value. (See testimony by Eugene L. Stewart, representing the UAW before the United States International Trade Commission, August 19, 1975.) A subsequent U.S. Treasury Department investigation to determine whether foreign auto companies were in fact violating antidumping regulations was terminated with a decision to take no action, possibly because Volkswagen (VW) had just announced plans to build an assembly plant in the United States.

specialize in the production of those goods in which it is relatively most efficient, and the value of world output would be maximized. Trade barriers, with a few minor exceptions,* reduce the total living standard in each nation individually, although they raise the income of some producers' groups. Tariffs and quotas provide consumers with incentives to purchase from domestic producers goods that could potentially be obtained at lower cost from abroad. Also, trade barriers allow greater exploitation of any domestic monopoly power that may exist by shielding both companies and unions in the protected industries from foreign competition.

Reduction of trade barriers, while desirable in the long run, may lead to serious short-run adjustment costs. Workers' employment, location, and job training decisions are influenced by current market values and opportunities; if demands shift suddenly because of public policy changes, temporary unemployment in affected industries could be substantial. The duration of unemployment depends on the fraction of total employees displaced in a given geographical locality or profession, the degree of industry specificity of employee skills and the experience, costs of mobility, and the private costs to displaced workers of remaining unemployed.† Losses in production resulting from such temporary unemployment need to be weighed against the long-run gains in efficiency

---

The U.S. Motor Vehicle Manufacturers' Association (MVMA) has consistently supported reduction of nontariff barriers and controls on the international flow of capital by all countries. (See "International Trade and Investment," position statement of the Motor Vehicle Manufacturers' Association of the United States, March 1974.)

*For example, a tariff may increase national income when a nation buys a significant fraction of the world output of a given commodity, and the world supply curve for that commodity is upward sloping. In that case, a nation can improve its terms of trade by imposing a tariff that lowers import demand. It is unlikely that this example applies to the automobile industry; the importance of scale economies in automobile production suggests that unit costs of imported automobiles would not decline and might even increase if the United States increased trade barriers. Other arguments for tariffs, such as the "infant industry" argument and the argument that domestic production needs to be protected for national security reasons, are clearly inapplicable to the U.S. automobile industry.

†If unemployment benefits are generous relative to wage opportunities in new employment, employees will have an incentive to prolong the time spent in searching for a new job. In the automobile industry, state unemployment benefits and supplemental unemployment benefits (SUB) provided by the auto companies under union contracts amount to 90 percent of an employee's previous salary for one year; this provides a powerful incentive to former employees to wait to be rehired rather than to search for alternative employment in a different location or at least a lower wage.

The fact that unemployment benefits may prolong unemployment does not make them poor public policy. Individuals' losses from temporary elimination of income can be catastrophic. It is worth some price in reduced output for this economy as a whole to insure workers against such losses.

INTRODUCTION

from reduced trade barriers to obtain a measure of the net gains from tariff or quota reduction.

(It should be noted that the unemployment effects we are measuring result only from demand shifts. Trade barrier changes that reduce employment demand in one industry should lead to a compensating increase in employment demand in other industries if macro policies maintain the same level of aggregate demand, while, if macro policies are contractionary, demand for labor in the economy will fall even if trade policies are becoming more restrictive. We are not measuring the costs of unemployment attributable to a general insufficiency of demand throughout the economy.)

Trade barriers imposed by the United States against imports of foreign automobiles are relatively insignificant compared both to U.S. trade barriers in some other manufacturing industries and to barriers foreign countries impose against the U.S. automobile industry. The U.S. import tariff on passenger automobiles is 3 percent;* all major automobile-producing countries impose higher tariffs on imports from the United States.

"Nontariff" barriers (NTBs) are also higher in foreign countries; examples of NTBs are excise taxes on the weight and horsepower of automobiles imposed by many European countries. These taxes act as trade barriers only because of the importance of economies of scale in the production of automobiles. Weight and horsepower excise taxes do not discriminate between European and U.S. automobiles of equal characteristics. In the absence of scale economies, U.S. manufacturers could design models specially for sale in Europe. However, since scale economies are important,† and automobiles manufactured in the United States are heavier and more powerful, on the average, than automobiles manufactured in Europe, the weight and horsepower excises may legitimately be viewed as trade barriers.

Recent pollution and safety regulations on new automobiles imposed by the U.S. government may also be viewed as nontariff barriers if (1) there are scale economies in redesigning automobile engines and bodies to meet the required pollution standards and to install the necessary safety equipment; (2) these standards require different technology than the standards imposed by governments in other countries; and (3) U.S. manufacturers find adjustment to the new technology easier than foreign manufacturers. We have seen no evidence indicating that current U.S. pollution and safety regulations are, in practice, sig-

---

*The base to which the tariff is applied is derived from an estimate of the sum of foreign production costs and an assumed profit markup. As this base is less than the retail sales price, the effective tariff rate as a fraction of the retail sales price of an imported automobile is somewhat lower than 3 percent.

†See Chapter 5 for a discussion of economies of scale in automobile production. Our data indicate that minimum efficient scale is larger in the production of small cars than in the production of larger cars more common in the U.S. market.

nificant barriers to imports. (Our views on the relative unimportance of pollution and safety regulations as trade barriers were formed in part from consultations with experts on the automobile industry, including an engineer and several truck company executives.)

The research results presented in this book aim at developing evidence useful for assessing (1) the net welfare gain from the removal of U.S. tariffs on imported automobiles, and (2) the net welfare gain (or loss) from imposition of higher tariffs on a quota.

In the former case, welfare gains to consumers from lower prices of imported automobiles have to be balanced against adjustment costs from temporary unemployment increases in the domestic automobile industry. In the latter case, consumer welfare would be reduced. The change in adjustment costs is probably insignificant during normal periods because workers are diverted to the automobile industry from many sources, and there is no evidence that the impact of job reduction would be great in any single sector experiencing a decline in demand. However, we may view tariff increases or a quota imposition as a policy designed to reduce adjustment costs from unemployment in the automobile sector when the U.S. automobile industry is suffering a slump brought about by factors other than reduction of trade barriers. In particular, tariff increases and/or quotas may be viewed as a potential solution to the abnormally high unemployment in the automobile industry typical of recession periods, such as 1974 and 1975. If so, policy makers should know both the total impact of a given tariff increase on domestic output and short-run employment and the relative magnitudes of short-run gains from higher employment and long-run losses from higher foreign car prices.

If we know the demand curves for domestic and foreign automobiles, we may view a quota as equivalent to a tariff yielding the same reduction in foreign new car purchases, except for income distribution effects, which depend on how quota allocations are determined among importers, and how the revenue from tariffs collected is spent. Both quotas and tariffs may be viewed as policies that raise the price of new imported automobiles by a given percentage. Thus, we analyzed both policies with a similar methodology, which is designed to estimate the demand, production, and welfare changes resulting from an exogenous change in the price of foreign cars. To obtain our final results, we performed a series of studies on aspects of the domestic and foreign automobile industries. These studies are presented in separate chapters of the book.

Computation of net welfare changes from tariff changes required us to estimate (1) the demand curves for foreign and domestic automobiles, with special reference to the relative price elasticity of substitution; (2) the effects of a change in prices of imported automobiles on domestic auto prices; (3) the shape of cost curves in automobile production; (4) comparative costs of producing automobiles at optimal scale in different countries; (5) the magnitude and timing of the effects of changes in domestic output on domestic employ-

INTRODUCTION

ment in the automobile industry; and (6) the expected adjustment costs per displaced worker from increased unemployment in the automobile industry.

These estimates are provided in separate studies of demand, pricing behavior, cost curves, international comparative advantage, demand for labor, and unemployment adjustment costs in the automobile industry. Chapter 2 provides background data on trade barriers, and changes in production, consumption, and trade among nations and regions that have been major producers and consumers of automobiles since World War II. Chapter 3 provides estimates of demand for foreign and domestic automobiles from time series and cross section data, and from a new model of market share demand developed by CRA. The time series results use price indexes we created for foreign and domestic car prices from historical data on price and characteristics of models sold in the United States. Chapter 4 presents some econometric estimates of the effects of import competition on domestic auto prices. Chapter 5 presents our estimates of the shape of automobile cost functions based, in part, on data supplied to us by sources in the U.S. automobile industry. Chapter 6 is a study of international comparative advantage in automobile production. Chapter 7 reviews the basic institutional features of the auto industry labor market and presents an econometric analysis of the effect of output changes on the demand for labor.

In Chapter 8 we use the results of the empirical research described in Chapters 3 through 6 to calculate the welfare gains and losses from trade policy changes.* Chapter 9 reviews the major findings of the study, and briefly discusses policy implications.

---

*The welfare estimates of the adjustment costs of unemployment rely on studies of the effects of worker displacement on earnings supplied to us by the Center for Naval Analyses (CNA), Public Research Institute. See Louis S. Jacobson, *Earnings Losses of Workers Displaced from Manufacturing Industries*, Public Research Institute, Center for Naval Analyses, Arlington, Va., Professional Paper 169, November 1976; Louis S. Jacobson, "Estimating the Lags in Earnings for Displaced Workers in the Steel Industry," in James Jondrow et al., *Removing Restrictions on Imports of Steel*, PRI 75-2, Public Research Institute, Center for Naval Analyses, Arlington, Va., May 1975.

CHAPTER

2

**TRADE BARRIERS AND
PRODUCTION, CONSUMPTION,
AND WORLD TRADE IN
MAJOR AUTOMOBILE
MARKETS, 1950-75**

This chapter outlines the basic facts of production, consumption, and international trade of passenger cars in different regions of the world. Trends in tariff barriers and their relationship to the observed flow of trade are reported. We conclude with a more detailed discussion of trends in U.S. imports and a general overview of the implications of current trends for future patterns in production and trade.

The United States is currently the leading producer of passenger cars in the world and also has the largest number of new car sales, both total and per capita. However, the U.S. share of both consumption and production has declined steadily since the end of World War II. Postwar recovery in West Germany, Japan, France, and Italy has been accompanied by a spectacular growth in automobile production, consumption, and exports, especially in Japan; output of automobiles in the United Kingdom and Canada has also grown faster than U.S. output. The Canadian growth is a direct result of the 1965 Canadian-U.S. Automotive Products Trade Act, which eliminated tariffs on automotive products between the United States and Canada. That agreement was followed by establishment by U.S. companies of a number of production facilities in Canada selling to both Canada and the United States.

Among the major automobile-producing nations—the United States, Japan, West Germany, the United Kingdom, France, Italy, and Canada— only the United States is a net importer of finished automobiles. U.S. imports from West Germany and Japan grew rapidly in the 1960s and early 1970s, while U.S. exports, except for exports to Canada, are negligible. The latter have been greatly outweighed in quantity by U.S. imports from Canada, in the past ten years.

U.S.-owned companies have been very active in overseas markets through foreign investments rather than through exports. Automobiles manufactured abroad by U.S.-owned companies account for almost 100 percent of local pro-

duction in Canada, and for a significant share of output in the United Kingdom and West Germany. U.S. companies also have production facilities in many developing countries and jointly own automobile production facilities in Japan. Japanese, British, French, German, Italian, and Swedish companies also have production facilities abroad; only Fiat among the non-U.S. companies produces automobiles in a foreign country with significant domestic production (France).

All major countries, and most small ones, impose some tariffs against imports of finished automobiles. Tariffs have been declining in general since the end of World War II. The United States and Japan, with tariffs of 3 percent and 6.4 percent, respectively, have the lowest rates of any major producing countries. The European Economic Community (EEC) external tariff is 11 percent; tariffs have been eliminated within the EEC and are being phased out between the EEC and the European Free Trade Area (EFTA). Most developing countries impose much higher duties, which serve, in many cases, to encourage the development of small-scale local assembly facilities. Nations outside of North America, Europe, and Japan currently purchase only a small fraction of the world's output of new passenger cars. Automobile sales in some of the developing nations can be expected to grow rapidly in future years.

The world automotive market may be viewed as consisting of three major producing and consuming regions: North America, Japan, and Europe. Tariffs have been eliminated within North America and are being lowered toward zero among countries within Europe. North America currently imports significant numbers of automobiles from Europe and Japan and exports very few. Japanese exports to Europe are significant but are much smaller than Japanese passenger car exports to North America. Automobiles produced and consumed in North America have significantly different characteristics than automobiles produced and consumed in Europe and Japan; for the most part American cars are bigger, heavier, more powerful, and less fuel-efficient. Automobiles produced by North American companies in Europe and Japan have "European" rather than "American" characteristics.

Buyers of small cars are a growing minority in the United States and Canada. As this minority grows, local demand will support domestic production at efficient scale of an increasingly large number of small car models, manufactured either by U.S. companies or by Japanese or European firms building new plants in North America. If Europe and Japan are to export to North America under such circumstances, they can no longer rely on product differentiation; for large-volume sales, production costs would need to be sufficiently lower in Europe and Japan than in the United States to outweigh the sum of transport costs and tariffs. Paradoxically, the growth of small-car demand in North America, though increasing imports from Europe and Japan in the short run, may ultimately greatly reduce imports as the quality and diversity of small cars manufactured in North America increase.

LOCATION OF PRODUCTION AND CONSUMPTION

Motor vehicle production is highly concentrated in several geographic areas; in 1974, of all motor vehicles, 92 percent were produced in Europe, North America, and Japan. The major producing nations—the United States, Japan, West Germany, France, the United Kingdom, Italy, and Canada—accounted for 77.9 percent of all production (Production is defined as output of fully assembled vehicles. In many developing countries where final automotive assembly plants are located, all major components, including bodies, engines, and transmissions are imported from one of the major producing nations. Final assembly accounts for a small fraction of value added in the automobile industry.

TABLE 2.1

World Production of Motor Vehicles
(thousands of vehicles)

	1950	1960	1970	1974
Africa	–	113	323	369
Morocco			25	27
South Africa	–	113	298	342
Asia	47	534	5,381	7,040
India	15	52	83	88
Japan	33	482	5,289	6,552
Europe*	1,999	6,481	13,362	15,175
France	358	1,369	2,750	3,463
West Germany	306	2,055	3,842	3,100
Italy	128	645	1,854	1,773
United Kingdom	785	1,811	2,098	1,937
North America	8,418	8,353	9,670	11,947
Canada	391	398	1,194	1,525
United States	8,006	7,903	8,284	10,071
South America		222	745	1,336
Argentina	–	89	220	286
Brazil	–	133	416	858
Oceania	127	326	474	605
Australia	127	326	474	489
World	10,592	16,389	29,955	36,472

*Includes USSR.

Source: U.S. Motor Vehicle Manufacturers' Association, *Motor Vehicle Facts and Figures* (Detroit, successive issues).

TABLE 2.2

Automobile Production by Major Producing Nations
(thousands of units)

	1950	1960	1970	1972	1974
United States	6,665.9	6,674.8	6,546.8	8,823.9	7,290.3
Canada	230.0	325.8	940.4	1,147.3	1,187.9
Japan	1.6	165.1	3,178.7	4,022.3	3,931.9
West Germany	216.1	1,674.3	3,129.1	3,166.0	2,839.6
France	257.3	1,175.3	2,458.0	2,993.0	3,041.3
United Kingdom	522.5	1,352.7	1,641.0	1,921.3	1,534.1
Italy	101.3	595.9	1,719.7	1,732.4	1,630.9

Sources: Society of Motor Manufacturers and Traders, Ltd., *The Motor Industry of Great Britain* (London: 1951, 1961, 1971, 1972, 1973); and *Ward's Automotive Yearbook* (Detroit: Ward's Communications, 1975).

Thus, the data understate the fraction of output produced in the major producing countries.)

Table 2.1 presents the level of motor vehicle production in major geographic regions in selected years from 1950 to 1974. (The data in Table 2.1 include all motor vehicles: trucks and buses as well as passenger cars. Since private passenger cars account for a large share of the total, the output shares and growth patterns reported would probably not be very different for private passenger cars alone.) It can be seen from Table 2.1 that the U.S. share of world motor vehicle production declined from 75.6 percent in 1950 to 27.6 percent in 1974.

Table 2.2 shows automobile production by the major producing nations between 1950 and 1974. The United States remains the world's leading producer, despite a rather sharp decline in output between 1972 and 1974. Japan, the second largest producer today, experienced extremely rapid growth of its automobile industry during the 1950s and 1960s; between 1950 and 1972, its output of passenger cars increased by a multiple of over 2,500. West Germany, France, and Italy also experienced very strong growth in that period, while output in the United Kingdom and Canada increased at a somewhat slower, though still robust, pace. The decline in output experienced by the United States in 1974 was part of a worldwide slump in the automobile industry. Among the major producing nations, only Canada and France increased their automobile output between 1972 and 1974.

TABLE 2.3

New-Car Registrations in Leading Consuming Nations
(in thousands of units)

	1950	1960	1970	1974
United States	5,061	6,577	8,398	8,701
Japan	17	145	2,379	2,287
West Germany	150	970	2,107	1,693
France	168	613	1,297	1,525
Italy	80	381	1,364	1,281
United Kingdom	143	811	1,127	1,274
Canada	*	541	636	885

*Not available.

Sources: "New Car Registrations by Makes in U.S., 1922 Through 1973," *Automotive News Almanac 1974*, pp. 20-21; U.S. Motor Vehicle Manufacturers' Association, *World Motor Vehicle Data 1973* (Detroit, 1973), pp. 118-22; Society of Motor Manufacturers and Traders, *The Motor Industry of Great Britain* (London, 1975).

TABLE 2.4

Passenger Car Production, Consumption, Imports, and Exports in Leading Producing Nations, 1974
(thousands of units)

Country	Output	Registrations	Imports	Exports	Sales Plus Inventory Change
United States	7,290	8,701	2,573	601	9,262
Japan	3,948	2,283	44	1,727	2,265
France	3,041	1,530	395	1,750	1,686
West Germany	2,840	1,693	575	1,713	1,702
Italy	1,631	1,272	330	686	1,275
United Kingdom	1,534	1,269	378	569	1,343
Canada	1,188	869	868	1,061	995
Australia	401	n.a.*	n.a.	n.a.	n.a.
Sweden	326	264	179	164	341

*Not available.
Source: U.S. Department of Commerce, "The Automotive Industry in 1974: An International Survey," Staff Report, Office of Economic Research, April 1975.

The pattern of growth across countries in consumption of automobiles has, for the most part, mirrored the growth in production. Table 2.3 presents data on new-car registrations in the major producing nations between 1950 and 1974. The United States remains the leading consuming nation, although new-car registrations grew much less rapidly in the United States between 1950 and 1974 than they did in Japan, West Germany, France, the United Kingdom, and Italy. Growth in per capita consumption of automobiles has been especially rapid in Japan, West Germany, and Italy. The United States' relative share of world consumption is greater than its relative share of world production; it is the world's leading importer of automobiles. The leading exporters are West Germany, Japan, and France.

Table 2.4 summarizes total production, sales, exports, and imports of the nine leading producing nations in 1974. It shows the United States as the leading importer among the major producing nations, with Canada a distant second. France, Japan, and West Germany are the three leading exporters; France, West Germany, Canada, and Sweden export over 50 percent of their production. Imports account for over 50 percent of domestic sales in Canada and Sweden, and for over 25 percent in the United States, France, Italy, the United Kingdom, and West Germany. Only in Japan are imports an insignificant proportion of domestic sales. It should be noted that most of the U.S. and Canadian exports are to Canada and the United States, respectively. If Canada is excluded, U.S. export sales are negligible. (A discussion of the growth of U.S.-Canada trade since the 1965 U.S.-Canada Automotive Products agreement is presented below.)

Table 2.5 outlines the pattern of trade among the major producing nations in 1973 in somewhat greater detail. The matrix in Table 2.5 gives a breakdown of exports from each major producing nation to the other major producers, the rest of Europe, and other nations. The major producing nations and other European countries purchase 85.4 percent of the exports of the leading producers; the nations in Table 2.5 thus account for most of the world's automobile trade. The first row of Table 2.5 shows that almost all U.S. exports are to Canada. Japan's major export market is the United States; the leading export markets for West Germany, France, and Italy are the nonproducing nations in Europe. (This included minor producers like Sweden, and countries with some local assembly plants—for example Spain, Belgium.) West Germany also sells large numbers of automobiles to the United States. (In 1972, West Germany was the largest source for the United States of automobiles imported from outside North America. Japanese sales in the United States have since outdistanced German sales.) One-third of Japan's exports are to the "rest of the world," mostly in Asia. Japanese exports are also reasonably high in European countries; in "other Europe," they outsell the United Kingdom, Italy, and, by far, the United States.

Table 2.6 shows some history of the growth of exports in the major producing nations. France, Italy, and West Germany emerged as major exporters

TABLE 2.5
Automobile Trade Flows Between Major Producing Nations, 1973
(imports/exports in thousands of autos)

Importer	United States	Canada	Japan	West Germany	France	U.K.	Italy	Imports from Big 7
United States	–	874.2	583.9	688.7	12.6	64.7	52.5	2,276.7
Canada	452.4	–	75.2	46.1	5.9	15.0	7.2	601.8
Japan	11.4	0.0	–	18.9	0.4	0.9	0.6	32.2
West Germany	3.9	0.0	32.6	–	257.3	13.5	146.7	454.0
France	0.4	0.0	16.7	147.0	–	13.3	108.8	286.2
United Kingdom	0.7	0.0	80.2	69.1	156.0	–	61.6	367.6
Italy	0.2	0.0	0.8	125.4	211.6	61.8	–	399.8
Other Europe	9.7	0.6	231.6	970.9	500.0	213.6	190.7	2,117.1
Rest of World	30.5	17.5	429.9	137.5	196.2	216.0	88.2	1,115.8
Total	509.2	892.3	1,450.9	2,203.6	1,340.0	598.8	656.3	7,651.1

Exporter

Source: Society of Motor Manufacturers and Traders Ltd., *The Motor Industry of Great Britain, 1974* (London, 1974).

TABLE 2.6

Exports of New Passenger Cars by Major Producing Nations
(in thousands of units)

	1950	1960	1970	1972	1974
United States[a]	120	177	39	34	84
Canada[a]	24	17	37	41	27
Japan	b	7	726	1,407	1,727
France	89	492	1,061	1,240	1,298
West Germany	67	841	1,935	2,098	1,883
Italy	20	198	632	659	686
United Kingdom	398	570	690	628	565
Total (top 7 producers, excluding trade between U.S. and Canada after 1970)	718	2,302	5,120	6,107	6,600

[a]1970-74 do not include trade between Canada and the United States.
[b]Less than 1,000 units.
Source: Society of Motor Manufacturers and Traders Ltd., *The Motor Industry of Great Britain* (London, 1951, 1961, 1971, 1972, 1973, 1975).

in the 1950s and continued to expand export sales rapidly in the 1960s. Japanese automobile exports were not a major factor in Europe and North America until the 1960s, when they experienced a spectacular growth, which continued after 1970, more than doubling between 1970 and 1974. Exports of non-North American major producers more than tripled during the decade of the 1950s, and then more than doubled in the 1960s.

While U.S. exports of finished automobiles are insignificant, U.S. companies have major investments in automobile manufacturing facilities in foreign countries. All automobile production in Canada in 1972 was by U.S.-owned firms. (Volvo has recently built an assembly plant in Nova Scotia. However, U.S.-owned firms still account for almost all automobile production in Canada.) U.S. auto companies also account for a significant share of local output in the United Kingdom and West Germany with models manufactured in those countries; recently U.S. companies have been jointly manufacturing automobiles in Japan with Japanese firms.

Other nations whose automobile manufacturers produce significant numbers of vehicles in foreign countries include West Germany, France, the United Kingdom, and Italy. Japanese firms have some scattered production in developing countries. Only Italy's Fiat, among the non-U.S. firms, produces passenger cars in another major producing country (France).

Table 2.7 summarizes data on passenger car output by non-domestic-owned companies in selected countries. It can be seen that foreign-owned companies account for all local production of finished automobiles in Argentina, Australia, Belgium, Brazil, Canada, Chile, the Philippines, Portugal, South Africa, Switzerland, and Venezuela, and for over one-third of total automobile output in France, Spain, the United Kingdom, and West Germany.

The growth of multinational corporations has important implications for the pattern of trade in automobiles. Companies that have developed and designed a given type of automobile can produce it anywhere in the world without major design changes; in addition these companies can market autos in foreign countries with the advantages of both experience in automobile manufacturing and revenue from domestic sales not available to new companies. Thus in the long run "European-style" cars can be produced in the United States, and "American-style" cars can be produced in Europe if the pattern of labor cost differences, productivity differences, transport costs, trade barriers, and scale economies in production make such changes economical. For example, Volvo recently built a plant in Canada, and Volkswagen is planning to construct one in the United States. Also, both Datsun and Toyota are considering the possibility of building plants in the United States when their volume has grown sufficiently to make such operations economical.

TRADE BARRIERS

All countries have tariffs against imported automobiles, but the rates vary greatly. In addition, many countries impose special taxes on vehicle characteristics that have the effect of discriminating against vehicles produced in the United States.

The United States and Japan have the lowest tariffs, 3 percent and 6.4 percent, respectively. The EEC common external tariff is 11 percent on finished automobiles; there are no tariffs between EEC members. Canada's external tariff is 15 percent. There are no tariffs on automobiles traded between the United States and Canada. (The 1965 U.S.-Canada Automotive Products Agreement eliminated duties on imports of motor vehicles and parts for use as original equipment in the manufacture of motor vehicles but did maintain some restrictions. See the following section on U.S.-Canada trade for details.)

Most developing countries and other nonproducers impose much higher tariffs on imported automobiles. For example, India's tariff is 100 percent, Thailand's is 80 percent, Indonesia's is 200 percent, Nigeria's ranges from 33.33 percent to 150 percent, and Iran's ranges from 25 percent to 50 percent.

Table 2.8 lists tariff rates, in 1974 and before the Kennedy Round of tariff negotiations (PKR), for a sample of major countries, including producers and nonproducers. Tariff rates imposed by the major producers have been, in general,

TABLE 2.7
1972 Passenger Car Output by Nondomestic Companies

	Company Owned By			
Production in	United States	Japan	West Germany	France
Argentina	61,893	–	–	49,591
Australia	307,034	–	–	–
Belgium	532,335	–	90,706	142,997
Brazil	148,711	–	265,947	–
Canada	1,137,832	–	–	–
Chile	672	654	–	4,042
France	536,615	–	–	–
Italy	–	–	–	–
Japan	236,164[b]	–	–	–
Mexico[c]	77,333	17,054	53,684	14,460
Philippines[c]	4,540	3,602	3,002	365
Portugal	13,924	18,274	7,865	9,084
South Africa[c]	72,486	19,667	26,650	8,741
Spain	62,962	–	–	126,491
Sweden	–	–	–	–
Switzerland	17,186	–	–	–
United Kingdom	994,572	–	–	–
United States	–	–	–	–
Venezuela	47,640	–	7,228	7,674
West Germany	1,307,330	–	–	–

declining since the 1930s. The U.S. tariff fell from a peak of 10 percent to 3 percent after the Kennedy Round. Japanese and European tariffs also have been falling. Table 2.9 summarizes changes in tariffs of some of the major producing nations.

In addition to tariffs, nations impose a wide variety of fees, excise taxes, use taxes, value-added taxes, and other charges on purchasing, owning, and operating private passenger automobiles. Though these taxes and fees do not by law distinguish among automobiles produced in different nations, they may be viewed as discriminatory if they in fact impose higher costs on owners and users of vehicles produced in some nations than on the owners and users in

PRODUCTION, CONSUMPTION, AND WORLD TRADE 17

Company Owned By				
United Kingdom	Italy	Total Foreign	Total	Percent Foreign
–	76,321	187,805	200,885	93.5[a]
25,655	–	332,689	332,689	100.0
81,503	36,015	883,556	922,287	95.8[a]
–	–	414,658	415,164	99.8[a]
–	–	1,147,280	1,147,280	100.0
1,356	15,728	23,452	23,452	100.0
–	648,956	1,185,571	2,992,959	39.6
–	–	–	1,732,379	0.0
–	–	236,164	4,022,289	5.9
–	–	162,531	163,673	97.3[a]
5	1,906	11,994	11,994	100.0
12,835	12,819	77,840	77,840	100.0
13,649	17,388	158,581	182,961	86.7[a]
34,199	41,567	265,219	600,557	44.2
–	–	–	317,962	0.0
–	–	17,186	17,186	100.0
–	–	994,572	1,921,311	51.8
–	–	–	8,828,175	0.0
2,933	3,308	63,783	63,783	100.0
–	12,996	1,320,326	3,521,540	37.5

Note: "Output" refers to the finished automobile. The degree of vertical integration of the industry varies from country to country. Some nations produce literally from scratch while in others production takes the form of assembly from imported parts.

[a]Production in these countries is essentially 100 percent foreign-owned but appears as less due to nonidentification of some producers.

[b]Represents production by Isuzu and Mitsubishi, which are partly owned by General Motors and have joint production with Chrysler, respectively.

[c]Represents sales by companies owned by nation in each column, regardless of where vehicle is produced.

Source: "1972 World Vehicle Production," *Ward's Automotive Reports Yearbook 1973*, p. 85.

TABLE 2.8
Current and Pre-Kennedy-Round Tariffs, Selected Countries
(percentage of price of auto)

Country	PKR Tariff	1974 Tariff	
Austria	20	20	free against EFTA[a]
Denmark	15	11	free against EFTA
EEC[b]	22	11	
Finland	14-15	8	free against EFTA
Greece	26.0	19.64	2.60% against EEC
Iceland	90	90	
Ireland	75	75	22.2% against United Kingdom
Malta	70	70	55% against EEC
Norway	10	8	
Spain	68	68	
Sweden	15	10	free against EFTA
United Kingdom	22	11	7.5% against other Commonwealth
Yugoslavia	30	30	
Argentina	14	14	
Brazil	70-105	70-105	
Chile	imports prohibited		
Canada	17.5	15	free against U.S. and U.K.
United States	6.5	3.0	free against Canada
Australia	45	35	
Indonesia		200	
Japan	20-40	6.4	
India	100	100	British preferential tariff of 20% being phased out
Nigeria	33.33-150	33.33-150	
South Africa	45-100	45-100	
Iran	25-50	25-50	
Egypt	100-200	100-200	

Note: Where ranges of tariffs are listed in the table, the tariff level is based on some measurable automobile characteristic—for example, weight or engine displacement.

[a]EFTA nations include Austria, Denmark, Finland, Ireland, Norway, and Sweden. Denmark and Ireland are joining the EEC.

[b]EEC original members are Belgium, France, West Germany, Italy, Luxembourg, and Netherlands. EEC tariffs against new members—United Kingdom, Denmark, and Ireland—are being phased out.

Source: Motor Vehicle Manufacturers Association, *1974 Digest of Import Duties for Motor Vehicles Levied by Selected Countries* (Detroit, 1974).

TABLE 2.9

History of Tariffs on Passenger Cars, Selected Major Producers
(percentage of price of auto)

Country	1930	1940	1950	1960	1968[a]	1973
United States	10	10	10	7.5	5.5	3
Japan	50	70	40	35–40	35–40	6.4
France	46	n.a.[b]	n.a.	30	22	11
United Kingdom	33.3	33.3	33.3	30	17.5	11
Germany	c	c	35	13–16	22	11

[a]Pre-Kennedy Round tariff.
[b]Not available.
[c]In this period, Germany imposed specific tariffs, which varied by weight.
Source: U.S. Motor Vehicle Manufacturers Association, *1974 Digest of Import Duties for Motor Vehicles Levied by Selected Countries* (Detroit, 1974).

others. In particular, taxes based on weight, horsepower, engine displacement, and wheelbase discriminate against the bigger, more powerful automobiles that have been produced in the United States in the postwar period.

Some examples of such nontariff barriers are the following:[1]

1. France imposes an annual "vignette" tax on cars based on age and fiscal horsepower. The fee ranges from 30 to 1,000 francs ($6.75 to $225).

2. Germany imposes an annual road use tax based on engine displacement of 14.40 marks per cubic centimeter of cylinder capacity. The German tax at October 1, 1975 exchange rates amounted to $127 per year for a 1975 model U.S. subcompact, $227 per year for 1975 compacts, $318 per year for a 1975 intermediate or full-size U.S. auto, $88 per year for a 1975 Volkswagen Beetle, $110 per year for a 1975 Volvo 242-S, and $72 per year for a 1975 Fiat 128. If we convert to present value terms and express as a fraction of the delivered price to Europe, we estimate that the tax applied to 1975 models would raise the price of a Volvo by 14 percent, a Fiat by 19 percent, a Volkswagen Beetle by 23 percent, a U.S. subcompact by 25 percent, a U.S. compact by 39 percent, a U.S. standard by 43 percent, and a U.S. intermediate by 46 percent.*

---

*In making the present value calculation, we assumed that the car was owned for ten years and applied a discount rate of 10 percent. The base price to which the present discounted cost of the tax was applied to compute a percentage increase in price was the sum of the 1975 list price in the United States and international freight rates between the U.S. east coast and Amsterdam in June 1975 for U.S. cars, and the difference between

3. Italy imposes a higher sales tax on autos with more engine displacement (18 percent for cars over 2,000 cubic centimeters; otherwise 12 percent) and an annual road tax based on fiscal horsepower. Almost all autos produced in the United States in 1975, including the Chevrolet Vega, qualified for the higher sales tax rate, while Volkswagen, Volvo 242, and Fiat qualified for the lower rate.

4. The Netherlands imposes an annual car tax based on weight of 13 guilders per kilogram. The annual Dutch tax amounts to $42 on a 1975 Volkswagen Beetle, $43 on a 1975 Fiat 128, $55 on a 1975 model U.S. subcompact, $62 on a 1975 Volvo 242, $75 on a 1975 model U.S. compact, $86 on a 1975 model U.S. intermediate, and $95 on a 1975 model U.S. standard. Converting to present value terms, the tax is equivalent to a percentage sales tax of 8 percent on a 1975 Volvo 242, eleven percent on a 1975 Volkswagen, eleven percent on a 1975 model subcompact, twelve percent on a 1975 model U.S. intermediate, 13 percent on a 1975 model U.S. standard, and 16 percent on a 1975 Fiat 128. Thus, the Dutch tax is not especially discriminatory against U.S. cars.

5. Greece imposes a special luxury tax on sales of more expensive cars (an added 25 percent on cars valued at over $1,800 U.S.).

6. Sweden imposes a transactions tax based on weight of 1.90 Kroner per kilogram, and an additional 240 kroner per kilogram for every full 50 kilograms over 1,600 kilograms, up to 1,800 kilograms. The Swedish tax is equivalent to a percentage sales tax of 11 percent on a 1975 Volvo 242, fourteen percent on a 1975 Volkswagen Beetle, 14 percent on a 1975 model U.S. subcompact, 16 percent on a 1975 Fiat 128, seventeen percent on a 1975 model U.S. compact, 21 percent on a 1975 model U.S. intermediate, and 24 percent on a 1975 model U.S. standard.

7. Japan has an automotive tax based on displacement and wheelbase: up to 360 cubic centimeter displacement, $12.50; 360-999 cubic centimeter, $50.00; 1,000-1,499 cubic centimeter, $58.33; 1,500-1,999 cubic centimeter, $66.67; for 2,000 cubic centimeters and over, the tax is $150 if the wheelbase is less than 3.038 meters, and $250 if the wheelbase is greater than 3.038 meters. The Japanese tax is equivalent to an annual tax of $67 on a 1975 Toyota Corolla, $150 on a 1975 Toyota Corona, U. S. subcompacts, compacts, and intermediates, and $250 on 1975 model U.S. standards. Japan also has an annual road tax based on cubic centimeters and wheelbase; the annual road tax is the same on all the above cars as the automotive tax. Taking the present discounted

---

U.S. list price and freight rates for European cars. The U.S. cars used in the calculation are Chevy Vega 4 (subcompact), Chevy Nova 6 (compact), Chevelle V-8 (intermediate), Impala V-8 (standard).

The same method was used for estimating the comparative percentage impact of NTBs on U.S. and foreign-car prices in other countries.

value of the sum of the two taxes, we compute that they amount to a 21 percent tax on 1975 model U.S. intermediates, a 25 percent tax on 1975 model compacts, a 27 percent tax on a 1975 Toyota Corolla, a 29 percent tax on a 1975 model U.S. subcompact, a 33 percent tax on a 1975 model U.S. standard, and a 41 percent tax on a 1975 Toyota Corona. One reason the percentage tax on U.S. cars relative to Japanese cars is relatively low is that the transport costs to Japan make the delivered prices net of excise taxes of U.S. cars to Japan before tax very high relative to prices net of tax of Japanese cars.

The above examples illustrate that many European countries impose special taxes that increase the local price of cars imported from the United States relative to European-made cars. In addition, many developing countries have special taxes that discriminate, in practice, against U.S. exports. Further, many tariff schedules in nonproducing nations vary explicitly with either weight, engine displacement, or other characteristics correlated with size and power.

Trade barriers may have an important effect in limiting U.S. exports overseas. The differential tariff schedules, which make it cheaper to export vehicles with the same production cost from Europe to the United States than from the United States to Europe, may have contributed to past decisions by U.S.-based multinational automobile companies to invest in facilities for producing small cars in Europe. European tariffs and nontariff barriers certainly make it more difficult to export full-size U.S. cars, though it is not clear there would be many sales in Europe of such cars, even in the absence of barriers.

U.S.-CANADA AUTOMOBILE TRADE

Trade between the United States and Canada in finished automobiles has expanded greatly since the conclusion of the U.S.-Canada Automotive Products Agreement in 1965, which reduced trade barriers in the automobile industry between the two countries. The United States has become a net importer of automobiles from Canada, although the trade "deficit" in finished automobiles has been to some degree conterbalanced by a trade "surplus" in imported parts. (Beginning in either 1974 or 1975, depending on which of two data sets is used, the surplus on original motor vehicle parts exceeded the deficit on finished motor vehicles.) Exports to the United States account for the majority of automobiles produced in Canada, while exports to Canada account for less than 10 percent of automobiles produced in the United States. Trade between the United States and Canada did not contribute to a worsening of the slump in the U.S. automobile industry in 1974 and 1975; during those two years, U.S. exports to Canada increased and U.S. imports from Canada declined. This section reviews briefly the principal features of the U.S.-Canada Automotive Products Agreement and presents statistics on U.S.-Canada trade before and after the agreement.

The U.S.-Canada Automotive Products Agreement affected the production location choice within North America for the major U.S. companies. Prior to the agreement, Canada imposed a 17.5 percent tariff on automobile imports from the United States, while the United States imposed a 6.5 percent tariff on imports from Canada. (These tariffs are equal to the pre-Kennedy Round external tariffs on automobile imports of the two countries. Canadian and U.S. automobile import tariffs against other countries have since been lowered to 15 percent and 3 percent, respectively.) The barriers encouraged companies to produce most automobiles sold in Canada within Canada, even though the protected Canadian market was too small to support production of a wide range of models at minimum efficient scale. Elimination of tariffs between the two countries has aided in the achievement of scale economies in production by making it economical for companies to produce some models in Canada and others in the United States for sale in both countries. The goal of achieving scale economies through specialization of production was a specific objective of the agreement.

The agreement sought:[2]

> a) the creation of a broader market for automotive products within which the full benefits of specialization and large-scale production can be achieved; b) the liberalization of United States and Canadian automotive trade in respect of trade barriers and other factors tending to impede it, with a view of enabling the industries of both countries to participate on a fair and equitable basis in the expanding total market of the two countries, and c) the development of conditions in which market forces may operate effectively to attain the most economical pattern of investment, production and trade.

Under the agreement, the United States (Canada) accords duty-free treatment to imports from Canada (the United States) of motor vehicles and parts for use as original equipment in the manufacture of motor vehicles. However, the agreement has a number of limitations that maintain restrictions on trade in automotive products between the two countries:

1. Some special purpose vehicles remain subject to tariffs by both the United States and Canada.

2. The agreement does not apply to replacement parts or parts sold in the after-market for servicing vehicles. In addition, trailers, tires, and tubes are subject to tariffs even if sold as original equipment.

3. The agreement is limited to products containing less than 50 percent foreign material, by value of material, where foreign material is defined as material produced in countries other than Canada and the United States. (This limit was 60 percent for motor vehicles until January 1, 1968.) The effect of

this limitation is to prevent European and Japanese manufacturers from exporting automobiles to Canada through the United States, avoiding the higher Canadian tariff.

4. The agreement contains a number of special restrictions to prevent the absence of tariffs from reducing automobile output in Canada. The Canadian manufacturer must meet certain qualifications in each relevant defined class of motor vehicles to import duty-free. First, the agreement is limited to manufacturers established in the base year, with the Canadian government holding the right to allow, or to prevent, other companies from importing duty free. (In practice, this means only the Big Four U.S. manufacturers can import to Canada duty-free. Under the agreement, Canada will retain the right to impose tariffs on automobiles produced at the future Volkswagen plant in the United States, even if the automobiles are made using mostly U.S.-manufactured parts.) Second, the manufacturer must maintain the same ratio as in the base year from between vehicles within a given class sold in Canada. (Classes of vehicles including passenger cars, buses, and commercial vehicles.) The output-to-sales ratio within Canada must be at least .75 for the manufacturer to be eligible to import duty free. Third, the manufacturer must maintain, by class of vehicle, the same amount, in absolute dollar terms, of "Canadian value added" in production as achieved during the base year period. The restrictions taken together mean that the agreement as a whole, while enabling manufacturers to realize scale economies by producing fewer models with greater output per model in Canada, prevents manufacturers from achieving the same objective by switching a larger fraction of their total output for sale in North America to the United States. (Along with the agreement, Canadian manufacturers submitted letters of undertaking to the government of Canada, assuring an increase each model year in Canadian value added in the production of motor vehicles and original parts. The increase was to be approximately 60 percent of the growth in sales each year, plus an additional $241 million increase in Canadian value added by the end of model year 1968. The letters of undertaking in effect guaranteed that Canadian value added would remain at least as great as it was before the agreement.)

Table 2.10 presents data on U.S.-Canada trade in finished automobiles between 1961 and 1975. The table shows that both U.S. exports to Canada and Canadian exports to the United States increased dramatically beginning in the year of the Agreement, 1965. Prior to 1965, trade between the United States and Canada in finished automobiles was practically nil. U.S. imports from Canada grew much more rapidly than U.S. exports to Canada after 1966; the trade deficit reached a peak of 455,000 vehicles in 1972. However, while the U.S. automobile industry was declining in 1974 and 1975, exports to Canada were increasing and imports from Canada decreasing.

TABLE 2.10

U.S.-Canada Trade in Finished Automobiles
(thousands of units)

| Year | Factory Sales from U.S. Plants ||| Factory Sales from Canadian Plants ||| Net U.S. Trade Balance with Canada[b] |
	Domestic	Exports to Canada	Total[a]	Domestic	Exports to United States	Total[a]	
1961	5,402	16	5,418	332	0	332	+16
1962	6,753	17	6,770	433	0	433	+17
1963	7,444	17	7,461	521	0	521	+17
1964	7,554	15	7,569	533	10	543	+5
1965	9,101	47	9,148	677	34	711	+13
1966	8,337	122	8,459	494	161	655	−39
1967	7,070	246	7,316	355	326	681	−80
1968	8,407	289	8,696	359	480	839	−191
1969	7,806	286	8,092	315	677	992	−391
1970	6,187	246	6,433	207	682	889	−436
1971	8,122	352	8,474	258	780	1,038	−428
1972	8,352	382	8,734	263	837	1,100	−455
1973	9,079	476	9,555	323	862	1,185	−386
1974	6,721	500	7,221	317	802	1,119	−302
1975	6,073	549	6,622	272	713	985	−164

[a] Total excludes exports outside of North America. These exports have been of trivial magnitude.
[b] U.S. exports to Canada minus U.S. imports from Canada.

Sources: Successive issues of *Automotive News Almanac*, table entitled "Motor Vehicle Sales from Plants in U.S. and Canada." Source of *Automotive News Almanac* data is the U.S. Motor Vehicle Manufacturers Association. Canadian export data from 1963 to 1969 supplied directly by U.S. Motor Vehicle Manufacturers Association.

TABLE 2.11

U.S.-Canada Trade in Original Equipment Motor Vehicle Parts in Terms of Transfer Values
(millions of dollars)

Year	U.S. Output Total	Exports to Canada	(Percent)	Canadian Output Total	Exports to United States	(Percent)	Net U.S. Trade Balance with Canada*
1960	9,092	306	(3.37)	234	1	(0.43)	305
1961	10,166	299	(2.94)	224	1	(0.45)	298
1962	12,654	405	(3.20)	305	6	(1.97)	399
1963	14,562	533	(3.66)	406	18	(4.43)	515
1964	15,094	559	(3.70)	462	45	(9.74)	514
1965	19,467	719	(3.69)	641	90	(14.04)	629
1966	18,892	819	(4.34)	856	302	(35.28)	517
1967	16,808	927	(5.52)	971	391	(40.27)	536
1968	19,464	1,314	(6.75)	1,341	656	(48.92)	658
1969	20,764	1,658	(7.99)	1,453	795	(54.71)	863
1970	17,058	1,587	(9.30)	1,338	920	(68.76)	667
1971	22,458	1,887	(8.40)	1,716	1,213	(70.69)	674
1972	24,253	2,146	(8.85)	2,066	1,504	(72.80)	642
1973	29,235	2,569	(8.79)	2,276	1,731	(76.05)	838
1974	29,138	3,128	(10.74)	2,203	1,563	(70.95)	1,565

Note: Transfer values are transactions values reported by U.S. manufacturers.
*U.S. exports to Canada minus U.S. imports from Canada.
Source: Ninth Annual Report of the President to the Congress on the Operation of the Automotive Products Trade Act of 1965 (Washington, D.C.: Government Printing Office, 1976), Tables 81, 82, 85, and 86.

TABLE 2.12

U.S.-Canada Trade in Motor Vehicle Parts as Reported by U.S. Department of Commerce
(millions of U.S. dollars)

Year	U.S. Exports to Canada	U.S. Imports from Canada	Net U.S. Trade Balance with Canada*
1964	603	88	515
1965	759	159	600
1966	969	458	511
1967	1,103	588	515
1968	1,563	957	606
1969	1,814	1,208	606
1970	1,644	1,331	313
1971	2,019	1,692	327
1972	2,456	2,146	310
1973	2,816	2,750	66
1974	3,332	2,552	780
1975	3,711	2,600	1,111

*Exports minus imports.

Source: United States International Trade Commission, *Automotive Trade Statistics 1964-1975*, Series A: Using Official Statistics of the United States Department of Commerce for U.S. Imports and U.S. Exports (Washington, D.C.: Government Printing Office, May 1976).

In recent years, most automobiles produced in Canada have been exported to the United States, while most automobiles sold in Canada have been imported from the United States. Thus, the objective of achieving specialization of production appears to have been realized. (If Canadians are purchasing a diverse range of vehicle models, and scale economies require output of any given model to be large relative to total sales in Canada, one would expect that a relatively small number of models would be produced in Canada, mostly for export, and that most automobiles for Canadian consumption would be produced in the United States.)

The total change in the U.S. trade balance with Canada in motor vehicle sector products depends both on change in imports and exports of finished automobiles, and in imports and exports of automobile parts. The U.S.-Canada Agreement lowered trade barriers on both finished vehicles and original equipment motor vehicle parts.

Available sources of published statistics give widely divergent estimates of the magnitude of net trade flows between the United States and Canada in

TABLE 2.13

U.S.-Canada Trade Balance in Motor Vehicles and Parts in Transfer Values (millions of U.S. dollars)

	Motor Vehicles				
Year	Passenger Automobiles	Trucks and Buses	Total	Parts	Total
1960	67	10	77	305	382
1961	49	8	57	298	355
1962	50	8	58	399	457
1963	26	14	40	515	555
1964	16	15	31	514	545
1965	53	21	74	629	703
1966	-54	-56	-110	517	407
1967	-144	-77	-221	536	315
1968	-518	-162	-680	658	-22
1969	-791	-250	-1,041	863	-178
1970	-860	-186	-1,046	667	-379
1971	-1,022	-168	-1,190	674	-516
1972	-1,011	-158	-1,169	642	-527
1973	-841	-131	-972	838	-134
1974	-894	13	-881	1,565	684

Source: Ninth Annual Report of the President to the Congress on the Operation of the Automotive Products Trace Act of 1965 (Washington, D.C.: Government Printing Office, 1976), Table 101.

motor vehicle sector products. The two major sources of data are the annual reports of the President to the Congress on the Operation of the Automotive Products Trade Act of 1965 and Department of Commerce data reported by the International Trade Commission. The sources differ in the methods used to value intercountry shipments; the former source uses transfer prices reported by the manufacturers while the latter uses customs values that are developed by adding set overhead and markup rates to production cost estimates. (The choice of a value of shipment figure can be a problem because many of the intercountry parts shipments are within a company rather than being arms-length transactions.) Also, the International Trade Commission data may underestimate U.S. exports because the U.S. customs service has no incentive to measure correctly the volume of exports; many may go through unreported.

TABLE 2.14

U.S.-Canada Trade Balance in Motor Vehicles and Parts as Reported by U.S. Department of Commerce
(millions of U.S. dollars)

Year	Motor Vehicles Passenger Automobiles	Other	Total	Parts	Total
1964	27	13	40	516	555
1965	36	21	57	600	657
1966	-91	-25	-116	511	395
1967	-263	-73	-336	515	179
1968	-646	-168	-814	606	-209
1969	-1,079	-235	-1,314	606	-707
1970	-1,181	-227	-1,408	314	-1,095
1971	-1,451	-251	-1,702	327	-1,374
1972	-1,517	-116	-1,633	310	-1,322
1973	-1,351	54	-1,297	67	-1,230
1974	-1,321	212	-1,109	780	-329
1975	-1,087	213	-874	1,111	237

Source: United States International Trade Commission, *Automotive Trade Statistics, 1964-1975*, Series A: Using Official Statistics of the United States Department of Commerce for U.S. Imports and U.S. Exports (Washington, D.C.: Government Printing Office, May 1976), Tables 1D, 6D, 7D, 8D.

In the president's report, U.S. exports are estimated by using official Canadian import data.

Tables 2.11 through 2.14 summarize the available data from the two sources in both trade in parts and the overall U.S.-Canada motor vehicle sector trade balance. Tables 2.11 and 2.12 both show that the United States has had a trade surplus with Canada in original equipment motor vehicle parts both before and after the U.S.-Canada Automotive Products Agreement. While the data show a rapid growth in trade after the agreement, they do not show any dramatic shift in the growth of the U.S. trade surplus after 1965. Both sets of data show U.S. imports from Canada beginning to decline and the U.S. trade surplus beginning to grow sharply after 1973, but the timing of the changes is not exactly the same. The U.S. trade surplus reported by the president's report is consistently higher than the trade surplus reported by the International Trade Commission.

Table 2.13 summarizes the total net trade balance in motor vehicle sector products between the United States and Canada from the two sources. Both

sources show a small trade surplus before 1965 changing to a substantial deficit after 1965, because of the growth in the trade deficit in finished motor vehicles. The growing surplus in parts, combined with a decline in the deficit in finished automobiles, led to a switch to a net surplus in 1974, according to the president's report, and a switch to a net surplus in 1975, according to the International Trade Commission data.

Summarizing this brief survey of U.S.-Canada trade, we find that trade did accelerate sharply after adoption of the U.S.-Canada Automotive Products Agreement in 1965. U.S. imports of finished motor vehicles from Canada grew much faster than U.S. exports of finished motor vehicles to Canada. The U.S. trade surplus in motor vehicle parts became considerably smaller than the U.S. trade deficit in finished motor vehicles. The trade picture shifted greatly in 1974 and 1975 with U.S. imports of both parts and finished automobiles from Canada declining and U.S. exports of parts and automobiles rising, giving the United States, in 1975, a net trade surplus with Canada in motor vehicle sector products for the first time since 1965.

AUTOMOBILE IMPORTS IN THE UNITED STATES: A BRIEF HISTORY

In this section, we briefly review the history of import penetration in the United States and present some broad explanations for the observed trends. More detailed discussion of changes in shares and prices, along with econometric estimates of demand equations designed to measure foreign-car to domestic-car prices, is presented in Chapter 3.

U.S. automobile imports can be divided into two distinct categories: imports from Canada and imports from outside North America. As all automobiles produced in Canada are by U.S. firms and since the type of cars purchased by Canadians do not differ significantly from the type of cars purchased by Americans, the volume of Canadian imports is determined primarily by production location decisions of U.S. firms and not by changes in tastes and income of U.S. consumers. On the other hand, European and Japanese cars, including autos made in Europe by U.S. companies, are significantly different from U.S. cars. Changes in the share of overseas imports purchased reflect changes in income, taste, and gasoline prices in the United States, as well as changes in the relative price and availability of foreign models and in the availability of close substitutes by U.S. manufacturers.

For the remainder of this section, we shall use the word "import" to refer to purchases of foreign automobiles produced outside of North America.

Automobile imports to the United States were almost negligible before the middle 1950s. There have always been some sales of European luxury cars like the Mercedes-Benz and the Rolls-Royce, and imported sports cars; these never have amounted to a significant share of U.S. car purchases, either in numbers or value, whatever their publicity as glamour cars. Large-scale imports

of foreign cars began after 1955 with penetration first by Volkswagen, and later by small French imports. These imports, benefiting from the absence of a U.S.-made small car and from the 1957-58 recession, expanded sales rapidly, capturing over 10 percent of new-car sales in the United States by 1958.

Import shares then declined sharply, falling to under 5 percent by 1962. The main reasons behind the decline in import shares were the failure of some of the French imports, in particular the Renault Dauphine, the introduction by U.S. manufacturers of compact models, including Corvair, Falcon, and Valiant, and the recovery from the recession, which lessened the public demand for small cars. Throughout the 1960s, cars sold in the United States became bigger and more powerful as incomes rose and real gas prices fell; at the same time U.S. manufacturers abandoned the small-car field to foreign competitors. While the share of small cars sold declined, the share of imports rose throughout the 1960s. The entry of new models from Japan was a major factor in the import growth. Toyota's initial attempt to enter the U.S. market with the Toyopet flopped in 1959; the Toyopet was too small and underpowered by U.S. standards. The second generation of Japanese models, introduced by Toyota and Nissan in 1965, was much more successful. The Japanese models were slightly bigger and more powerful than Volkswagens and comparable in price. Initially, Japanese imports were sold mainly in California; by the end of the decade they had established nationwide dealer networks that were growing from a solid base. Volkswagen sales peaked in 1970 and subsequently began to decline. Sales of Japanese imports continued to grow.

The U.S. automobile industry underwent major changes in the first half of the 1970s. The recessions of 1970-71 and 1974-75, the introduction of increasingly stringent antipollution regulations, and the sharp increases in gasoline prices altered the magnitude and pattern of demand. The gasoline price increases and fears of shortage and the decline in real income during two recessions encouraged a shift to smaller, more economical cars. The pollution regulations led to a temporary decline in fuel efficiency of U.S. cars. (That this shift was temporary is borne out by 1975 EPA data on fuel economy in new U.S. cars.)[3] This decline was particularly marked in U.S. small cars; the inferiority of U.S. small cars in fuel economy compared to Japanese and German competitors accentuated the shift to imports.

Detroit responded to the huge shift to imports in 1970 by introducing in 1971 two new subcompact models, Vega and Pinto. Import shares declined briefly in 1971 and then began to grow again in 1972. Increases in relative import prices following the revaluation of the German mark in 1969 and the devaluation of the U.S. dollar relative to German and Japanese currencies after 1971 did not halt the shift to imports. (The data we have developed show that, while the quality-adjusted ratio of foreign-to-domestic prices did increase in 1973 and 1974, the increase was not as large as might be expected from the

size of the devaluation or from measures of unadjusted prices. See Chapter 3 for a full explanation.)

Foreign-car shares increased moderately in 1974 and sharply to an all-time high in 1975. The year 1974 saw increases both in the relative price of foreign cars and in gasoline prices. In 1974, buyers shifted both to U.S. compacts and to imports.

In the first five months of 1975, buyers shifted away from U.S. compacts and toward imports; the share of full-size U.S. cars increased. List-price compar-

TABLE 2.15

Foreign-Car Sales and Small-Car Shares as Fraction of U.S. Market

Year	Import Share of New-Car Sales	Small-Car[a] Share of New-Car Sales	Imports as Percent of Small-Car Shares
1955	0.72	n.a.[b]	—
1956	1.53	n.a.	—
1957	3.26	n.a.	—
1958	7.86	n.a.	—
1959	10.11	15.69	64.44
1960	7.58	30.47	24.88
1961	6.47	35.38	18.29
1962	4.89	29.23	16.73
1963	5.10	25.56	19.95
1964	6.00	22.32	26.88
1965	6.11	21.77	28.07
1966	7.31	21.42	34.13
1967	9.18	23.75	38.65
1968	10.48	24.94	42.02
1969	11.24	22.80	49.30
1970	14.67	31.33	46.82
1971	13.16	34.28	38.39
1972	14.58	35.18	41.44
1973	15.15	29.04	52.17
1974	15.74	32.36	48.64
1975	20.73	36.02	57.55

[a]"Small car" is defined to be a car shorter than 190 inches.
[b]Not available.
Source: Computations from raw data in *Automotive News Almanac*, annual issues.

FIGURE 2.1

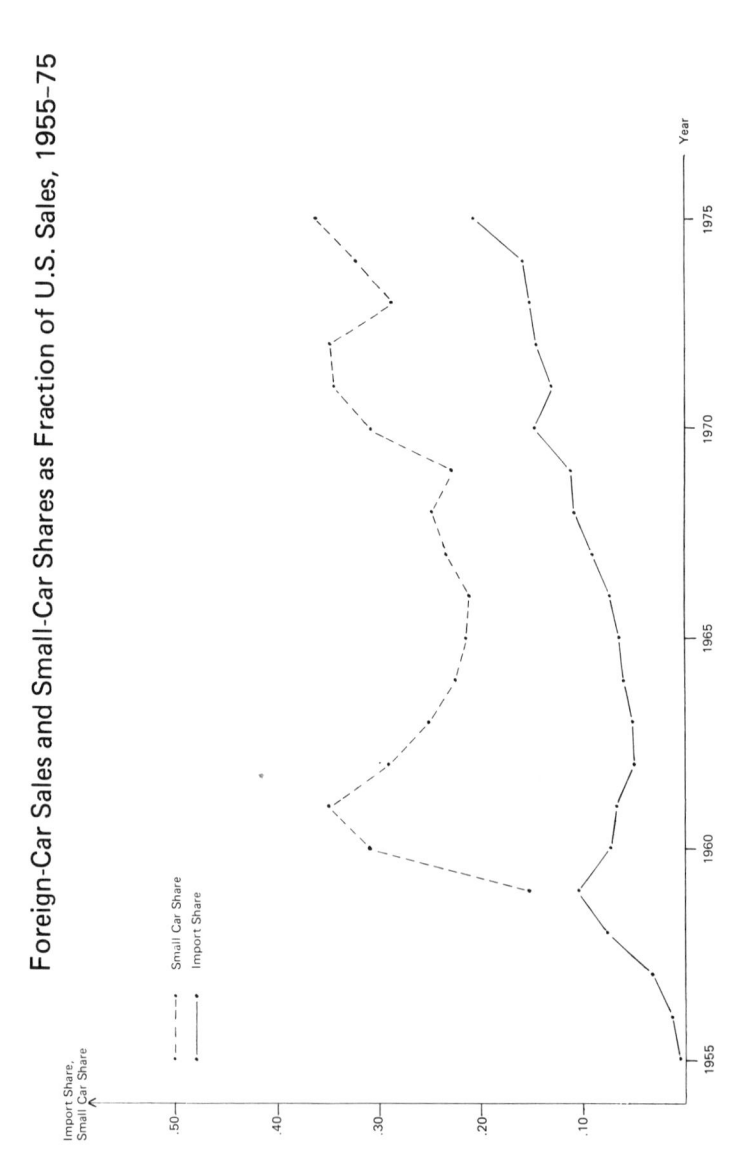

Foreign-Car Sales and Small-Car Shares as Fraction of U.S. Sales, 1955–75

Source: Successive issues of *Automotive News Almanac*, table entitled "Motor Vehicle Sales from Plants in U.S. and Canada." Computed from raw data in *Automotive News Almanac*, various issues.

isons show that U.S. compacts and subcompacts increased in price relative to imports between 1974 and 1975. U.S. small cars did improve in fuel economy, especially models introduced in midyear, but it is possible that the public was not aware of these improvements in the early months of 1975. Most of the growth in imports in the early 1970s was in the small economical cars—Toyota, Datsun, and, in early 1975 Volkswagen. However, slightly larger, more luxurious imported models providing better handling, better fuel economy, and much higher prices than U.S. compacts were also growing in sales in the early 1970s. Imports in this category include BMW, Volvo, Saab, Audi, and Peugeot. In addition, sales of captive imports (models produced by U.S. companies in foreign countries), including Capri, Opel, and Dodge Colt, were growing, and new imported models were introduced. Imports other than the big three (Volkswagen, Toyota, Datsun), while remaining a small fraction of all U.S. new car sales in 1975, had grown as a proportion of total imports in the previous five years.

The import share reached a peak of over 20 percent in the first five months of 1975. However, in early 1976 import shares declined to their lowest level since 1971. The fall in import shares in 1976 was due to three main factors: (1) the recovery of the U.S. economy, which led to a big increase in domestic-car sales; (2) a shift of the U.S. buying public back toward bigger cars as fears of a gasoline shortage faded and expected large gas price increases failed, for a time, to materialize; and (3) a sharp increase in the relative supply cost of European cars. The sales decrease of Volkswagen was especially sharp, while Japanese imports continued to grow.

Table 2.15 and Figure 2.1 show annual changes in import shares and small-car shares between 1955 and early 1975. The small-car share was computed from the sample of models we used to estimate foreign and domestic price indexes. Coverage in this sample of models is more than 95 percent complete (by sales). We defined a small car as one less than 190 inches long; by this definition, all imports except the larger Mercedes-Benz are small cars. Domestic "compacts" are sometimes small cars and sometimes not; for example, Dodge Dart and Plymouth Valiant were small cars in the mid-1960s but not afterward.

Table 2.15 and Figure 2.1 show that both the small-car share and import share reached a peak in the first five months of 1975. Import shares have grown steadily since 1962, with the exception of a brief decline in 1971 and an increase in the rate of growth in 1975. The small-car share was low throughout the mid-1960s; in 1970, relative sales of small cars increased sharply and have continued to grow in every year except the boom year 1973.

The picture that emerges until 1976 is one of a steadily growing role of auto imports in the United States. Imports captured a large share of small-car sales in the 1960s and have grown along with the relative growth in small-car sales since 1970. A number of major structural changes affecting U.S. automobile sales have occurred since 1955, including the initial entry of low-price European imports (especially Volkswagen) as a large-scale competitor, the first

wave of U.S. small cars in the late 1950s, the growth of the Japanese automobile industry, and the movement to small cars that accompanied the national economic problems, high gas prices, and antipollution regulations of the 1970s. Further structural changes are likely. In 1976, General Motors began marketing a new minicar (the Chevette), Volkswagen decided to build an assembly plant in Pennsylvania, and Japanese manufacturers were reported also considering establishing production facilities in the United States. Even with the 1976 shift to bigger cars, small cars will continue to be a significant factor in the U.S. market in the coming years and may become much more important if new policies to encourage energy conservation raise the relative price of big cars. The ability of the U.S. manufacturers to introduce models competitive with the popular imports and the willingness of foreign manufacturers to establish production facilities in the United States will significantly affect the extent of future import penetration in the United States.

NOTES

1. For more details, see Motor Vehicle Manufacturers Association, *1974 Digest of Import Duties for Motor Vehicles Levied by Selected Countries* (Detroit, 1974).
2. *Agreement Concerning Automotive Products Between the Government of the United States of America and the Government of Canada*, Article I.
3. See New York *Times*, September 23, 1975.

CHAPTER

3

RELATIVE PRICES AND THE DEMAND FOR DOMESTIC AND FOREIGN AUTOMOBILES

EFFECTS OF TARIFFS ON FOREIGN-CAR DEMAND

An increase in the tariff rate raises the cost of selling automobiles in the United States that are produced abroad. Thus, tariffs will raise the price of imported automobiles relative to that of domestically produced automobiles; the exact amount of the increase depends on exchange rate effects, on the ability of foreign manufacturers to absorb higher costs without raising prices,* and on the responses of domestic companies to an increase in the price of imports.

In the short run, this relative price change can be expected to increase the share of new-car sales of automobiles currently produced in the United States. In the long-run, it is possible that higher tariffs will also lead to changes in production location; the types of automobiles now produced in Europe and Japan might be produced in the United States under a different set of cost incentives.

In this chapter, we present results of econometric estimation of the effect of relative price changes on relative purchases of domestic and imported new cars in the United States. The estimates consider only the short-run effects of tariff changes, ignoring potential effects on location. (Possible location effects

---

*If other tariff and/or fiscal-monetary policies keep exchange rates and relative rates of inflation constant, and if foreign and domestic manufacturers are both on their long-run supply curves and if long-run supply curves are horizontal (that is, constant cost), then the percent increase in foreign-car price will be equal to the absolute increment in the ad valorem tariff rate times the ratio of the base to which the tariff is applied and the retail sales price.

are discussed in Chapters 5 and 6.) In our regressions, we define two "composite" goods—domestic automobiles and imported automobiles. Domestic and imported automobiles are viewed as close, but not perfect, substitutes.

Imported automobiles are, for the most part, smaller, lighter, and less powerful than domestic cars and have better fuel economy. Apart from measurable differences in physical and performance dimensions, imports also have different styling and handling characteristics, and different relative "status" attributes among different groups in the population in various parts of the country. It follows that imported and domestic automobiles can both have significant sales in the United States even if prices, adjusted for differences in physical dimensions and performance characteristics, are not the same.

The econometric evidence presented in this chapter gives some indication that U.S. consumers view imported and domestic automobiles as good substitutes for one another and are quite responsive to changes in relative prices. On the other hand, domestic and imported automobiles are clearly not perfect substitutes. Some imports sell for considerably higher prices than domestic cars with similar physical and technical performance characteristics; the proportionate price difference is higher for bigger cars. (In part, these differences result from differences in characteristics we could not measure quantitatively. In other words, domestic and imported automobiles are not perfect substitutes because they have different mixes of attributes.) At least some buyers consider imports to be more luxurious cars than domestic competitors within each size class. This conclusion is strengthened by econometric estimates presented below, which show a positive correlation between income and foreign-car share.

The second section of this chapter briefly outlines the welfare implications of different estimates of demand elasticities. In the next section, we briefly review past work on the demand for automobiles and comment on alternative ways of estimating share elasticities. The third and fourth sections present the results of time series and cross-section demand estimates of the effect of relative price changes on relative sales of imported and domestic autos.

The fifth section presents an alternative set of estimates derived by using a new model of consumer choice among competing differentiated durable goods developed by CRA for the purpose of estimating the effect of relative price changes on the market shares of different types of automobiles. The sixth section reviews the principal results.

The appendixes at the end of the chapter provide more detailed discussion of methodology used. Appendix 3.A details how price indexes for imported and domestic automobiles were constructed, while Appendix 3.B discusses the methods used to construct a relative annual cost of ownership and operation index for foreign and domestic automobiles, which combines new car-prices and gasoline costs. In Appendix 3.C, we present in detail alternative specifications of time series econometric estimates of the import share equations from the

RELATIVE PRICES AND DEMAND

third section. Finally, Appendix 3.D presents a theoretical discussion of the CRA market share model used to derive the estimates presented in the fifth section.

WELFARE IMPLICATIONS OF PRICE ELASTICITIES

Policies that artificially raise the price of imported automobiles reduce net welfare to the extent that buyers are diverted to commodities that are less valued, at the initial prices. (Consumer welfare will be further reduced because of the higher prices paid by buyers still purchasing imported cars. This part of the loss to foreign-car buyers, however, will be counterbalanced by an increase in tariff revenues; it represents a straight income transfer from foreign-car buyers to taxpayers, if the extra revenue substitutes for other taxes.) Higher prices of foreign new cars will cause some buyers to purchase domestic models instead, and others to defer purchase of a new car.

If the market for domestic automobiles is competitive, and if long-run cost curves for automobile production are horizontal, an increase in the price of imported autos caused by a tariff increase will not affect the price of domestic autos. (If short-run supply curves are upward sloping because plants are being run near capacity, then the rise in domestic demand caused by a tariff will lead to a temporary increase in the domestic price.) In the long run, the price of domestic autos will depend only on production and selling cost, including a normal return to investors. On the other hand, if the market is not perfectly competitive, then a tariff that raises the price of imports may also lead to an increase in the domestic price. This rise in the domestic price will affect the total deadweight loss,* as buyers are diverted away from new domestic-car purchases to other expenditures, and will cause an income transfer from buyers of U.S. cars (at post tariff prices) to factors of production in the domestic automobile industry. (Econometric estimates of the effects of import price changes on domestic price changes are presented in Chapter 4 below. The consequences of these effects for the measurement of welfare changes are discussed in Chapter 8.)

Policies that lower imported-car prices may lead to temporary adjustment costs in the domestic automobile industry. The adjustment costs depend on the responsiveness of domestic new-car purchasers to prices of imported cars. As the prices of imports fall, sales of imports will rise; some of the new sales will be shifts away from domestic new cars, while others will be part of an increase in the total market for new cars brought about by the lower import price.

---

*We use the term "deadweight loss" to refer to the loss to new-car buyers from higher prices that is not matched by an income gain to sellers or to taxpayers.

These relationships can be viewed in the context of a simple two-equation model of automobile demand:

$$F = f(P_F, P_D, X) \qquad (3.1)$$

$$D = d(P_F, P_D, X) \qquad (3.2)$$

where:
- D = new domestic-car sales,
- F = new foreign-car sales,
- P_F = price of a foreign car,
- P_D = price of a U.S. car, and
- X = a set of exogenous variables affecting new car demand (including possibly current stock, income, and unemployment rate).

Assuming domestic competition, we can trace a downward-sloping demand curve for foreign cars from Equation 3.1 for any given levels of P_D and X. The slope of the demand curve for foreign cars depends on the substitutability between foreign and domestic cars and between foreign cars and other goods. Figure 3.1 traces out a demand curve for foreign cars, under the assumption that demand is linear.

In Figure 3.1, Q_{F_0} and P_{F_0} are the annual sales and price of foreign cars before a tariff increase, and Q_{F_1} and P_{F_1} represent annual sales and price of foreign cars after the increase. The tariff change is equal to $P_{F_1} - P_{F_0}$. The shaded area ABC measures the deadweight loss from the tariff increase; it is approximately equal to the difference between what consumers would have been willing to pay for the forgone foreign-car purchases and what they would have to pay in the absence of tariffs. The area $P_{F_1}ABP_{F_0}$ represents the income transfer from foreign-car purchasers to taxpayers. It can easily be seen that if a flatter demand curve is drawn through the initial point, Q_{F_0}, the deadweight loss from the tariff increase $P_{F_1}P_{F_0}$ is greater. For a set of straight-line demand curves, the deadweight loss from a given tariff is greatest if point A lies along the line OP_{F_1}—that is, if the slope of the demand curve is such that the tariff reduces import demand to zero. For a flatter slope, the deadweight loss is lower because the flatter slope indicates that consumers do not value the same number of forgone foreign cars as much as they do when the demand curves are steeper. If the demand curve is horizontal (that is, if foreign cars and domestic cars are perfect substitutes), then the net deadweight loss is zero. (However, the dead-

FIGURE 3.1

Welfare Loss from Tariff on Imported Cars: Pure Competition in Domestic Production

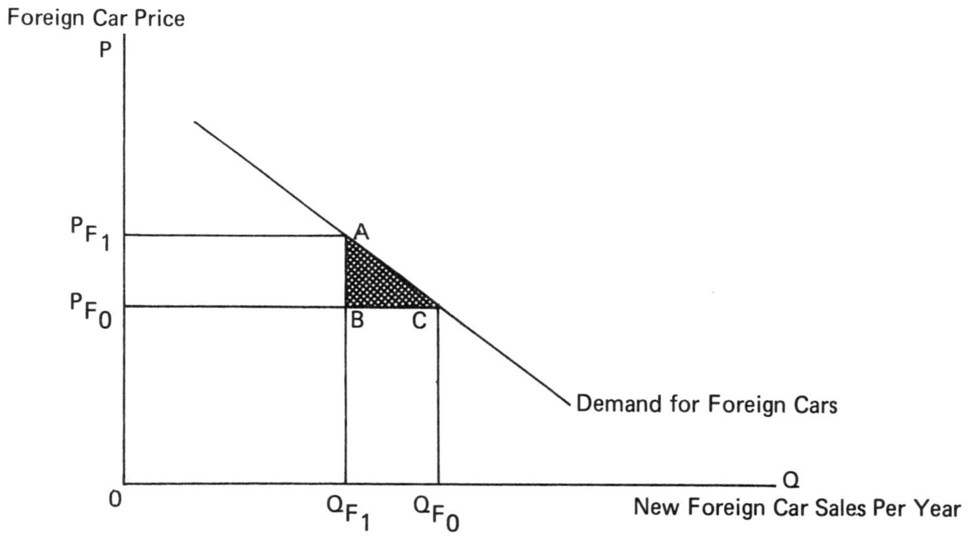

Shaded area ABC is deadweight loss from tariff.

Source: Computed from raw data in *Automotive News Almanac*, various issues.

weight loss is positive if foreign cars are perfect substitutes for domestic cars and would be cheaper without trade barriers. Under such circumstances, the deadweight loss can be computed from the area under the demand curve for all automobiles between the foreign supply price and the domestic supply price.)

A flatter slope implies a greater elasticity of demand in absolute terms for foreign cars at the point Q_{F_0}. For small tariff changes, the greater the elasticity of demand, the bigger will be the deadweight loss from a tariff. The reverse is true for quotas; for any given quota, the deadweight loss will be greater for inelastic demand curves for foreign cars. (We can also see this relationship from observation of Figure 3.1. If a quota limits foreign-car sales to Q_{F_1}, the area ABC will be greater, the steeper the demand curve; for steeper demand curves, the point A is higher along the line $Q_{F_1}A$.)

If domestic-car price is a function of foreign-car price, the measurement of welfare loss is somewhat more complicated. Still, the deadweight loss from a tariff is greater if the elasticity of substitution between foreign and domestic cars is greater. With high substitutability, foreign cars play an important role in constraining domestic-car prices; thus an upward shift in the foreign curve caused by a tariff has a relatively larger effect on the domestic price than in the case where domestic and foreign cars are not good substitutes.

The loss from labor adjustment costs from lower tariffs depends on $\partial Q_D/\partial Q_F$, the change in domestic sales resulting from a given change in foreign-car prices. The bigger $\partial Q_D/\partial Q_F$, the bigger is the employment gain (loss) from higher (lower) imported-car prices.

In the econometric work reported in this chapter, we estimate a market share equation of the form:

$$\log(F/D) = A_0 + A_1 \log(P_F/P_D) + A_2 \log X \qquad (3.3)$$

where:

F/D = the ratio of foreign-to-domestic new-car sales,
P_F/P_D = the relative price ratio of foreign-to-domestic autos,
X = a vector of exogenous variables affecting automobile demand, and
A_0, A_1, and A_2 are constants.

The form of the equation assumes that the change in the share of foreign-car sales depends only on the change in the ratio of domestic-to-foreign car prices; it is unaffected by whether the ratio changes because foreign-car prices are rising or because domestic-car prices are falling. We estimate changes in the total market demand for foreign and domestic cars when tariffs change by combining our estimates of share elasticities with estimates of the total market

elasticity of demand for automobiles with respect to a change in the average price of new cars, as derived in numerous previous studies of the demand for automobiles (The findings of these studies are briefly reviewed in the next section.)

We can write Equations 3.1 and 3.2 in constant elasticity form as follows:

$$\log F = b \log P_F + c \log P_D \tag{3.4}$$

$$\log D = g \log P_F + h \log P_D \tag{3.5}$$

where:
- b = the own price-elasticity of foreign-car demand,
- c = the cross price-elasticity of foreign-car demand,
- g = the cross price-elasticity of domestic-car demand,
- h = the own price-elasticity of domestic-car demand,
- b and h are expected to be negative, and
- c and g are expected to be positive.

The welfare loss to consumers from tariffs depends on the value of b; the employment gain (loss) depends on the value of g. The elasticity of foreign to domestic sales with respect to the foreign and domestic price ratio, which we label A_1 in Equation 3.3, is equal to $(b - g)$ and also is equal to $(h - c)$. The log of the ratio of foreign-to-domestic sales in Equations 3.4 and 3.5 is ($\log F - \log D$). The relative price of foreign cars can increase by one percent either by a 1 percent increase in P_F, or by a 0.99 percent decrease in P_D*. The increase in ($\log F - \log D$) with respect to a unit increase in $\log P_F$ is $(b - g)$; the unit increase in ($\log F - \log D$) with respect to a one-unit decrease in $\log P_D$ is $(h - c)$. Thus, the elasticity of F/D with respect to P_F/P_D is equal to $(b - g) = (h - c)$.

It can also be shown that the absolute value of b, the elasticity of foreign-car demand with respect to foreign-car price, is directly proportional to the absolute value of g, the elasticity of domestic-car demand with respect to foreign-car price, in the neighborhood of any initial level of domestic and foreign sales, D and F, for a given value of the total market elasticity of demand for automobiles.

Let $T = F + D$ represent total sales of automobiles.
Then,

---

*For infinitesimal changes, a given percentage change in (P_F/P_D) is equal to the same percentage increase (reduction) in $P_F (P_D)$.

$$\frac{\partial T}{\partial P_F} = \frac{\partial F}{\partial P_F} + \frac{\partial D}{\partial P_F}. \quad (3.6)$$

Since

$$b = \frac{P_F}{F} \times \frac{\partial F}{\partial P_F} \text{ and } g = \frac{P_F}{D} \times \frac{\partial D}{\partial P_F}$$

we can write Equation 3.6 as

$$\frac{\partial T}{\partial P_F} = \left(\frac{F}{P_F} \times b\right) + \left(\frac{D}{P_F} \times g\right). \quad (3.7)$$

Multiplying both sides of Equation 3.7 by $\frac{P_F}{T}$, we obtain

$$\epsilon_{TP_F} = \frac{P_F}{T} \frac{\partial T}{\partial P_F} = \left(\frac{F}{T} \times b\right) + \left(\frac{D}{T} \times g\right) \quad (3.8)$$

where ϵ_{TP_F} is the elasticity of total sales with respect to foreign-car price. We can write ϵ_{TP_F} as

$$\epsilon_{TP_F} = \epsilon_{T,P} \times \epsilon_{P,P_F} = \epsilon_{T,P} \times \frac{F}{T} \quad (3.9)$$

where

$\epsilon_{T,P}$ = the elasticity of total sales with respect to average car price, and
$\epsilon_{P,PF} = \frac{F}{T}$ = the elasticity of average price with respect to foreign-car price.

Substituting Equation 3.9 into Equation 3.8, we obtain

$$\frac{F}{T} \epsilon_{TP} = b \frac{F}{T} + g \frac{D}{T}$$

or, rearranging terms,

$$b = \epsilon_{TP} - \left(\frac{D}{F} \times g\right). \quad (3.10)$$

Since b is negative and g is positive, Equation 3.10 shows that the absolute value of b is directly proportional to the absolute value of g. If we know both $(b - g)$ and ϵ_{TP}, we can use Equation 3.10 to compute the implied values of b and g.

The relationship between b and g indicates that, for higher estimates of the elasticity of relative sales with respect to relative price, both the increase (reduction) in the deadweight loss from higher (lower) tariffs, and the domestic

auto industry employment increase (decrease) from higher (lower) tariffs, will rise (with the exception, noted above, that the net welfare loss from a tariff that reduces imports to zero is lower for greater demand elasticities).

If we convert b and g into estimated average slopes by multiplying them by the ratios (F/P_F) and (D/P_F), respectively, taken at the means of the observations, then both the consumer surplus change and the employment change are directly proportional to g.*

Thus, in general, a finding of higher price elasticities of substitution will imply bigger total welfare changes from changes in tariffs. However, the magnitude of the elasticity estimate may not greatly affect the sign of the net welfare change. For the introduction of any given quota below current import consumption, the employment effect will be the same for any demand elasticity; the deadweight loss from the quota will be greater for less elastic demand.

These conclusions do not imply that the choice between quota or tariff policies should depend on the elasticity of demand. For any estimated demand elasticity, there exists a quota level equivalent, in effect, to any given tariff. For higher demand elasticities, the quota equivalent to a given tariff will be smaller.

The welfare change depends on the timing as well as the final magnitude of consumer buying changes in response to price changes. If the change in share slowly approaches an equilibrium level, both the present value of the deadweight loss and the labor adjustment effects will be smaller than if adjustment is instantaneous. Simulations of net welfare changes using alternative plausible estimates of a simple lag structure are presented in Chapter 8.

ESTIMATING IMPORT DEMAND: PREVIOUS RESEARCH AND ALTERNATIVE APPROACHES

Most previous research on automobile demand has focused on estimation of equations for total sales, which do not distinguish among types of car purchased. While the literature on total demand for automobiles is extensive, only a few previous studies have attempted to model changes in market shares by type of car sold.

The work on total automobile demand has estimated the effect of changes in income, a price index series, a variable for credit conditions, and a lagged

---

*The area of the welfare triangle in Figure 3.1 is equal to $(½)\Delta P_F \Delta Q_F$, which equals $(½)\Delta Q_F/\Delta P_F \times (\Delta P_F)^2$. While the employment loss is proportional to g, the welfare loss from an employment reduction may be more than proportional to g if the duration of unemployment rises when more workers are laid off within a given geographic region in a short time.

sales or stock variable on total new automobiles purchased.[1] These studies have generally estimated price elasticities in the neighborhood of -1 and income elasticities ranging from 1.5 to 4. The time series studies have been facilitated by the existence of long data series on new-car purchases in the United States dating back to the 1920s. While the appropriate way of computing an automobile price index from existing information has been a subject of continued dispute, the price elasticities estimated in econometric studies of aggregate new-car demand have been fairly consistent, even though different methods of constructing a new-car price index were used.[2]

Previous research on estimating the market share of different automobile manufacturers and/or car types has been much less extensive than the research on total automobile demand, and, in general, it has been less successful in obtaining statistical estimates of price effects that are consistent with economic theory. Cowling and Cubbin estimated a negative relationship between market shares and quality adjusted prices using time series data from England for 1956-68.[3] Cowling and Cubbin estimated firm sales as a function of lagged sales, quality adjusted price, and advertising expenditures; their findings implied a short-run price elasticity of individual manufacturers' demand of -1.9497, and a long-run price elasticity of -7.06. On the other hand, Triplett and Cowling, applying similar methods to U.S. data, were unable to detect a negative relationship between changes in individual manufacturers' market shares over time and changes in the residuals from hedonic price regressions of those manufacturers' models.[4] We are aware of only one study that specifically estimates U.S. demand for imports, an unpublished paper by McMenamin, Pinard, and Russell.[5] While this paper obtains negative coefficients for demand elasticities for imports, the results are suspect, in our view, for several important reasons.*

---

*The authors used quarterly data on automobile imports and prices. No correction was made for quality changes, and it is not clear whether appropriate changes were made for the mix of models sold. The authors used unit value export price indexes at the lowest level of aggregation; it is not clear whether the aggregation within the "motor vehicle sector" is at the level of four-digit industries—that is, automobiles and trucks—or at the individual-make level. For example, if Volkswagen sales fluctuated while Mercedes sales remained stable, the study might detect a downward-sloping demand curve for imports from Germany because the average price of a German export is falling as VW sales increase; the authors do not report whether the index is constructed for fixed weights of VW and Mercedes sales. The authors report a small, finite, negative price elasticity for Canadian imports without comment, even though Canadian imports are in fact cars made by the same manufacturers as U.S. cars and are not notably different in characteristics. If U.S. manufacturers decide to locate production of relatively cheaper and more popular models in Canada, average price will fall and Canadian imports will rise, but this indicates nothing about the likely effect of a tariff on imports from Canada.

There are three alternative methods we have used to estimate price elasticity of demand for imported cars; the third approach is a new method CRA has developed. The first two approaches rely on correlating differences in the mix of domestic and imported automobiles purchased with differences in import prices relative to domestic prices; the third uses the distribution of current purchases of individual automobile models to infer a distribution function of consumer tastes for automobile characteristics; this estimated taste distribution is then used to forecast shares of the same models when relative prices of different models change.

The two traditional approaches are time series analysis and cross-section analysis. Each has benefits and drawbacks as an estimation method using currently available data.

For the time series analysis, we lacked published data giving separate price indexes for foreign and domestic cars. We created such price indexes using regressions for adjacent years of prices of individual models, both foreign and domestic, on physical characteristics and a time dummy. We used one-year-old transaction prices from past issues of the automobile *Red Book*, published by National Market Reports, Inc., as a proxy for actual new-car prices, rejecting the alternative of using new-car list prices as a proxy variable. Previous researchers have shown that the relationship between transactions prices and list prices of new cars has varied widely over time; in addition, relative discounts on foreign and domestic models have not been constant over time.[6] Unfortunately, one-year-old transactions prices are not an ideal proxy for new-car prices either; the ratio between new-car transactions prices and one-year-old transactions prices will change if the market is in disequilibrium. Despite these problems, our estimated price index for domestic cars mirrors closely the Bureau of Labor Statistics (BLS) index of new-car prices since 1960.

The other difficulty with the time series approach is that fluctuations in the quality adjusted ratio of domestic to foreign-car prices have been small relative to other changes in the market that have influenced import shares. Some of these other changes are not easily quantified. They include changes in the availability of close domestic substitutes for imports; the growth in imported-car dealer networks with its consequent spread of information and reduction of servicing costs; changes in the available variety and quality of foreign models, especially since the introduction of Japanese cars in the late 1960s; and changes in environmental and safety regulations, which have impacted new-car purchase prices and fuel costs.

Despite problems of model specification and data construction, we have found strong evidence of a significant price effect on import shares. Our estimated time series equations, and their interpretation, are presented in the next section.

The cross-section method of estimating import share demand relies on those differences in import and domestic car prices across states that can be

inferred from data on freight charges. Freight on imports is lowest on the two coasts and highest in the midwest; freight on domestic cars is lowest in the midwest (near Detroit) and highest on the coasts. Also gasoline prices vary across states because of differences in the gasoline tax. The problem with the cross-section data is that we do not have actual relative prices, nor do we know the extent to which differences in availability of service affect differences in ownership costs. Where import shares are small, ownership costs may vary inversely with the size of the share.

The cross-section results yield evidence of a very high price elasticity of substitution between domestic and imported automobiles. Our estimated cross-section equations and their interpretation are presented in the section beginning on page 65.

The third approach, which we will call the CRA hedonic market share model, uses data on prices, characteristics, and sales of different automobiles in a given year. A function is estimated describing the distribution of consumer tastes for characteristics implied by revealed purchases. This consumer taste distribution function can then be used to forecast the market shares of each automobile if prices and/or characteristics of some of the models offered by manufacturers change. As an example, a tariff increase will raise the price of imported automobiles; only consumers with a relatively greater preference for the characteristics offered by inputs will continue to purchase them. Estimates derived by using the hedonic market share model are presented in the section beginning on page 71.

A fourth possible approach, not pursued in this study, is to conduct a survey questionnaire that asks actual or prospective automobile purchasers how they would respond to changes in relative automobile prices. The questionnaire approach was used by Market Facts, Inc. in a recent study of imported-car purchases performed under contract to the U.S. Department of Labor.[7] We show in the section beginning on page 71 that the findings from applying CRA's hedonic market share model are very close to the results implied by the survey responses reported by Market Facts.

ECONOMETRIC ESTIMATES OF IMPORT SHARE DEMAND FROM TIME SERIES DATA

In this section, we present econometric evidence from time series data showing that the share of new-car sales accounted for by imports is very sensitive to the relative price of foreign and domestic cars. Although our long-run price elasticity estimates are quite sensitive to changes in specification, the short-run one-year estimates are closely clustered between –1.5 and –2, indicating that a 1 percent increase in the ratio of imported-to-domestic prices would lead to slightly less than a 2 percent reduction in the ratio of imported-to-domestic

new-car sales. The short-run price elasticity estimates, and the lower bound of the long-run price elasticity estimates, are very close to the estimates derived from the CRA hedonic market share model shown in the next section.

The wide range in the long-run price elasticities presented below can be explained by the fact that price changes have not been the principal determinant of changes in the share of imported cars sold in the United States in the past 15 years. It has not been possible to quantify precisely the contribution of all of the other relevant variables. In particular, the coefficient of lagged share in the estimated equations, which determines the relationship between the implied short-run and long-run price elasticities, is very unstable, varying with which other exogenous variables are included in the equation to explain the upward trend of foreign-car sales.

In our equations, we use the ratio of foreign-to-domestic new-car sales as the dependent variable. The independent variables used in different specifications include a relative price index of foreign-to-domestic cars compiled from sales price, fuel economy and gasoline price data, personal income per capita, personal income per capita relative to per capita income in the previous year, unemployment, the price of gasoline, a time trend variable, the number of years since the introduction of Japanese cars, and the ratio of foreign-to-domestic new-car sales in the previous year. We also tried a number of alternative measures of the availability and competitiveness of imported cars, including the relative number of imported makes available, the ratio of number of imported-car to domestic-car dealers, and a measure of the relative market coverage of imported to domestic autos, which all proved to be uncorrelated with import new-car sales. Descriptions of the construction of these additional variables, and a full review of equation specifications not reported in this section, are provided in Appendix 3.C.

Construction of Price Indexes

We constructed price indexes of domestic and foreign prices by using hedonic regression analysis (While the Bureau of Labor Statistics and a number of independent researchers have compiled indexes of new-car prices in the United States in recent years, we were unable to find any source that had compiled separate price indexes for domestic and foreign automobiles.) We estimated a series of regressions for adjacent years of the form

$$\log P = a_0 + \sum_{i=1}^{n} a_i C_i + bY \qquad (3.11)$$

where:
P = price of an auto of vintage $(t-1)$ in year t, and
C_i = physical characteristics of the auto, and

Y = dummy for most recent year, which is equal to 0 in year t and 1 in year $(t+1)$.

The coefficient of Y thus represents the percentage change in price of a one-year-old automobile between years t and $(t + 1)$, after correcting for changes in physical characteristics. Estimating a set of these adjacent-year regressions, we compile a chain index from annual percentage changes in price of models of vintages 1959 through 1973 in the years 1960 through 1974.[8] We performed separate sets of regressions for domestic and foreign cars.

The price data used are retail prices for one-year-old cars from National Market Reports Inc.'s *Red Book: Region A*. We did not use list prices because we believe that changes in list prices are a poor indicator of changes in transactions prices actually paid by consumers. Discounting practices have not been constant over time or across types of automobiles. Data on new-car transactions prices were not available. While movements in one-year-old transactions prices may be a better indicator of movements in new-car transactions prices than movements in new-car list prices, they are not a perfect measure. Problems are caused if the ratio of new-car to one-year-old prices changes over time, which may occur either if there is a change in the demand for new cars relative to used cars, even recent ones, causing the equilibrium price gradient to become flatter or steeper,* or if the market is in temporary disequilibrium. The latter may occur if there is a sharp rise in demand for foreign cars that is not immediately reflected in an increase in new-car prices; then, a temporary shortage in the supply of foreign cars may cause the one-year-old price to be bid up early in the model year, above its equilibrium level relative to the supply price of new cars. (In effect, we are describing a simple example of the identification problem. The rise in the one-year-old price reflects an upward shift in demand, rather than an increase in the cost of production. To correct for this, we adjusted our price indexes for relative changes in foreign-to-domestic prices that occurred during the model year. The exact methods used are described in Appendix 3.A.)

For characteristics data, we used information on physical dimensions supplied in successive issues of *Automotive News Almanac* for domestic and foreign models. Characteristics used in the hedonic regression include weight, headroom, length, horsepower, brake area, turning circle, and dummy variables for hard-top, automatic transmission, power steering, power brakes, and

---

*For example, this could happen if rising incomes led to an increase in the percentage of people wishing to drive newer vintage cars, perhaps because of higher personal preferences for reliability and higher time costs, at given prices. This would reduce the price of used cars relative to new cars. The same thing would happen if repair costs increased relative to new car production costs.

RELATIVE PRICES AND DEMAND 49

station wagons. The use of physical dimensions data can be justified if performance is a reasonably stable function of physical dimensions. This may not always be true; for example, although weight in any year is generally positively correlated with quality of ride and luxuriousness of an auto, technology changes may in some years have reduced the weight for given values of performance dimensions.[9]

The models used in compiling the indexes are domestic and foreign models for which one-year-old prices were available in the spring issue of the *Red Book* and for which characteristics data were available from annual issues of *Automotive News Almanac*. Where different body types and engine types of a given model were listed, we chose the body and engine types for which we believed sales were greatest.[10]

Table 3.1 shows the chain indexes for foreign and domestic car prices we developed from the hedonic regressions. The base year is 1960 = 100 for domestic cars. For 1959-60 models in 1960-61, we estimated another regression including both foreign and domestic cars and a foreign-car dummy; we estimated in that year that imports were 9.9 percent more expensive than domestic autos with the same characteristics. We then developed separate chain indexes of foreign and domestic prices from the base year 1960 using adjacent year regressions as described above. The adjusted foreign-to-domestic price ratio in column 4 is computed by taking the ratio of column 3 to column 2. Column 5, the actual foreign-to-domestic price ratio, is computed as the ratio of simple sales weighted averages of foreign and domestic prices in each year. Column 5 is not a price index; the average price of foreign cars may rise, for example, if the mix of imported cars bought shifts to relatively more expensive models. Column 5 does show, however, that imports are no longer at the cheaper end of the spectrum to the extent that they were 15 years ago, although the average domestic model is still more expensive.

The quality adjusted ratio of import prices to domestic prices (Column 4) fell about 12 percent between 1960 and 1961, reached a trough at 0.93 in 1964, and then after a sharp rise to 1.098 in 1965, fell again to 0.90 in 1967. After 1967, the import price ratio increased steadily to 1.119 by 1971, dropped to 1.00 by 1973, and then jumped over 20 percentage points to 1.217 by 1974. (Changes in prices of one-year-old imports do not correspond exactly to movements in new-car list prices in recent years. List prices of imports began rising between the 1972 and 1973 model years, reflecting the dollar devaluation of late 1971; however, used-car transactions prices did not rise to reflect the effects of the devaluation until after 1973.) The sharp rise in import prices after 1973 coincided with the jump in the price of gasoline and the fears of fuel shortage that accompanied the 1973-74 oil embargo.

Figure 3.2 depicts the movement of quality adjusted import and domestic prices of autos between 1960 and 1974 computed from our hedonic regression

TABLE 3.1

Domestic and Imported Car Price Indexes
(1960 domestic = 100.0)

(col. 1) Year	(col. 2) Domestic Price Index Deflated by CPI for All Goods	(col. 3) Import Price Index Deflated by CPI for All Goods	(col. 4) Import-to-Domestic Price Ratio	(col. 5) Unadjusted Ratio of Average Import Price to Average Domestic Price
1960	100.0	109.9	1.099	0.6888
1961	84.8	82.3	0.971	0.6836
1962	93.6	94.8	1.011	0.6713
1963	91.9	92.0	1.001	0.6795
1964	93.6	87.0	0.930	0.6332
1965	85.9	94.3	1.098	0.7358
1966	85.7	81.7	0.953	0.6196
1967	84.7	76.4	0.902	0.6524
1968	82.8	79.7	0.963	0.7152
1969	78.5	79.6	1.013	0.7738
1970	63.0	64.1	1.018	0.7105
1971	68.0	76.1	1.119	0.8202
1972	69.5	73.3	1.054	0.7622
1973	66.7	66.7	1.000	0.7850
1974	78.0	94.9	1.217	0.8665

Source: CRA hedonic regressions.

equations. In general, big swings in import and domestic prices have coincided, but the relative movements of the two have differed. Import prices fell relatively more quickly than domestic prices between 1960 and 1961. Both import and domestic prices declined in the middle 1960s, but the timing differed; import prices were relatively lower than domestic prices between 1966 and 1968. Both import and domestic prices rose between 1973 and 1974; however, the increase in import prices was much sharper.

Real gasoline prices (adjusted for Consumer Price Index, CPI) declined throughout almost the entire period, reaching a low point of 85.9 in 1972 (1967 = 100.0). The gas price index then rose to 88.7 in 1973 and jumped to 108.3 in 1974, a high for the entire sample period. The increase in gasoline prices may have encouraged a shift to imports after 1973.

FIGURE 3.2

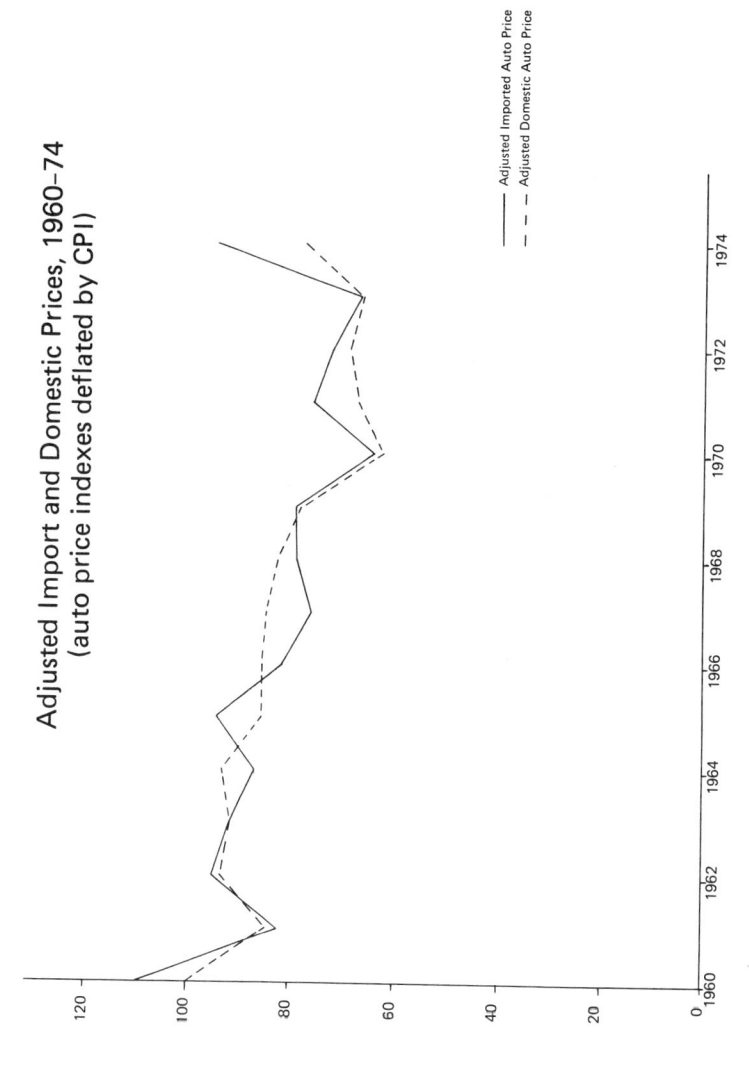

Adjusted Import and Domestic Prices, 1960–74
(auto price indexes deflated by CPI)

——— Adjusted Imported Auto Price
– – – Adjusted Domestic Auto Price

Source: Table 3.1, Columns 2 and 3.

TABLE 3.2

Comparison of Imported-to-Domestic Car Relative Price and Total Cost Indexes

(Col. 1) Year	(Col. 2) Import-to-Domestic Price Ratio	(Col. 3) Import-to-Domestic Gas Cost Ratio	(Col. 4) Import-to-Domestic Total Cost Ratio
1960	1.099	0.608	0.985
1961	0.971	0.473	0.853
1962	1.011	0.535	0.907
1963	1.001	0.517	0.881
1964	0.930	0.566	0.851
1965	1.098	0.517	0.949
1966	0.953	0.589	0.860
1967	0.902	0.535	0.807
1968	0.963	0.622	0.874
1969	1.013	0.536	0.885
1970	1.018	0.513	0.865
1971	1.119	0.518	0.947
1972	1.054	0.483	0.890
1973	1.000	0.454	0.832
1974	1.217	0.542	0.981

Computed from separate indexes of domestic and import prices, gasoline price, and domestic and import mileage. For explanation of details of computation, see Appendix 3.B.

Sources: Import-to-Domestic Price Ratio from Table 3.1. Import-to-Domestic Gas Cost Ratio computed from gasoline price data supplied by U.S. Bureau of Labor Statistics and from mileage estimates reported in Thomas C. Austin and Karl H. Hellman, "Passenger Car Fuel Economy: Trends and Influencing Factors," paper presented to National Combined Farm Construction and Industrial Machinery and Fuels and Lubricants Meetings, Milwaukee, September 10–13, 1973. Import-to-Domestic Total Cost Ratio computed as ratio of imported and domestic total costs, which are computed as weighted averages, respectively, of the imported and domestic price and gas cost indexes.

We computed first-year total cost indexes for domestic and foreign automobiles by combining the price indexes with indexes of annual gasoline costs for domestic and foreign automobiles, using weights of .65 for selling price and .35 for annual gasoline costs in 1974. In deriving the weights, we assumed a 20 percent depreciation rate in the first year, a 5 percent interest rate, a gasoline price of $.55 per gallon, and average annual miles driven of 10,000 miles. The gasoline cost index was computed to be the ratio of the gasoline price divided by a mileage index. The mileage indexes were computed from historical estimates of mileage for automobiles of different weight classes provided in a paper by two

EPA researchers.[11] For imported cars, we used mileage for autos weighing 2,000 pounds, while for domestic cars we used mileage for autos weighing 4,000 pounds.

Table 3.2 compares the relative price index of domestic and foreign cars with the relative total cost index. Column (2) of Table 3.2 shows the relative price index from Table 3.1. Column (3) shows the relative gas cost index, while column (4) shows the combined relative total cost index. The imported to domestic gas cost index is approximately .5 for most years because imported cars have far superior fuel economy to domestic cars. The relative importance of the gasoline cost index as a component of total cost increased considerably between 1973 and 1974 because of the rise in the price of gasoline. Thus, although the import-to-domestic price ratio increased by 21.7 percent between 1973 and 1974, and the import-to-domestic gas cost ratio increased by 19.3 percent, the total cost ratio rose by only 17.9 percent because the superior fuel efficiency of imports became a more important component of the relative cost comparison.

Figure 3.3 compares the trends in the relative price index and the relative cost index between 1960 and 1974. It can be seen that the two indexes practically mirror each other, with the relative total cost index lower because of the superior fuel efficiency of foreign cars. The relative price of foreign cars rose faster than the relative total cost of imported cars between 1973 and 1974, the year of the big gasoline price increase.

Regression Results

Tables 3.3 and 3.4 present the results of some specifications of the time series regression. (In addition to the equations reported here, we also tried some two-stage least-squares estimates, using rough data on relative unit labor cost changes in Germany, Japan, and the United States as an instrument for the price variable. The "estimated price" variable performed poorly in all regressions.) In Table 3.3, the regressions shown use data for the years 1961-74, while the regressions in Table 3.4 exclude 1974 from the sample. (Because 1974 was a very unusual year, involving large increases in both the gasoline price and the imported-car price, several months of a serious gasoline shortage, and shortage of imported and small domestic new cars, it was thought that eliminating 1974 from the sample might alter the regression results. While some parameters did change significantly between the two sets of equations, the results for 1961-73 are for the most part qualitatively similar to the results for 1961-74. The dependent variable in all equations is the ratio of foreign-to-domestic new-car sales in a given calendar year; the corresponding price ratio variable is an estimate of midyear prices of one-year-old cars, which we use as a proxy for new-car transactions prices. Where the total cost index is used in place of the price index in an equation, the price used to compute total cost is based on the same

FIGURE 3.3

Comparison of Relative Price Index and Relative Total Cost Index

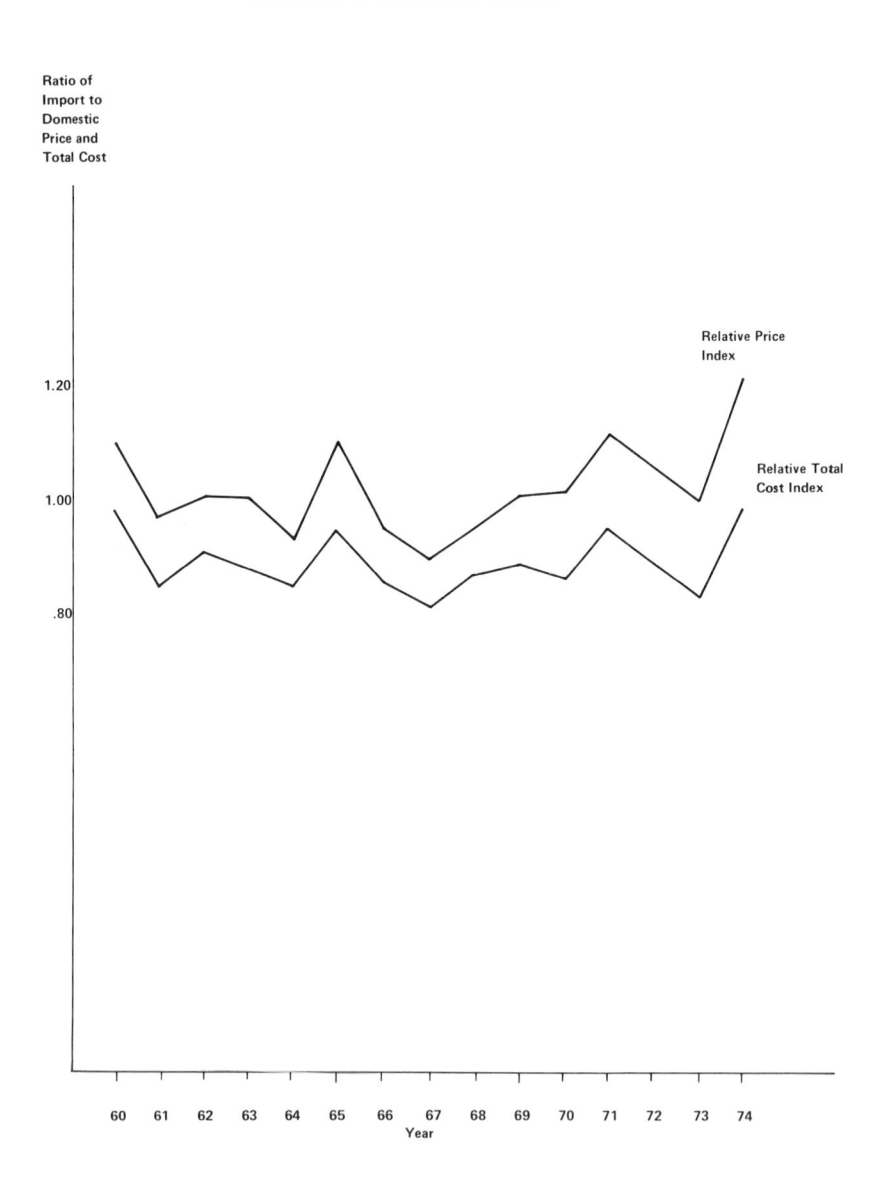

Source: Table 3.2, columns 2 and 4.

TABLE 3.3

Time Series Regression Results: Alternative Specifications, 1961–74

Equation (3.3.1)

LOG (FDSALE) = 0.00140 + 0.917 LOG (FDSALE$_{-1}$)
 (0.012)   (10.078)

 −1.515 LOG (FDPRICE) + 0.882 LOG (INCOME)
 (3.405)   (3.450)

 R^2 = .9509 ρ = −.130   *OBS:* 1961–74

 S.E.E. = *.1323*

Equation (3.3.2)

LOG (FDSALE) = −0.0278 + 0.821 LOG (FDSALE$_{-1}$)
 (0.222)   (4.693)

 −1.298 LOG (FDPRICE) + 0.978 LOG (INCOME) − 0.427 LOG (GPRICE)
 (2.234)   (3.303)   (0.643)

 R^2 = .9546 ρ = −0.150   *OBS:* 1961–74

 S.E.E. = *.1365*

Equation (3.3.3)

LOG (FDSALE) = 0.202 + 0.347 LOG (FDSALE$_{-1}$)
 (1.518) (1.349)

 −1.166 LOG (FDPRICE) + 0.423 LOG (INCOME) + 0.107 JAPAN
 (2.968)   (1.539)   (2.383)

 R^2 = .9615 ρ = 0.030   *OBS:* 1961–74

 S.E.E. = *.1108*

Equation (3.3.4)

LOG (FDSALE) = 0.320 + 0.281 LOG (FDSALE$_{-1}$)
 (2.414) (1.129)

(continued)

(Table 3.3, continued)

$$-1.211 \text{ LOG (FDPRICE)} + 0.148 \text{ JAPAN} + 0.673 \text{ LOG (GPRICE)}$$
$$(2.362) \qquad\qquad (4.059) \qquad (1.245)$$

$$R^2 = .9571 \qquad \rho = 0.100 \qquad OBS: 1961\text{-}74$$

$$S.E.E. = .1139$$

Equation (3.3.5)

$$\text{LOG (FDSALE)} = 0.247 + 0.358 \text{ LOG (FDSALE}_{-1})$$
$$(1.503) \ (1.331)$$

$$-1.328 \text{ LOG (FDPRICE)} + 0.119 \text{ JAPAN}$$
$$(2.512) \qquad\qquad (2.296)$$

$$+ 0.309 \text{ LOG (INCOME)} + 0.345 \text{ LOG (GPRICE)}$$
$$\ (0.867) \qquad\qquad\quad (0.512)$$

$$R^2 = .9622 \qquad \rho = 0.044 \qquad OBS: 1961\text{-}74$$

$$S.E.E. = .1156$$

Equation (3.3.6)

$$\text{LOG (FDSALE)} = 0.0282 + 0.875 \text{ LOG (FDSALE}_{-1})$$
$$(0.227) \ (8.055)$$

$$-1.754 \text{ LOG (FDPRICE)} + 1.017 \text{ LOG (INCOME)} - 2.404 \text{ LOG (RELINC)}$$
$$(3.252) \qquad\qquad\quad (3.282) \qquad\qquad\quad (1.149)$$

$$R^2 = .9468 \qquad \rho = 0.016 \qquad OBS: 1961\text{-}74$$

$$S.E.E. = .1318$$

Equation (3.3.7)

$$\text{LOG (FDSALE)} = 0.0638 + 0.814 \text{ LOG (FDSALE}_{-1})$$
$$(0.604) \ (8.506)$$

$$-1.895 \text{ LOG (FDCOST)} + 1.036 \text{ LOG (INCOME)}$$
$$(3.967) \qquad\qquad\quad (4.010)$$

(continued)

(Table 3.3, continued)

$R^2 = .9576$ $\rho = -0.100$ *OBS:* 1961-74

S.E.E. $= .1198$

Equation (3.3.8)

LOG (FDSALE) = 0.223 + 0.342 LOG (FDSALE $_{-1}$)
             (1.799) (1.417)

-1.454 LOG (FDCOST) + 0.571 LOG (INCOME) + 0.0939 JAPAN
(3.262)   (1.947)   (2.175)

$R^2 = .9646$ $\rho = 0.068$ *OBS:* 1961-74

S.E.E. $= .1046$

Equation (3.3.9)

LOG (FDSALE) = 0.108 + 0.742 LOG (FDSALE $_{-1}$)
             (0.977) (6.773)

-2.279 LOG (FDCOST) + 1.242 LOG (INCOME) -2.894 LOG (RELINC)
(4.177)   (4.205)   (1.620)

$R^2 = .9592$ $\rho = 0.047$ *OBS:* 1961-74

S.E.E. $= .1131$

(t-statistics are in parenthesis in all equations.)

Variable Definitions (and Sources): FDSALE = ratio of foreign-to-domestic new-car sales (*Automotive News Almanac*, successive issues). FDSALE-1 = ratio of foreign-to-domestic new-car sales in previous year. FDPRICE = ratio of import price index to domestic price index (CRA hedonic regressions, Table 3.1). FDCOST = ratio of import total cost index to domestic total cost index (Table 3.2). INCOME = real per capita disposable personal income (*U.S., Economic Report of the President*, 1975). GPRICE = real price index of gasoline (from unpublished data provided by Consumer Price Indexes Branch of the U.S. Bureau of Labor Statistics). JAPAN = trend variable for number of years since mass entry of Japanese imports; before 1965 = 1, after 1966 = year $-1965 + 1$. RELINC = ratio of per capita disposable income to per capita disposable income of previous year. ρ = serial correlation coefficient.

TABLE 3.4

Time Series Regression Results: Alternative Specifications, 1961-73

Equation (3.4.1)

LOG (FDSALE) = 0.206 + 0.888 LOG (FDSALE$_{-1}$)
 (1.526) (10.788)

−2.001 LOG (FDPRICE) + 1.135 LOG (INCOME)
(4.458)   (4.497)

R^2 = .9590 ρ = −0.050   *OBS:* 1961-73

S.E.E. = *.1114*

Equation (3.4.2)

LOG (FDSALE) = 0.230 + 0.597 LOG (FDSALE$_{-1}$)
 (2.230) (4.947)

−1.580 LOG (FDPRICE) + 1.534 LOG (INCOME) −1.260 LOG (GPRICE)
(4.373)   (6.661)   (2.750)

R^2 = .9841 ρ = −0.240   *OBS:* 1961-73

S.E.E. = *.0879*

Equation (3.4.3)

LOG (FDSALE) = 0.292 + 0.503 LOG (FDSALE$_{-1}$)
 (2.153) (1.980)

−1.692 LOG (FDPRICE) + 0.788 LOG (INCOME) + 0.0734 JAPAN
(3.724)   (2.473)   (1.589)

R^2 = .9709 ρ = −0.100   *OBS:* 1961-73

S.E.E. = *.1034*

Equation (3.4.4)

LOG (FDSALE) = 0.311 + 0.284 LOG (FDSALE$_{-1}$)
 (1.979) (1.072)

(continued)

(Table 3.4 continued)

$$-1.218 \text{ LOG (FDPRICE)} + 0.148 \text{ JAPAN} + 0.682 \text{ LOG (GPRICE)}$$
$$(2.232) \qquad\qquad (3.834) \qquad\quad (1.182)$$

$R^2 = .9512 \qquad \rho = 0.100 \qquad OBS:\ 1961\text{-}73$
$$S.E.E. = .1206$$

Equation (3.4.5)

$$\text{LOG (FDSALE)} = 0.176 + 0.731 \text{ LOG (FDSALE}_{-1})$$
$$\qquad\qquad\qquad\quad (1.282)\ (3.010)$$

$$-1.589 \text{ LOG (FDPRICE)} - 0.0462 \text{ JAPAN}$$
$$(4.258) \qquad\qquad\qquad (0.642)$$

$$+ 1.888 \text{ LOG (INCOME)} - 1.735 \text{ LOG (GPRICE)}$$
$$\ (3.150) \qquad\qquad\quad (1.979)$$

$R^2 = .9853 \qquad \rho = -0.250 \qquad OBS:\ 1961\text{-}73$
$$S.E.E. = .0915$$

Equation (3.4.6)

$$\text{LOG (FDSALE)} = 0.344 + 0.949 \text{ LOG (FDSALE}_{-1})$$
$$\qquad\qquad\qquad\quad (2.202)\ (11.863)$$

$$-1.912 \text{ LOG (FDPRICE)} + 1.066 \text{ LOG (INCOME)} + 4.181 \text{ LOG (RELINC)}$$
$$(4.685) \qquad\qquad\qquad (4.600) \qquad\qquad\qquad (1.491)$$

$R^2 = .9750 \qquad \rho = -0.220 \qquad OBS:\ 1961\text{-}73$
$$S.E.E. = .1077$$

Equation (3.4.7)

$$\text{LOG (FDSALE)} = 0.312 + 0.744 \text{ LOG (FDSALE}_{-1})$$
$$\qquad\qquad\qquad\quad (2.870)\ (9.949)$$

$$-2.573 \text{ LOG (FDCOST)} + 1.373 \text{ LOG (INCOME)}$$
$$(6.286) \qquad\qquad\qquad (6.327)$$

$R^2 = .9748 \qquad \rho = -0.0100 \qquad OBS:\ 1961\text{-}73$
$$S.E.E. = .0852$$

(continued)

(Table 3.4 continued)

Equation (3.4.8)

LOG (FDSALE) = 0.342 + 0.551 LOG (FDSALE $_{-1}$)
             (3.020) (2.561)

   -2.310 LOG (FDCOST) + 1.140 LOG (INCOME) + 0.0400 JAPAN
   (4.673)   (3.481)   (0.959)

   $R^2 = .9779$ $\rho = -0.030$ *OBS:* 1961-73

                   S.E.E. $= .0857$

Equation (3.4.9)

LOG (FDSALE) = 0.416 + 0.796 LOG (FDSALE $_{-1}$)
             (3.401) (10.636)

   -2.474 LOG (FDCOST) + 1.306 LOG (INCOME) + 3.234 LOG (RELINC)
   (6.434)   (6.343)   (1.467)

   $R^2 = .9833$ $\rho = -0.150$ *OBS:* 1961-73

                   S.E.E. $= .0818$

---

t-statistics are in parenthesis in all equations.
For variable definitions and sources, see Table 3.3.

estimate of midyear prices of one-year old cars, the fuel economy estimates are for model-year cars of the corresponding calendar year, and the gasoline price estimates are averages for the same year. The lagged sales ratio is included in all the equations; some of the specifications indicate that import shares in any year change very slowly from the share in the previous year.

The equations are estimated by generalized least squares to correct for serial correlation; the original value of ρ, the serial correlation coefficient, was selected by trial and error to minimize the standard error of the estimate.

The coefficient of FDPRICE, the ratio of import to domestic quality-adjusted prices, is the short-run elasticity of relative import demand with respect

to relative import price. The long-run elasticity can be computed by the following formula:

$$\text{L.R. elasticity} = \frac{(\text{S.R. elasticity})}{(1 - m)}$$

where:
m = the coefficient of LOG (FDSALE$_{-1}$) in Equations (3.3.1) to (3.3.9) and Equations (3.4.1) to (3.4.9).

The long-run elasticity gives the change in FDSALE in response to an initial change in FDPRICE in long-run equilibrium; this is large relative to the first-year change when the one-year lagged sales coefficient is high.*

Tables 3.5 and 3.6 give the implied short-run and long-run relative price elasticities computed from each of the estimated equations reported in Tables 3.3 and 3.4, respectively. From Table 3.5, we can see that the short-run price elasticity is fairly stable with respect to changes in specifications; it varies between -0.945 and -1.754. The estimated relative price elasticities are slightly higher when the 1974 observation is eliminated from the equation; Table 3.6 shows that they vary between -1.218 and -2.001. However, the long-run elasticity estimate is very sensitive to specification changes because of the instability of the coefficient of lagged relative sales; it ranges from a low of -1.436 to a high of -18.253 for the equations for the years 1961-74 and from a low of -1.701 to a high of -37.490 for the equations for the years 1961-73.

The lower relative price elasticities are reported in equations that include a time trend variable, JAPAN, for years after 1966. The time trend is strongly correlated with the lagged import-to-domestic sales ratio. Thus, the coefficient of the lagged sales ratio in the equations that *exclude* the time trend may be *biased upwards*, leading to an upward bias in the measure of the absolute size of the long-run relative price elasticity in those equations. (On the other hand, if a higher ratio of imported domestic sales causes the import-to-domestic price ratio to increase, by exerting pressure on domestic firms to keep prices down, there may be some upward bias to the coefficient of FDPRICE, or a downward

---

*Where FDCOST, the ratio of the import to domestic total cost index, is used in place of FDPRICE in an equation, the implied short-run elasticity with respect to price is equal to the product of the elasticity of relative sales with respect to relative price and the elasticity of relative cost with respect to relative price. As price is approximately 65 percent of total cost (see Appendix 3.B for the computation), a 1 percent increase in price is equal to about a .65 percent increase in total cost, when gasoline costs are constant.

TABLE 3.5

Implied Short-Run and Long-Run Relative Price Elasticities* from Time Series Regressions, 1961–74

Equation	Short-Run Elasticity	Long-Run Elasticity	Price Variable	Other Independent Variables
3.3.1	−1.515	−18.253	FDPRICE	INCOME
3.3.2	−1.298	−7.251	FDPRICE	INCOME, GPRICE
3.3.3	−1.166	−1.786	FDPRICE	INCOME, JAPAN
3.3.4	−1.211	−1.684	FDPRICE	JAPAN, GPRICE
3.3.5	−1.328	−2.069	FDPRICE	JAPAN, INCOME, GPRICE
3.3.6	−1.754	−14.032	FDPRICE	INCOME, RELINC
3.3.7	−1.232	−6.624	FDCOST†	INCOME
3.3.8	−0.945	−1.436	FDCOST†	INCOME, JAPAN
3.3.9	−1.481	−5.740	FDCOST†	INCOME, RELINC

$$\text{Long-Run Elasticity} = \frac{\text{Short-Run Elasticity}}{1 - \frac{\partial \text{LOG(FDSALE)}}{\partial \text{LOG(FDSALE)}_{-1}}}$$

*Elasticity of foreign-to-domestic sales ratio with respect to foreign-to-domestic price ratio.
†Where FDCOST was used as the price variable in an equation, the formula

$$\frac{d\text{LOG(FDSALE)}}{d\text{LOG(FDPRICE)}} = \frac{d\text{LOG(FDSALE)}}{d\text{LOG(FDCOST)}} \cdot \frac{d\text{LOG(FDCOST)}}{d\text{LOG(FDPRICE)}} \cong .65 \frac{d\text{LOG(FDSALE)}}{d\text{LOG(FDCOST)}}$$

was used to translate the relative total cost elasticity into an estimated elasticity with respect to relative sales price.
Source: CRA time-series regressions.

TABLE 3.6

Implied Short-Run and Long-Run Relative Price Elasticities* from Time Series Regressions, 1961–73

Equation	Short-Run Elasticity	Long-Run Elasticity	Price Variable	Other Independent Variables
3.4.1	-2.001	-17.866	FDPRICE	INCOME
3.4.2	-1.580	-3.921	FDPRICE	INCOME, GPRICE
3.4.3	-1.692	-3.404	FDPRICE	INCOME, JAPAN
3.4.4	-1.218	-1.701	FDPRICE	JAPAN, GPRICE
3.4.5	-1.589	-5.907	FDPRICE	JAPAN, INCOME, GPRICE
3.4.6	-1.912	-37.490	FDPRICE	INCOME, RELINC
3.4.7	-1.672	-6.531	FDCOST†	INCOME
3.4.8	-1.502	-3.345	FDCOST†	INCOME, JAPAN
3.4.9	-1.608	-7.882	FDCOST†	INCOME, RELINC

$$\text{Long-Run Elasticity} = \frac{\text{Short-Run Elasticity}}{1 - \frac{\partial \text{LOG(FDSALE)}}{\partial \text{LOG(FDSALE)}_{-1}}}$$

*Elasticity of foreign-to-domestic sales ratio with respect to foreign-to-domestic price ratio.
†Where FDCOST was used as the price variable in an equation, the formula

$$\frac{d\text{LOG(FDSALE)}}{d\text{LOG(FDPRICE)}} = \frac{d\text{LOG(FDSALE)}}{d\text{LOG(FDCOST)}} \cdot \frac{d\text{LOG(FDCOST)}}{d\text{LOG(FDPRICE)}} \approx .65 \frac{d\text{LOG(FDSALE)}}{d\text{LOG(FDCOST)}}$$

was used to translate the relative total cost elasticity into an estimated elasticity with respect to relative sales price.
Source: CRA time-series regressions.

bias to the absolute size of the short-run and long-run relative price elasticity. The impact of imports on domestic auto prices is discussed in Chapter 4.) The cross-section results reported in the following section are consistent with the higher group of estimates of relative price elasticity reported here, while the results from CRA's hedonic market share model shown in the next section are close to the lower elasticity estimates.

Very high income elasticities are reported in Equations (3.3.1), (3.3.2), (3.3.6), (3.3.7), and (3.3.9), and in Equations (3.4.1), (3.4.2), (3.4.5), (3.4.6), (3.4.7), (3.4.8), and (3.4.9). In these equations, income may also be serving as a partial proxy for time trend; import shares and income have both grown over time. Inclusion of the time trend variable JAPAN for years after 1966 lowers the estimated income elasticity in the equations for the sample years 1961-74. Still, import shares are found to be positively related to income in the long run. This result suggests a view of imported cars as a "luxury" good.*

The variable RELINC, the ratio of per capita disposable income in one year to per capita disposable income in the previous year, has a negative coefficient in Equations (3.3.6) and (3.3.9). RELINC is low during a temporary recession; import shares appear to be high during those periods (such as 1970 and 1975, as well as 1958). It appears that import new-car purchases are less sensitive to short-run income swings than domestic purchases.† The econometric findings are consistent with behavior of buyers of luxury American cars during the 1975 recession; sales of Buicks and Cadillacs increased between early 1974 and early 1975, as did import sales, while sales of most domestic models fell sharply. One possible explanation is that high-income buyers are less sensitive to recessions; this is consistent with the perception of imports as "luxury" goods.

---

*It may appear paradoxical to view imports, which are smaller and more fuel-efficient for the most part than domestic cars, as a luxury good. However, many imports are purchased as "second cars" by families already owning a standard American car. Demand for second cars is income elastic; also, a new import is a more luxurious second car than the alternative of a used domestic car. Finally, within each size class, as we have shown above, imports are generally somewhat more expensive, adjusted for physical characteristics, than domestic competitors. For evidence from earlier years showing that buyers of new foreign cars had higher incomes than buyers of new American cars, see Fabian Linden, "The Market for Foreign Cars," *Conference Board Record* 10, [June 1973] : 62-64.

†However, it should be noted that the coefficient RELINC is positive in equations for which the 1974 observation is missing. Thus, RELINC may only be picking up the increase in the import share as income declines in one year, 1974. On the other hand, the fact that 1974 is the only year in the sample in which a major decline in real income occurred suggests that the 1961-73 sample is not adequate to test the potential effect of a recession on the share of imported cars.

The variable JAPAN is a trend variable that picks up the sharp growth in import shares after 1965; this growth coincided with the introduction of popular Japanese imports beginning around 1966. The coefficient of JAPAN from the regressions for 1961-74 shows a 10 to 15 percent annual growth of the import sales ratio after 1965, which is independent of all other explanatory factors. (JAPAN measures a growth trend in the import share between 1966 and 1974, which is not adequately explained by other variables. If the equation is to be used for forecasting purposes, it is clearly inappropriate to extrapolate equations including JAPAN in future periods.)

Finally, the coefficient of the variable GPRICE, the real price of gasoline, is unstable and sometimes has the wrong sign in the equations in which it appears. We expect the import share to increase with higher gasoline prices because imports get better gas mileage than domestic cars; the relative lifetime cost of owning an import (compared to a U.S. car) falls as the price of gas rises. However, relative fuel costs change not only with changes in the price of gas but also with relative changes in automobile fuel efficiency. (For example, the relative cost of domestic automobiles may have risen in the early 1970s because of the reduction in fuel economy of all cars caused by the introduction of antipollution devices.) In addition, multicolinearity in the sample and the absence of a large number of degrees of freedom make it impossible to test precisely the relative impact on changes in share of changes in long-run income, in the short-run rate of growth of income, and in the price of gasoline.

Our results all indicate significant price substitutability between domestic and imported new cars. The short-run relative price elasticity estimates range from -1 to -2. Long-run price elasticities are higher for all specifications, and significantly higher for some specifications, reflecting lagged adjustment to the final share level. Differences in estimates of the lag coefficient cause our estimates of the long-run effect of a given relative price change to be somewhat imprecise, though it may be argued that estimates in the high range are biased upward.

ECONOMETRIC ESTIMATES OF IMPORT SHARE DEMAND FROM CROSS-SECTION DATA

In this section, we present econometric estimates of the relative price elasticity of import demand derived from equations relating relative foreign and domestic new-car sales across states to interstate differences in price.

Import shares vary greatly across states; they are much greater on the east coast and the west coast than in the midwest. We do not have data on differences in transactions prices of new-car sales (or used-car sales) in states. However, it is likely that the main source of interstate price variation is differences in freight charges. We have constructed estimates on price differences across states in 1974 by combining estimates of average list prices of domestic and foreign cars sold in 1974 with data we have collected on freight charges.

For domestic freight charges, we used Buyers' Guide Reports, *New Car Prices, 1975*. This source has a table of freight charges, by state, which takes a weighted average of the model-type freight charges, using as weights the national sales in 1974 of each model type. Although assembly plants are located throughout the country, freight charges are always imposed as a function of cost of transportation from Detroit.* For foreign-car freight charges, we used data on Volkswagen freight charges to different states supplied by Volkswagen of America. We were unable to obtain similar data from Datsun and Toyota; however, a Toyota representative informed us that the port of entry prices for Toyota were the same on the east coast as in California; a similar pattern was true for Volkswagen. Thus, it is reasonable to assume that the Volkswagen freight charge data are roughly comparable to the numbers that would apply to low-price Japanese imports.

Table 3.7 shows the foreign-car shares and estimated domestic and foreign freight charges by state. Cursory examination of the numbers reveals a strong negative correlation between foreign-car shares and relative foreign-to-domestic prices derived by this method. This relationship is confirmed econometrically.

Table 3.8 presents the results of our best estimated equations for the ratio of foreign-to-domestic new-car sales. The relative price elasticity of the import sales ratio is -18.188, approximately equal to the highest value of long-run elasticity estimated in the time series equations. The import share is also positively correlated with the percent of the population aged 20 to 29, per capita income, and the price of gasoline. Other variables we tested and found uncorrelated with the import sales ratio were the percentage of population in urban area, the percent of the population residing in U.S. census-defined Standard Metropolitan Statistical Areas (SMSAs), and the median education level of the population. We also estimated equations omitting Michigan and other auto-producing areas; these omissions had little effect on the results.

---

*This policy is not entirely out of line with pricing based on actual costs. Even for cars assembled in California, the major components (that is, bodies, engines, and so on) need to be shipped from Detroit.

TABLE 3.7

Import Shares by States, 1974, Compared to Freight Charges

State	Import Share (in percent of new car sales)	EST Domestic Freight (in dollars)	EST Foreign Freight (in dollars)
Alabama	12.86	204.98	98
Arizona	20.21	292.34	60
Arkansas	11.40	202.92	89
California	32.49	292.34	60
Colorado	26.47	258.59	145
Connecticut	24.28	187.70	56
Delaware	14.94	176.10	70
D.C.	16.61	n.a.	104
Florida	15.85	249.00	104
Georgia	15.32	193.48	104
Idaho	23.83	292.34	60
Illinois	9.26	85.34	130
Indiana	8.26	154.21	84
Iowa	9.13	173.62	130
Kansas	12.38	216.23	133
Kentucky	10.01	112.14	90
Louisiana	11.90	235.02	98
Maine	19.62	202.86	76
Maryland	18.19	171.37	104
Massachusetts	20.11	200.59	76
Michigan	6.22	41.34	84
Minnesota	9.91	170.98	130
Mississippi	12.16	212.98	98
Missouri	10.75	161.71	127
Montana	18.95	270.39	60
Nebraska	10.95	193.38	133
Nevada	22.06	292.34	60
New Hampshire	23.00	196.02	76
New Jersey	17.42	181.25	56
New Mexico	19.11	281.22	136
New York	15.59	183.19	56
North Carolina	16.06	143.33	104
North Dakota	8.53	206.01	130
Ohio	9.57	89.50	90
Oklahoma	n.a.	228.26	109
Oregon	33.09	292.34	60
Pennsylvania	13.80	177.47	70
Rhode Island	19.91	194.77	76

(continued)

(Table 3.7 continued)

State	Import Share (in percent of new car sales)	EST Domestic Freight (in dollars)	EST Foreign Freight (in dollars)
South Carolina	16.28	193.08	104
South Dakota	8.62	196.02	130
Tennessee	11.92	190.16	98
Texas	12.99	242.72	109
Utah	23.43	290.36	60
Vermont	26.24	183.17	76
Virginia	17.79	176.92	104
Washington	30.38	292.34	60
West Virginia	10.61	130.49	104
Wisconsin	9.03	76.84	130
Wyoming	19.31	254.55	145

Sources: Import Shares from *Automotive News Almanac* 1975, Est. Domestic Freight computed from data in Buyer's Guide Reports, *New Car Prices* 1975 (Milwaukee: DMR Publications). Est. Foreign Freight from data supplied by Volkswagen of America.

It may be argued that 1974 was an unusual year because of the oil embargo and the subsequent increase in the price of gasoline. Therefore, we also estimated cross-section import share equations using 1973 data. Table 3.9 shows that the coefficient from the 1973 regression are almost the same as the coefficients from the 1974 regression. The only major difference between the two sets of estimates is that the income coefficient, which is positive in the 1974 equation, is negative (though not statistically significant) in the 1973 equation. The estimated relative price elasticity is very high, and almost the same, in both sets of equations.

Import shares across states have been quite stable in recent years. Table 3.10 presents regional rankings of import shares in 1968 and in 1974. The Pacific coast, mountain states, and New England had the largest import shares in both 1968 and 1974; imports were least popular in the midwest (including the Great Lakes region). Column 3 of Table 3.10 indicates that there has been no general tendency for imports to grow faster in the regions where shares were low in 1968; in fact, two of the fastest-growing regions have been New England and the mountain states.

Both theoretical considerations and comparison with the time series results suggest the possibility that the absolute value of the price elasticity estimated in Equation (2) is biased upward. Low foreign-car sales in states with higher relative foreign-car prices may in part reflect the reluctance of some

TABLE 3.8

Cross-Section Regression Results, 1974

Equation (3.8.1)
FDSALE = 3.136 − 0.0501 FDPRICE + 0.0253 PC2029
       (5.429)(7.624)   (2.599)

   + 0.0000211 PCAPI + 0.00582 PGAS
       (1.412)   (0.874)

   $R^2 = .6590$ $F(4,42) = 20.294$ *S.E.E. = .0635*

Equation (3.8.2)
LOG (FDSALE) = 63.424 − 18.188 LOG (FDPRICE)
              (6.156) (8.643)

   + 1.845 LOG (PC2029) + 0.271 LOG (PCAPI)
     (2.992)   (0.910)

   + 1.490 LOG (PGAS)
     (0.971)

   $R^2 = .7103$ $F(4,42) = 25.745$ (t-statistics are in parentheses)

   S.E.E. = .2748

Variable Definitions (Sources): FDSALE = Ratio of foreign-to-domestic new-car registrations, 1974 (constructed from data in *Automotive News Almanac*, 1974 and 1975). FDPRICE = Ratio of estimated average delivered list prices of new foreign cars to average delivered list prices of new U.S. cars (*Sources*: average list prices from *Automotive News Almanac*, 1974 and 1975); domestic freight charges from Buyer's Guide Reports, *New Car Prices 1975*, (Milwaukee, DMR Publications, 1975), import freight charges from data supplied on the telephone by Volkswagen of America. PC2029 = Percent of population between ages 20 and 29: *U.S., Census of Population: 1970, General Population Characteristics—United States Summary*. PCAPI = Per capita income, 1973: *Survey of Current Business*, April 1974. PGAS = Price of gasoline, December 1974: *Platt's Oil Price Handbook and Oilmanac*, (New York: McGraw-Hill, 1974).

---

consumers to purchase automobiles that are not locally popular and for which adequate service facilities are not available. In other words, the relevant import price variable for buyer decisions, which includes both sales price and money and time costs of repair and maintenance, may be systematically higher in states with lower imported-car sales. Thus, small differences in desired purchases caused by price differentials may be magnified by availability problems in the states with somewhat higher prices. If so, the differences in foreign shares across states associated with differences in relative prices may provide too high an estimate of the nationwide change in sales that would occur in response to a small change in the foreign-to-domestic price ratio.

TABLE 3.9

Cross-Section Regression Results, 1973

Equation ((3.9.1)

FDSALE = 2.878 −0.0471 FDPRICE + 0.0214 PC2029
         (5.664) (8.480)   (2.558)

   −0.000000993 PCAPI + 0.0128 PGAS
   (0.071)   (2.264)

$R^2 = .7003$ S.E.E. $= .0544$ $F(4,42) = 24.535$

Equation (3.9.2)

LOG (FDSALE) = 63.317 − 17.614 LOG (FDPRICE)
               (6.881) (9.426)

   + 1.613 LOG (PC2029) − 0.138 LOG(PCAPI) + 2.079 LOG (PGAS)
   (2.896)   (0.476)   (2.084)

$R^2 = .7388$ S.E.E. $= .2478$ $F(4,42) = 29.692$

(t-statistics are in parentheses in both equations.)

Variable Definitions (Sources): FDSALE = Ratio of foreign-to-domestic new-car registrations, 1973, constructed from data in *Automotive News Almanac*. FDPRICE = Ratio of estimated average delivered list prices of new foreign cars to average delivered list prices of new U.S. cars.

Sources: Averages list prices from *Automotive News Almanac*, 1974 and 1975; domestic freight charges from Buyer's Guide Reports, *New Car Prices* (Milwaukee: DMR Publications, 1975); Import freight charges from data supplied on the telephone by Volkswagen of America. PC2029 = Percent of population between ages 20 and 29 (*Census of Population. 1970, General Population Characteristics: −United States Summary*); PCAPI = Per capita income, 1973 (*Survey of Current Business*, April 1974); PGAS = Price of gasoline, July 1973: *Platt's Oil Price Handbook and Oilmanac* (New York: McGraw-Hill, 1973).

It is also possible that other factors, possibly patriotism, could be causing the relatively higher domestic sales in the midwest. However, the data do not reveal any obvious correlation between political attitudes and/or related socioeconomic variables (such as the rural/urban population mix) and imported auto shares.

In conclusion, our cross-section estimates show a very high price elasticity of substitution between domestic- and foreign-made automobiles. For reasons noted above, this price elasticity may overstate the actual effect of an overall import price increase brought about by a tariff change. We view the cross-section results as upper-bound estimates of the price elasticity.

TABLE 3.10

Import Shares by Region

Region	Import Share 1968 (percent of New Car Sales)	Import Share 1974 (percent of New Car Sales)	Import Share Ratio (1974/1968)
Southeast	10.14	15.09	1.4882
Pacific Coast	21.52	32.24	1.4981
Southwest	9.48	13.81	1.4568
Mountain	13.11	23.95	1.8269
New England	12.86	21.52	1.6734
Mid-Atlantic	10.39	15.65	1.5063
Great Lakes	6.16	8.64	1.4026
Midwest	5.56	10.30	1.8525
Border	7.73	10.48	1.3558
Total	10.48	15.74	1.5019

Note: States in each region are *Southeast*: Alabama, Florida, Georgia, Mississippi, North Carolina, South Carolina, Tennessee, Virginia; *Pacific Coast*: Alaska, California, Oregon, Washington; *Southwest*: Arizona, Arkansas, Louisiana, Nevada, New Mexico, Texas; *Mountain*: Colorado, Idaho, Montana, Utah, Wyoming; *New England*: Connecticut, Maine, Massachusetts, New Hampshire, Rhode Island, Vermont; *Middle Atlantic*: Delaware, D.C., Maryland, New Jersey, New York, Pennsylvania; *Great Lakes*: Illinois, Indiana, Michigan, Minnesota, Ohio, Wisconsin; *Midwest*: Iowa, Kansas, Nebraska, North Dakota, South Dakota; and *Border*: Kentucky, Missouri, West Virginia.

Source: Automotive News Almanac, 1969, 1975.

ECONOMETRIC ESTIMATES OF IMPORT SHARE DEMAND FROM CRA HEDONIC MARKET SHARE MODEL

The CRA hedonic market share model is a new technique of demand analysis used here to provide an alternative set of estimates of the impact of changes in imported car prices on the import share of new-car sales. The technique yields general predictions of the effects of changes in prices and characteristics of any set of automobile models on the market shares of individual models. The predictions of the share changes for individual models are then summed to obtain the predicted change in the share of a class of models resulting from any relative price changes.[12]

The input data used are the price, selected characteristics, and new-car sales in a given time period of a set of automobile models. (For the share estimates to be reasonable, market coverage of the set of automobile models in-

cluded should be almost complete. This condition was met in the sample used, which excluded only a few specialty cars that accounted for less than 1 percent of all sales in the sample period.) The characteristics include available attributes that either contribute to, or are correlated with, the quality of a car. Available characteristics data for recent years include both the physical dimensions from *Automotive News Almanac* used in the hedonic price regressions in the section beginning on page 46 and performance data collected by the U.S. Department of Transportation and the U.S. Environmental Protection Agency. The physical characteristics data include number of cylinders, headroom, height, horsepower, legroom, length, gas tank capacity, transmission type (automatic or manual), turning circle, weight, and width. The performance variables used were acceleration and fuel economy (miles per gallon). The sample period was the five-month period between April 1974 and August 1974; this period was selected to include the part of the 1974 model year subsequent to the period of acute gasoline shortage.

The estimating technique assumes that individual consumers have varying demand for automobile characteristics, including price, because of differences in income, use patterns, and personal tastes. In the absence of differences in consumer preference, we would not expect the product differentiation in the automobile market that is in fact observed.

The utility of individual consumer i from purchase of model j can be denoted as

$$U_j^i = U(C_j, P_j, \alpha^i) \tag{3.12}$$

where C_j is a vector of characteristics of model j, P_j is the price of model j, and α^i is a set of parameters mapping C_j and P_j into U_j^i. P_j can be viewed as representing the reduction in consumption of other goods implied by the choice of model j.* If the utility function is linear we can write $U_j^i \sum_{l=1}^{N} \alpha_l^i C_{jl} - P_j$ where the α_l^is represent consumer i's marginal rates of substitution between the N characteristics ($l = 1, \ldots, N$) and price. The α^is are different because of differ-

---

*The approach outlined here does not start with a utility function for all goods and a budget constraint, as in the usual presentation of consumer demand theory, but instead focuses directly on the choice among discrete alternatives. It can be shown that the model can be derived directly from the standard formulation of consumer choice theory by assuming either the separability of utility between the items of interest and other goods or that prices of all other goods remain constant in relative terms. (See Scott Cardell, Gilbert DeBartolo, and Zvi Griliches, "A Hedonic Share Demand Model with an Application to the Demand for Heat Pumps," unpublished paper, 1977.)

ences in tastes across individual consumers. Consumer i will choose a model k if

$$U_k^i(C_k, P_k, \alpha^i) \geq U(C_j, P_j, \alpha^i) \text{ for all } j. \tag{3.13}$$

We then define a set:

$$\Omega_k = [\alpha | U(C_k, P_k, \alpha) = \max_j U(C_j, P_j, \alpha)]. \tag{3.14}$$

That is, Ω_k is the set of all α such that k is the utility maximizing choice. In other words, model k will be purchased by some consumers, and Ω_k defines the set of combinations of parameters of the utility function for which that model will be bought.

If we view α as a vector of random variables, we can generate a probability distribution among models:

$$Pr(k \text{ is chosen}) = Pr(\alpha \epsilon \Omega_k) \tag{3.15}$$

We then fit a simple functional form to describe the characteristics of the utility function (that is, the αs).

Recall that the distribution of αs reflects the distribution of consumer tastes for automobile characteristics. Let β represent a vector of sufficient statistics of the probability distribution of the αs. (For example, if the αs have a multinomial distribution, the β vectors include the mean and variance for each α and the covariance for each pair of αs.) For any given set of models, with defined values of the C vector and P_j, we then have

$$Pr(\alpha \epsilon \Omega_k) = F_k(\beta; S_1) \ldots \tag{3.16}$$

where S_1 represents the set of prices and characteristics of the available set of models in time period 1. Equation (3.16) states that the probability that model k will be purchased depends both on the distribution of the parameters of the consumers' utility functions for characteristics, and on the price and characteristics of all available models.

The technique then seeks to find a vector, β^*, such that

$$F_j(\beta^*, S_1) = f_j \qquad j = 1, \ldots N \tag{3.17}$$

for all j, where j is an index describing the N models, and f_j is the observed market share of the jth model. In effect, the technique selects statistics describing a distribution of consumers' utility functions that reproduces the market shares of individual models actually observed. The selection process is done

by numerical methods; we have developed and programed an algorithm that solves Equation (3.17) for the β*s.

Imposition of a tariff on imported automobiles will, in the short run, change the prices of imported models. Thus, after a tariff we have a new set of available models, S_2, which is known. If consumer tastes are stable as prices are changing—that is, if β* remains the same when S_1 changes to S_2—it is appropriate to apply Equation (3.17) to solve for a new set of f_js. In other words, we apply the estimated taste distribution to a new set of available models to generate a new market share distribution. We then aggregate the individual market shares of all imported models to compute the new share of imports at the higher import prices.

Using this method, the effects of changes in import price on import share are simulated below. From the individual data points thus generated, we derive a relationship between import share and relative import price and can estimate for different points on the curve the price elasticity of demand for imports. We also provide estimates of the distribution by automobile type of increases (decreases) in domestic shares when import prices rise (fall).

The advantage of this technique is that it enables us to use detailed information on the product differentiation characteristics that make imports attractive to some new-car buyers. The technique provides estimates of the distribution across consumers of subjective tradeoffs among different characteristics and price, and thus it yields insights into the number of buyers who are just at the margin between purchasing a domestic car and purchasing an import, as well as how many are willing to pay a much higher price for an import. Further, the technique in principle will predict which individual import models will lose sales because of a tariff, as well as the aggregate import sales decline.

The estimates presented below should be viewed as preliminary estimates only. The expense of estimating the taste parameters has prohibited extensive testing of alternative model specifications within the scope of this project. In addition, the predictions derived from the model have not been validated by comparison with actual historical experience. Still, the results presented below seem quite plausible and are very similar both to the lower-bound estimates from the time series regressions presented in a preceding section of this chapter, and to a set of predictions of the impact of imported-car price increases on market shares derived by questionnaire techniques in a study by Market Facts, Inc.[13]

The estimate of the taste distribution for characteristics that we used to derive the share elasticities with respect to relative price changes used five characteristics variables: volume, passenger area, weight, turning circle, and gallons per mile. Volume is defined as the product of length, width, and height and is a proxy measure for a combination of total seating capacity and trunk space. Passenger area is computed as the product of headroom and legroom and represents a proxy for driver and front seat passenger comfort. Utility is positively

correlated with volume, passenger area, and weight. Utility is negatively correlated with turning-circle diameter (the smaller the turning circle, the more maneuverable the automobile) and with fuel consumption in gallons per mile. The variable "acceleration" was used in the first-run estimate but did not have the expected positive coefficient. (A possible reason that the acceleration variable does not have the expected positive coefficient is that, in this sample, acceleration is negatively correlated, all other things equal, with automatic transmission. Automatic transmission is probably a characteristic positively desired by many buyers but is not included in the estimated utility function, though prices are adjusted for inclusion or absence of automatic transmission. Thus, inclusion of automatic transmission as a variable in future research may both improve the sign of the acceleration coefficient and make the predictions slightly better.)

Table 3.11 summarizes statistical information on the estimated distributions of the marginal rates of substitution between characteristics and price. The form of the estimated distribution function is log-normal; the statistics reported in Table 3.11 were computed by taking exponents of the parameters of the normal distributions of the logs of the characteristics. As the distributions are log-normal, the mean and median of the distributions are not the same.

TABLE 3.11

Distribution of Estimated Marginal Values of Automobile Characteristics (dollars per unit)

(Col. 1)	(Col. 2)	(Col. 3)	(Col. 4)	(Col. 5)	(Col. 6)
				\multicolumn{2}{c}{95 Percent Consumer Consumer Taste Range[a]}
Characteristic	Median	Mean	Coefficient of Variation	Lower Bound[b]	Upper Bound[c]
VOL 2	2.3053	7.1149	2.9198	.12156	43.720
AREAG	5.1795	5.8383	0.5201	1.9849	13.515
WEIGHT	2.7782	3.1316	0.5201	1.0646	7.2497
TURN	−7.4435	−303.29	40.7345	−1,547.5	−.03581
GPM	−565.42	−637.33	0.5204	−1,475.34	−216.70

Variable Definitions: VOL2 = (.0001) x (LENGTH) x (WIDTH) x (HEIGHT) (in cubic inches). AREAG = (HEADROOM) x (LEGROOM) (in square inches). WEIGHT = weight (in lbs.). TURN = turning circle diameter (in feet). GPM = gallons per 100 miles.
[a]Range of values of marginal rates of substitution including 95 percent of consumers.
[b]2.5th percentile of consumer taste distribution.
[c]97.5th percentile of consumer taste distribution.
Source: CRA hedonic market share model.

The numbers reported in Column (2) of Table 3.11, the median of the distributions, give the marginal value of an additional unit of the characteristic in dollars, where the units of the characteristics are defined at the bottom of Table 3.11. For example, the coefficient attached to *VOL2* indicates that the median consumer is willing to pay $2.31 for an extra 10,000 cubic inches of volume. The coefficient attached to weight indicates that the median consumer is willing to pay an additional $2.78 for an additional pound.

The absolute value of the coefficient on gallons per mile is more than twice as high as it would be if it reflected the first-year savings from running a more fuel-efficient automobile and if those savings were computed using the same assumptions that were used in computing the total cost variable for the time series equations.[14] However, if the typical 1974 car buyer had a longer time horizon and expected real gasoline prices to continue to rise after 1974, the magnitude of the coefficient is certainly consistent with rational behavior.

The coefficient of GPM (gallons per mile) reported in Table 3.11 implies that a consumer would be willing to pay an additional $565.42 to obtain an automobile that used one less gallon of gasoline per 100 miles. At a price of gasoline of $.55 per gallon, a buyer who drove 10,000 miles per year would save $55 in the first year from a reduction in gas consumption of one gallon per 100 miles. When we apply the figures used in a preceding section of this chapter—a 20 percent depreciation rate and a 5 percent interest rate—an extra $565.42 in initial selling price would raise the fixed cost of owning a new automobile in the first year by $141.36, about 2.5 times the saving in gasoline cost. By these calculations, the savings in gasoline cost would equal the higher fixed cost if the owner drove 25,700 miles in the first year.

Two factors could account for this difference between the estimated utility of better mileage and the estimate of gasoline cost savings. First, the combined interest and depreciation as a fraction of price is much lower in subsequent years than in the initial year of ownership; if the buyer is not planning to sell the car in the first year and has a longer time horizon, the ratio of gasoline costs to fixed costs of ownership may be much higher than is implied by the above calculation. Second, in 1974, buyers may have been expecting gasoline prices to rise or may have feared future shortages and/or rationing because of the experience in the previous winter.

As an illustration of the first point, suppose the owner was planning to hold the auto for its entire lifetime. If autos last ten years and are driven 10,000 miles per year, the present discounted value of a saving on one gallon per 100 miles of gasoline can be computed as the discounted value of the sum of dollar savings each year. Again when we use a gasoline price of $.55 per gallon and a 5 percent discount rate, the present value of gasoline savings over the lifetime of an auto is computed to be $424.69, only slightly lower than the additional demand price of $565.42. If, in 1974, gasoline prices were expected to continue to rise more quickly than the consumer price index, then the estimated co-

efficient of gallons per mile reported in Table 3.11 appears consistent with rational behavior of new-car buyers.

The upper and lower bounds of the 95 percent range indicate the degree of dispersion in tastes for each characteristic among consumers. The most widely dispersed values are for the characteristic "turning circle"; this result appears to make some sense because some buyers place a very high value on a car that handles well and can get into small parking places, while other buyers have practically no use for that characteristic. The dispersion of the coefficient attached to gallons per mile reflects differences among buyers in annual miles driven, subjective discount rates relating current to future cost savings, expected length of ownership of an automobile, and expectations about future trends in gasoline prices and availability.

Table 3.12 compares the predicted shares consistent with the utility function estimated in the model with actual market shares of different automobile types. The model was estimated using two different price variables—the one-year-old price in August 1974 of 1974 models reported in National Market Reports, Inc., *Red Book* and the estimated new transactions price of 1974 models. The new transactions price variable was corrected by applying "typical" discount factors for different types of cars reported in the annual automobile buying issue of *Consumer Reports* (April 1974) to list prices reported in the 1974 issue of *Automotive News Almanac*.

The data reported in Table 3.12 show that the predicted shares from the model conform fairly closely to the actual shares; the model fits the data well. Predicted import shares are slightly higher than actual shares. One explanation for the "import bias" of the model may be the exclusion of automatic transmission from the characteristics used in the utility function; a much larger fraction of domestic than imported autos have automatic transmissions and North American buyers probably place a positive value on that. The exclusion of automatic transmission, in particular, may explain the fact that the share of domestic subcompacts is about 10 percent higher than the predicted share, as domestic subcompacts are closest to imports in all the other characteristics. (Alternatively, it is possible that many people simply prefer domestic autos to imported autos of equal characteristics because of "patriotism" or suspicion of foreign products, or that the preference for domestic autos reflects some unmeasured advantage such as better availability of service facilities.)

Table 3.13 summarizes the effects of fixed percentage changes in the price of all imported automobiles on market shares of different major subcategories of domestic and foreign autos. Column (3) of Table 3.13 provides estimates of the impact of a 10 percent increase in all import prices on market shares, while Column (4) estimates the effect of a (3/1.03) percent reduction (equivalent to the nominal import tariff rate as a fraction of after-tariff price)* of import prices.

---

*Actually, the tariff applies to "manufacturers' cost," which is smaller than transactions price. Thus, the effective tariff on manufacturers' price is slightly less than 3 percent.

TABLE 3.12

Comparison of Predicted Shares to Actual Shares by Automobile Type, April–August 1974

	Actual Share	Predicted Share: One-Year-Old Price	Predicted Share: Estimated New Transactions Price
Domestic autos			
Subcompact	.08792	.07900	.07767
Compact	.21413	.23299	.23701
Luxury small	.03397	.01825	.01822
Intermediate	.26943	.24582	.25633
Standard	.20846	.21383	.20902
Luxury standard	.05108	.05598	.06075
Specialty	.00299	.00215	.00223
All domestics	.86798	.84802	.86183
Imported autos			
Subcompact	.08013	.09624	.09080
Compact	.05340	.04449	.03744
Sports car	.01200	.00815	.00692
Luxury	.00444	.00321	.00336
All imports	.13197	.15209	.13852

Definition of Automobiles by Type:
Domestic subcompact: Gremlin, Pinto, Vega.
Domestic compact: Hornet, Javelin, Valiant, Dart, Maverick, Comet, Apollo, Nova, Camaro, Omega, Firebird, Ventura.
Domestic luxury small: Mustang II.
Domestic intermediate: Matador, Satellite, Coronet, Torino, Montego, Cougar, Century, Chevelle, Monte Carlo, Cutlass, LeMans, Grand Prix.
Domestic standard: Ambassador, Fury, Chrysler New Yorker, Dodge, Ford, Mercury, Thunderbird, Buick, Riviera, Chevrolet, Oldsmobile, Pontiac, Toronado.
Domestic luxury standard: Imperial, Lincoln, Mark IV, Cadillac, Eldorado.
Domestic specialty: Corvette.
Imported subcompact: Audi Fox, Marina, Colt, Datsun B210, Fiat 128, Fiat 124, Fiat XI/9, Honda, Mazda 808, Opel Manta, Renault, Subaru, Toyota Corolla, Toyota Corona, VW Beetle, VW 412, VW Dasher, Datsun PL 610.
Imported compact: Audi 100 LS, Capri, Mazda RX-4, Mazda RX-2, Mazda RX-3, Peugeot 504, Saab 99 LE, Toyota Celica, Toyota Mark II, Volvo 140 Series, Volvo 164, Datsun PL 710.
Imported sports car: MG, Jaguar, Triumph, Datsun 260 Z, Pantera, Porsche.
Imported luxury: BMW Bavaria, Mercedes Benz.
Source: CRA hedonic market share model.

TABLE 3.13

Effect of Proportionate Changes in Import Prices on Market Shares from CRA Hedonic Market Share Model

(Col. 1)	(Col. 2) Predicted Share: Base Case	(Col. 3) Predicted Share: Import Prices up 10 Percent (Percent Change)		(Col. 4) Predicted Share: Import Prices down (3/1.03) Percent (Percent Change)	
Domestic autos					
Subcompact	.07900	.08281	(+4.8)	.07777	(−1.6)
Compact	.23299	.24023	(+3.1)	.23409	(−1.1)
Luxury small	.01825	.01895	(+3.8)	.01802	(−1.3)
Intermediate	.24582	.25287	(+2.9)	.24347	(−1.0)
Standard	.21383	.21943	(+2.6)	.21188	(−0.9)
Luxury standard	.05598	.05716	(+2.1)	.05560	(−0.7)
Specialty	.00215	.00221	(+2.8)	.00214	(−0.5)
All domestics	.84802	.87366	(+3.0)	.83937	(−1.0)
Imported autos					
Subcompact	.09624	.08124	(−15.6)	.10083	(+4.8)
Compact	.04449	.03560	(−20.0)	.04725	(+6.2)
Sports car	.00815	.00647	(−20.6)	.00873	(+7.1)
Luxury	.00321	.00235	(−26.8)	.00353	(+10.0)
All imports	.15209	.12566	(−17.8)	.16034	(+5.4)

Note: Definition of automobiles by type same as in Table 3.12.
Source: CRA hedonic market share model.

The results in Table 3.13 are consistent with a priori expectations. The percentage changes in shares of domestic-car types corresponding to a given percentage change in the import price are greatest for the closest substitutes to imports—the subcompact, luxury small, and compact cars—while the percentage change in import shares is greater for compact imports than for subcompact imports. Compact imports are probably on the whole closer substitutes for typical domestic automobiles than subcompact imports. However, the percentage figures partially mask the fact that larger absolute changes in the shares of subcompact imports and intermediate and standard domestics occur in response to the relative price change because these automobiles account for a significant fraction of domestic and import sales, respectively. For example, the predicted

absolute increase in sales of domestic intermediates in response to an increase in the import price is greater than the predicted absolute increase in sales of domestic subcompacts. This result can be explained partially by shifts from imported compacts to domestic intermediates: For buyers of imported "compacts" such as Volvo and Audi, a medium-sized Buick or Oldsmobile may be perceived as a better substitute than a Pinto or Vega. It is likely that automobiles in the same price range are better substitutes than automobiles in the same size range. For example, while Volvo and Audi are smaller than domestic compacts, they are more expensive than most intermediate and some standards.

The relatively high percentage changes in imported sports car and luxury car sales reflect very small absolute changes in sales because these two categories account for a minor fraction of total sales.

Table 3.14 summarizes the relative price elasticities estimated from the price changes simulated in Table 3.13. The relative price elasticity is computed as the ratio *dLOG(FDSALE) / dLOG(FDPRICE)*, where *FDSALE* is the ratio of imported-to-domestic new-car sales, and *FDPRICE* is the ratio of imported-to-domestic new-car prices. The estimated relative price elasticity is slightly higher with a 10 percent increase in the import price than with a 2.91 percent decrease, suggesting that import shares will decline somewhat more rapidly with bigger increases in the relative import price.

Finally, Table 3.15 compares the findings from CRA's hedonic market share model with the findings from a survey conducted by Market Facts, Inc. under contract to the U.S. Department of Labor in the past year. The Market Facts survey asked buyers of imported cars how their automobile purchase decision would have been affected by increases of $500 and $1,000 in the price of all imports. Table 4.9 of the Market Facts report provides estimates of the percent of buyers who would have bought the same car, and the percent who would have either bought other cars or kept their used car, while Table 4.11

TABLE 3.14

Relative Price Elasticities for Simulated Changes in Import Prices

Change in Import Price	Relative Price Elasticity
+10 percent	−2.3154
−2.91 percent*	−2.1339

Note: Relative price elasticities defined as the expression dLOG(FDSALE)/dLOG(FDPRICE) where FDSALE is the ratio of foreign-to-domestic new-car sales and FDPRICE is the ratio of foreign-to-domestic new-car prices.

*or (3/1.03) percent.

Source: CRA hedonic market share model.

TABLE 3.15

Comparison of CRA Hedonic Market Share Estimates to *Market Facts* Estimates[a] of Effect of Price Increases for Imported Automobiles

(Column 1) Percent of Buyers Purchasing[b]	(Col. 2) $500 Increase Market Facts	(Col. 3) $500 Increase CRA	(Col. 4) $1,000 Increase Market Facts	(Col. 5) $1,000 Increase CRA
Same car	66	—	24	—
Others	34	—	76	—
Others: U.S.	26	26	59	44
Subcompact	9	4	20	7
Compact	6	7	12	13
Luxury small	4	1	9	1
Intermediate	2	7	5	12
Standard	4	5	8	9
Luxury	0	1	1	2
Specialty and other	0	0	1	0
Others: imported	8	—	17	—
Subcompact	5	—	9	—
Luxury small	2	—	5	—
Luxury	0	—	1	—
Specialty	0	—	1	—
Total imported	74	74	41	56

[a]Market Facts, Inc., *A Foreign Automobile Impact Study* (report submitted to U.S. Department of Labor, Washington, D.C. 20210, March 1976), Tables 4.9 and 4.11.

[b]Numbers do not always add up to 100 because of rounding.

of the Market Facts report provides a percentage breakdown of the type of car buyers shifting to another model would have purchased. We have combined Tables 4.9 and 4.11 of the Market Facts report into percentage estimates of the effects of $500 and $1,000 price increases on new car shares by counting only those buyers who would have still purchased a new car, and dividing the buyers who responded "don't know" to the questionnaire in proportion to the categories reported by those giving definite responses.* Columns (2) and (4) give the resulting predictions of the breakdown of new-car purchases per 100 initial buyers of foreign cars who are still purchasing a new car.

---

*The CRA hedonic market share model in its present form assumes the market size is fixed. While this assumption is clearly incorrect because buyers can keep their used car an additional year if new-car prices rise (or can reduce automobile ownership), the model

Columns (3) and (5) provide the corresponding estimates from the CRA hedonic market share model with $500 and $1,000 price increases, respectively. The CRA model does not identify the type of car purchased by any individual so it is not possible to predict how many people would have bought the same car; however, it is possible to predict the breakdown by car type of the increased domestic sales.

Table 3.15 shows a surprisingly close correspondence between the CRA and Market Facts predictions. For a $500 increase, the predicted shift to domestic cars implied by the two studies is exactly the same; however the breakdown is a bit different. CRA predicts relatively more sales of domestic intermediates, while Market Facts predicts a bigger shift to domestic subcompact and small luxury cars. For a $1,000 price increase, the substitution elasticity predicted by Market Facts is relatively greater; Market Facts predicts that 59 out of 100 buyers will shift to domestic cars, compared to only 44 out of 100 predicted by CRA. Again, Market Facts predicts a bigger shift than CRA to the categories subcompact and luxury small, while CRA predicts a bigger growth in the sales of domestic intermediates. (The CRA predictions show a relatively greater substitutability between autos of similar price classes, while the Market Facts predictions show, compared to CRA, a relatively greater substitutability between autos of similar size classes.)

In all, the first-run estimates from the CRA hedonic market share model seem quite plausible and are broadly consistent with the results of other research. The relative substitution elasticity is within the lower range of elasticity estimates in the time series demand analysis. The predicted effect of a moderate ($500) increase in import prices is exactly the same as the implied forecast from an actual market survey using a totally different approach. (The utility function estimated in the CRA hedonic market share model is a linear function of characteristics; thus, it is possible that the model does not predict as well for very large changes in prices as it does for small and moderate changes.) The breakdown of changes in domestic sales by category in response to a change in imported prices is reasonably plausible; percentage changes in forecasted sales are relatively greater for categories of automobiles that are generally viewed as better substitutes for imports. Further experimentation with different forms of the model specification holds the promise of yielding more reliable and persuasive results.

SUMMARY OF FINDINGS

Measurement of welfare effects of a tariff or quota change affecting automobile imports requires knowledge of the price elasticity of demand for im-

---

can yield useful forecasts of the effects of import price changes on import and domestic new-car sales if combined with estimates derived from other sources of the total market price elasticity of new-car demand. Estimates of the effects of a change in the price of automobile imports on domestic sales are provided in Chapter 8, below.

ported automobiles. In general, both consumer welfare losses for a given tariff increase and labor adjustment costs from a given tariff reduction are greater the higher the absolute value of the relative price elasticity of the ratio of imported to domestic automobile sales.

We estimate equations to explain variations in the import share from both time series and cross-section data, deriving separate sets of estimates of the effects of changes in the ratio of import-to-domestic prices on the ratio of import-to-domestic automobile sales. We also estimate the effect of import price changes on import shares by applying a new technique of analysis, the CRA hedonic demand model, which estimates a distribution function of demand for automobile characteristics from existing data on market shares of automobiles with different prices and characteristics and then applies the estimated function to predict the effect of price changes on market share changes.

Both the time series and cross-section equations explain a large proportion of the variance in import shares. Both yield coefficients indicating strong and statistically significant effects of relative price changes on import shares; the elasticities from the cross-section equations, however, were much higher. The implied long-run elasticities from the time series equations were sensitive to changes in specification because of the instability of the coefficient of lagged import share; the short-run elasticity estimates, however, were quite insensitive to changes in specification. The statistical findings from CRA's hedonic market share model, which suggest that the relative price elasticity of the import-to-domestic sales ratio is about -2, are consistent with the lower-bound, and more plausible, long-run demand elasticity estimates from the time series equations. The relative price elasticity of -18 estimated in the cross-section equation is close to some of the high long-run implied elasticity estimates from the time series equations. The cross-section equations may overestimate the relative price elasticity by understating the relative cost of ownership differences between domestic and imported automobiles in different states.

The finding of a positive income elasticity of import share demand in the time series equations and in some of the cross-section equations provides some support to a view of imported cars as more of a "luxury" good than domestic cars.

APPENDIX 3.A

Construction of Hedonic Price Indexes For Domestic and Imported Cars

This appendix provides the details of the data and methodology used in constructing the foreign-to-domestic auto price series used in the time series regression equations in Chapter 3.

To obtain the price ratio series, separate indexes of foreign and domestic prices are constructed from regression equations, which estimate the percentage change in price, adjusted for characteristics between adjacent years for foreign and domestic models, respectively. Below, we outline the method of construction of the index in some detail, reviewing the general method, the data sources, and how specific data and model choice problems are handled.

Estimation of Chain Indexes: Overview of Method

We first use individual model observations on 1960 and 1961 prices of 1959 and 1960 automobiles, both domestic and imported, to estimate a regression equation of the form

$$\log(P) = a_0 + a_1 C + a_2 DY + a_3 DF + a_4 DFPY$$

where P is one-year-old transactions price; C is a vector of automobile market characteristics, including weight, headroom, length, horsepower, brake area, turning circle, and dummy variables for the presence of automatic transmission, power steering, power brakes, disk brakes, and for station wagons; DY is a dummy for year (0 if 1960 price; 1 if 1961 price); DF is a dummy for foreign (0 if domestic; 1 if foreign); and $DFDY$ is the product of DF and DY (1 if foreign in 1961; 0 otherwise). The coefficient of DF gives the percentage price premium for imported cars in 1960, holding characteristics differences fixed. The price of domestic cars is then set equal to 100.00 in 1960, the price of imported cars equal to $100.00\,(1 + a_3)$ in 1960. Having obtained an estimate of the foreign-to-domestic price ratio for the initial year, separate regressions for subsamples of domestic and foreign models are estimated, using equations of the form:

$$\log(P) = a_0 + a_1 C + a_2 Y$$

for adjacent years from 1960-61 to 1973-74, where the variables are defined as above. We then compute the price index in year t as

$$H_t = H_{t-1}\,(1 + a_2)$$

where a_2 represents the characteristics adjusted percentage change in price between year $t - 1$ and year t, H_t is the price index in year t, and H_{t-1} is the price index in year $t - 1$.

The regression equations estimating price changes between adjacent years for individual models are all weighted by annual sales of each model. (The method used to handle the inconsistency between model year and calendar year—sales data are for calendar year—is discussed below.)

Data Sources

Specifications Data

The characteristics data used in the hedonic regressions are from successive issues of *Automotive News Almanac*, published annually. Table 3A.1 describes the variables used in the study. *Automotive News Almanac* gives separate listings of characteristics for imported and domestic models. Since we are using prices at time t and $t + 1$ for cars of vintage $t - 1$ and t, the characteristics data used, for example, for the 1960 to 1961 price change are data for 1959 and 1960 models, the models for which the price data are collected.

The descriptions of two of the variables—weight and horsepower—differ slightly between domestic and imported models. For construction of the changes over time in import prices relative to domestic prices, we are not greatly concerned about small changes in characteristics definitions as long as the definitions remain constant over time.

There is one major inconsistency in the *Automotive News* data. The horsepower variable is defined as gross horsepower for models of vintage 1971 and earlier, and as net horsepower beginning in 1972. This inconsistency creates a problem only in our estimate of the 1972-73 price change; for this year we created an "adjusted horsepower" variable for the 1972 models by regressing 1972 horsepower on 1971 horsepower and 1972 weight for models with the same engine displacement in 1971 and 1972. We then use this correction factor

TABLE 3A.1

Description of Variables

Specification	Domestic Description (Units)	Foreign Description (Units)
Weight	Curbweight (lbs.)	Unladen Weight (lbs.)
Headroom	Front seat to headliner (in.)	Front seat to headliner (in.)
Length	Overall length (in.)	Overall Length (in.)
Horsepower	Maximum brake horsepower at RPMs (net for 1971 and earlier; gross for 1972 and after)	Maximum horsepower at RPMs (net for 1971 and earlier; gross for 1972 and later)
Brake area	Effective brake area (square inches)	Effective brake area (square inches)
Turning circle	Turning circle diameter (feet)	Turning circle diameter (feet)

Source: Charles River Associates.

to convert the raw net horsepower measure for 1972 to a gross horsepower equivalent for all models in the sample. The conversion equation is

$$AJHSPOW = (1 - DY)(HSPOW) + DY*EXP[-2.5843 + (.8385 * LOG(HSPOW)) + .4513 \, LOG(WEIGHT)]$$

where DY is 1 in 1972, 0 in 1971; HSPOW is horsepower reported in *Automotive News*; WEIGHT is weight reported in *Automotive News;* and AJHSPOW is the gross horsepower equivalent. For 1971, $AJHSPOW = HSPOW$.

Estimation of Sales Data

The sales of each domestic model in the data base used in the hedonic regressions are supplied in tables entitled "New Car Registrations by Maker Models" in *Automotive News Almanac*. New-car registrations in a given calendar year are used as a proxy for sales in a given model year. This distortion in the data does not seriously affect our results because sales are used only as weights and not as dependent or independent variables in the equation. The purpose of weighting the equations by sales is to give more power in determining the coefficients to more popular automobiles; thus, changes in Impala prices impact the domestic price index much more heavily than changes in the price of a Corvette. As the relative sales of different models remain reasonably stable from year to year, the weights from using calendar-year instead of model-year sales are not inappropriate.

For sales data on imports, there is one imporant difference: New-car registrations in most years are available only for the top ten selling import models. For other foreign models, sales data are taken from a table in *Automotive News Almanac* entitled "Import Cars in Operation by Model Year." Where both measures are available to use as a proxy for new-car sales, we find that the number of model year cars of vintage t in operation at the end of year t is very close to the number of new registrations in year t for a given model or make.

Standard and Optional Equipment on Domestic Cars

Dummy variables are assigned to each model to control for automatic transmission, power steering, power brakes, or disk brakes. The respective dummy variables are assigned the value of unity if the attribute is present and the value of zero if the attribute is absent. For each model, the attribute is determined to be present only if the equipment is standard. (The price assigned to each model is consistent with the presence or absence of each of the attributes.)

Information on the attributes is supplied in *Automotive News Almanac* from a table entitled "Retail Delivered Prices of (Model-Year) U.S. Models." These tables list whether or not the first three abovementioned attributes are standard, optional or unavailable. For disk brakes, the retail delivered price lists in *Automotive News* contain notations indicating whether disk brakes are standard. Commonly, power brakes are listed as standard equipment, with a note in the margin stating that "power brakes (are) front disk." In these cases, the *Red Book* indicates either that both disk and power brakes are available or, for some models, that the brakes are power disk. In both cases, the attributes "power brakes" and "disk brakes" are assumed to be present. No distinction is made between models with front wheel disk brakes only and models with disk brakes on all four wheels; for both groups, a value of unity is recorded for the disk brake dummy.

Standard and Optional Equipment on Foreign Cars

Automotive News does not have a retail delivered price table for imported cars that lists standard or optional equipment. Instead, the specification table for imported models indicates whether disk brakes are present and whether automatic transmission is standard or optional equipment. When the table indicates that either front disk brakes or four-wheel disk brakes are equipment on the model, the attribute is recorded as being present. The automatic transmission attribute is recorded as being present only when the specification table indicates that it is standard equipment.

No mention of power steering or power brakes was found in either *Automotive News* or the *Red Book*. It is therefore assumed that these are not offered on imported models, and the dummy variables power steering and power brakes are not used in the foreign-car regressions.

Body Type for Domestic and Foreign Cars

Each model in the sample is assigned one of three body-type designations: sedan, hardtop, or station wagon. The body type is controlled for in the data base by the use of two dummy variables. One of the dummy variables assumes the value of 1 if the model is a hardtop and 0 otherwise; the other assumes the value of 1 if the model is a station wagon and 0 otherwise. If the model is a sedan, both dummy variables are 0.

The number of body types offered by automobile manufacturers is more diverse than the three mentioned above. There are, within each of three basic categories, different arrangements of seats and doors. There are also convertibles, limousines, hatchbacks, coupes, fastbacks, and roadsters. We group the variables

into three categories to avoid the use of an excessive number of dummy variables; it is, however, necessary to make some body-type distinction because some body types are significantly more expensive than others. The groups we use are (1) as sedans: two-door sedan, four-door sedan, roadster, limousine, and convertible; (2) as hardtops: two-door hardtop, four-door hardtop, coupe, fastback, hatchback, and hardtop sedan; and (3) as station wagon: two-seat station wagon and three-seat station wagon.

Prices of Domestic and Foreign Models

The prices in the data base are one-year-old retail prices taken from the *Red Book (Region A)*. For the years 1969 through 1974, the prices were taken from Edition no. 3 (April 1 to May 14); for the years 1960 through 1967 the prices were taken from Edition no. 4 (May 15–June 30). The data-base year 1968 has two sets of prices—one set from Edition no. 3 and one set from Edition no. 4. Thus, in any pair of years, prices from the same edition can be used. The prices are gathered by sampling dealers in the eastern region of the United States. Because of the measurement and publications lag, the prices in the spring *Red Book* actually reflect market conditions around January and February.

The prices appearing in the data base are adjusted to conform to the presence or absence of automatic transmission, power steering, power brakes and disk brakes. The *Red Book* supplies the necessary price adjustments; for example, the 1970 Ford Galaxie 500 eight-cylinder four-door sedan did not include automatic transmission, power steering, power brakes, or disk brakes as standard equipment. The 1971 *Red Book: Region A*, Edition no. 3 listed the price of a 1970 Ford Galaxie 500 eight cylinder four-door sedan with automatic transmission and power steering at $2,425, with $270 deducted for a standard three-speed transmission and $145 deducted for no power steering. We record the price of that model as $2,010, subtracting optional values from the *Red Book* price, and assigned values of zero to the dummies for automatic transmission, power steering, power brakes, disk brakes, hardtop, and station wagon.

Selection of Models for Inclusion in the Regression

Models are included in the regression if they appear in all of the data sources. For some of the excluded models, specifications data from *Automotive News* are unavailable; for others, the price of the model is not listed in the *Red Book*. Almost all of the models with significant sales are included in the sample.

The engine class (four-cylinder, six-cylinder, eight-cylinder) of the model chosen is that which we judge to have had the most sales. Most models offer

only one engine class. For those models that offer more than one class, *Ward's Automotive Yearbook* often specifies the sales of each model-engine class. For other models, the choice is made using the subtotals for six- and eight-cylinder cars within each make supplied in *Automotive News Almanac*. For a few models with large sales of both six- and eight-cylinder versions, both are included as separate observations and the sales breakdown from *Ward's Automotive Yearbook* is used for the weighting variable.

Selection of the body type of each model is based upon our judgment of what was probably the most popular-selling body type of each model. However, once a specific body type is selected for a particular model, that body type is assigned to the model for each year it appears in the data base. For example, if a four-door hardtop version of a model is initially chosen, each successive yearly price observation on that model is the price of a four-door hardtop in that model.

Selection of the makes of foreign cars is based on sales. The most popular foreign makes are included to the point where sales of the next most popular make are a small proportion of total sales of imports. Between 10 and 20 foreign makes are selected for each year, and one model is selected from each make. (Unlike the sales data for domestic cars, the sales data for foreign cars are broken down by make only, and not by model within make.)

Selection of the model within a make of foreign automobile is made in a manner similar to that of selection of body type. The initial selection is based on our knowledge of which model was the most popular. If our knowledge of the foreign make is scant, two guidelines are adopted in the selection. The first guideline is that the model be the most basic or cheapest offered within the make. The second guideline is to select the model that was offered for the most number of years. The model that best complies with these two guidelines is chosen.

Generally, all domestic models that appear in the specifications, sales, and price data sources are included in the data base. However, in some cases, a few models within a make are taken together as one model, and the sales data for those models are appropriately aggregated and assigned to the representative model; this is done whenever two or more models within a make have the same specifications. The model chosen to be the representative is the one that sold the most units over time. For example, Chevrolet offered the Biscayne, Belair, and Impala for all the data-base years, 1959-73. (Chevrolet introduced the Caprice in 1965.) In any year, the specifications for these three (four) models that appear in *Automotive News* are the same. They differ, however, in such luxury items as trim, upholstery, and gadgets. Data on these variables are unobtainable, however, and therefore the price could not be adjusted for them. For the purpose of calculating a price index, these models are represented by the Impala, which sold the most units during the entire time period studies. (In the early part of the period, Belair had the most sales. However, had we switched

TABLE 3A.2
Computation of Foreign-to-Domestic Relative Price Index

Year	DPRICE	FPRICE	CPIRATIO	RELFOR	DPRICE1	FPRICE1	FDPRICE
1960	100.00	98.47	0.964	1.115	96.4	105.8	109.9
1961	84.21	86.62	0.980	0.943	82.5	80.0	97.1
1962	94.18	94.98	0.978	1.004	92.1	93.3	101.1
1963	92.85	98.46	0.985	0.944	91.5	91.6	100.1
1964	95.95	94.25	0.984	0.946	94.4	87.7	93.0
1965	92.13	98.94	0.957	1.022	88.2	96.8	109.8
1966	91.29	84.73	0.992	1.025	90.6	86.2	95.3
1967	92.59	81.35	0.993	1.027	91.9	83.0	90.2
1968	94.79	86.48	0.988	1.056	93.7	90.2	96.3
1969	94.29	85.91	0.993	1.113	93.6	94.9	101.3
1970	85.78	92.60	0.927	0.943	79.5	80.9	101.8
1971	90.77	92.96	0.986	1.093	89.5	100.2	111.9
1972	95.58	97.50	0.989	1.034	94.5	99.7	105.4
1973	96.49	93.87	0.998	1.029	96.3	96.4	100.0
1974	100.43	128.03	1.045	0.955	104.9	127.8	121.7

Table 3A.2 (continued)

Variables:
DPRICE = domestic price index computed from CRA hedonic regressions
FPRICE = foreign price index computed from CRA hedonic regressions
CPIRATIO = ratio of July CPI to January CPI for new cars
Source: "Consumer Price Index," *Monthly Labor Review*, September issues 1960–74, Table 25.
RELFOR = amount by which foreign price changes relative to domestic price → beginning to middle of year. Computed by taking the ratio

$$\left(\frac{P_{VW\,(fall)}}{P_{VW\,(spring)}}\right) \Big/ \left(\frac{P_{Chevy\,(fall)}}{P_{Chevy\,(spring)}}\right)$$

where

$P_{VW\,(fall)}$ = price of a Volkswagen Beetle of vintage $t-1$ in fall of year t
$P_{VW\,(spring)}$ = price of Volkswagen Beetle of vintage $t-1$ in spring of year t
$P_{Chevy\,(fall)}$ = price of a full-size Chevy of vintage $t-1$ in fall of year t
$P_{Chevy\,(spring)}$ = price of a full-size Chevy of vintage $t-1$ in spring of year t

Source: Fall and spring Issues of National Market Reports, Inc., *Red Book*, Region A.
DPRICE1 = (DPRICE) × (CPIRATIO)
FPRICE1 = (FPRICE) × (CIPRATIO) × (RELFOR)
FDPRICE = foreign-to-domestic relative price index = (FPRICE1) / (DPRICE1)

from Belair to the more expensive Impala when Impala became the largest seller, we could have recorded a spurious price increase, as the price of the "representative" model would have been rising even if the prices of both alternatives remained the same.) The sales of these models are aggregated and assigned to the Impala; the price taken from the *Red Book* is the Impala price.

Estimation of Missing Values in the Data Base

Estimation of the Attributes for Standard Equipment

In a few cases, data are missing on automatic transmission and disk brakes for foreign models. When this occurs, the attributes of the model in the surrounding years are investigated and, if consistent, applied to the model in the intervening year. When the attributes in the surrounding years are inconsistent, or when the model is not offered in one of the surrounding years or when the attribute data are also missing in the surrounding years, the attribute is assigned by our best judgment.

Estimation of Missing Specifications Data

For some observations, one or more of the following specifications are missing: turning circle, horsepower, brake area, and headroom. The missing values are estimated by ordinary least-squares regression on the pooled data for the 15 years. Each of the specification variables that were fitted are regressed both on a constant and on the 13 variables from the original data base that are most significant in explaining the variance of the dependent variable, subject to the condition that none of the independent variables have missing values in the observations for which the dependent variable is missing.

Computing Relative Price Series

Table 3A.2 shows our computation of the foreign-to-domestic relative price index from the separate indexes developed in the hedonic regressions. Columns (1) and (2), labeled DPRICE and FPRICE, give the domestic and foreign price indexes from the regressions described in this appendix. These results give an estimate of annual price changes between successive winters. As our sales data give sales for the entire calendar year, it is better to use a midyear price estimate as a proxy for the price paid by the representative consumer in our time series demand equations. To make this correction, we multiplied DPRICE by CPIRATIO, the ratio of the Consumer Price Index for new automobiles in July to the CPI for new automobiles in January of the same year. Published

RELATIVE PRICES AND DEMAND

data from the Bureau of Labor Statistics are used to compute this ratio, which we interpret to be the ratio of midyear domestic prices to winter domestic prices. Since the price change is computed within a model year, adjustment for changes in characteristics do not have to be made. Multiplying Column (1) by CPIRATIO (Column (3)) gives the variable DPRICE1, an index of the movement in domestic price between successive midyear points.

To compute the change in foreign prices between midyear points, we multiply the original (winter) foreign price index by the midyear domestic price change (CPIRATIO) and by a variable measuring the relative change of domestic to foreign prices during the year. The latter variable, denoted as RELFOR in Column (4), is constructed by taking the ratio of the midyear to early-year prices of Volkswagen Beetles and full-size Chevrolets from fall and spring issues of the *Red Book*. In performing the comparison, we took care to use consistently defined models of Volkswagen and Chevrolet within each model year.

Columns (5) and (6) give the midyear domestic and imported car price indexes, denoted DPRICE1 and FPRICE1, respectively. The last column of Table 3A.2 gives our computations of the relative price series, the ratio of FPRICE1 to DPRICE1, which we label FDPRICE. FDPRICE is the relative price index variable used in the time series regression equations reported in Chapter 3.

APPENDIX 3.B

Construction of Relative Total Cost Index for Domestic and Imported Automobiles

This appendix show how the domestic and imported price indexes were combined with a gasoline price index and with estimates of changes in mileage of different types of automobiles to compute a relative total cost index for domestic and imported automobiles.

The index was constructed in two steps. In the first step, we combined the gasoline price index with estimates of mileage for domestic and imported automobiles to obtain gasoline cost indexes for domestic and imported automobiles. In the second step, we computed total cost indexes for domestic and imported automobiles by taking a weighted average of the respective price and gasoline cost indexes and then computed a relative total cost index as the ratio of the imported total cost index to the domestic total cost index.

The computations in the first step are shown in Table 3B.1. Column (2) of Table 3B.1 gives an index of real gasoline prices. Columns (3) and (4) provide indexes of mileage of domestic and imported automobiles, respectively, using estimated domestic mileage in 1974 as the base figure. The mileage indexes

TABLE 3B.1

Computation of Total Gas Cost Indexes

(Col. 1) Year	(Col. 2) Real Gas Price (1974 = 100)	(Col. 3) Estimated[a] DMILEAGE (1974 = 100)	(Col. 4) Estimated[b] FMILEAGE (1974 DMILEAGE = 100)	(Col. 5) Estimated DGAS Cost	(Col. 6) Estimated FGAS Cost
1960	96.29	111.71	183.78	86.20	52.39
1961	94.19	126.13	264.85	74.68	35.56
1962	93.66	124.32	232.42	75.34	40.30
1963	92.44	108.11	209.00	85.51	44.23
1964	90.85	116.22	205.40	78.17	44.23
1965	92.72	110.81	214.41	83.67	43.24
1966	92.14	110.81	188.28	83.15	48.94
1967	92.34	109.01	203.59	84.71	45.36
1968	89.85	108.11	173.88	83.11	51.67
1969	88.05	107.21	199.99	82.13	44.03
1970	83.84	108.11	210.81	77.55	39.77
1971	80.91	105.41	203.59	76.76	39.74
1972	79.29	100.00	207.21	79.29	38.27
1973	81.90	97.30	214.41	84.17	38.20
1974	100.00	100.00	184.68	100.00	54.15

[a]Mileage for autos weighing 4,000 lbs.
[b]Mileage for autos weighing 2,000 lbs.

Variable Definitions and Sources: Real Gas Price = Gasoline price index divided by consumer price index for all goods (*Source*: Computed from unpublished data provided by the Consumer Price Indices Branch of the U.S. Bureau of Labor Statistics). Estimated DMILEAGE = Estimated mileage index of domestic automobiles (*Source*: Computed from historical mileage estimates in Thomas C. Austin and Karl H. Hellman, "Passenger Car Fuel Economy: Trends and Influencing Factors," paper presented at National Combined Farm, Construction and Industrial Machinery and Fuels and Lubricants Meetings, Milwaukee, September 10–13, 1973). Estimated FMILEAGE = Estimated mileage index of imported automobiles (*Source*: Same as above). Estimated DGASCOST = Estimated gasoline cost index for domestic automobiles. Computed as Real Gas Price/Estimated DMILEAGE). Estimated FGASCOST = Estimated gasoline cost index for imported automobiles. Computed as (Real Gas Price/Estimated FMILEAGE).

TABLE 3B.2

Computation of Relative Total Cost Index from Price and Gas Cost Indexes

(Col. 1) Year	(Col. 2) Real DPRICE (1974 = 100)	(Col. 3) DGASCOST (1974 = 100)	(Col. 4) DCOST (1974 = 100)	(Col. 5) FPRICE (1974D = 100)	(Col. 6) FGASCOST (1974D = 100)	(Col. 7) FCOST (1974D = 100)	(Col. 8) FDCOST
1960	152.74	86.20	129.45	167.82	52.39	127.42	98.45
1961	129.54	74.68	110.34	125.69	35.56	94.14	85.32
1962	143.04	75.34	119.35	144.74	40.30	108.19	90.65
1963	140.37	85.51	121.17	140.47	44.23	106.79	88.13
1964	142.19	78.17	119.78	132.90	44.23	101.87	85.05
1965	131.22	83.67	114.58	144.03	43.24	108.75	94.91
1966	130.94	83.15	114.21	124.71	48.94	98.19	85.97
1967	129.40	84.71	113.76	116.76	45.36	91.77	80.67
1968	126.44	83.11	111.27	121.81	51.67	97.26	87.41
1969	119.97	82.13	106.73	121.58	44.03	94.44	88.49
1970	96.20	77.55	89.67	97.87	39.77	77.54	86.47
1971	103.80	76.76	94.34	116.11	39.74	89.38	94.74
1972	106.19	79.29	96.78	111.90	38.27	86.13	89.00
1973	101.83	84.17	95.65	101.84	38.20	79.51	83.19
1974	100.00	100.00	100.00	121.70	54.15	98.06	98.06

Variable Definitions and Sources: Real DPRICE = hedonic price index for domestic automobiles deflated by CPI for all goods and adjusted to make 1974 = 100 (*Source:* Table 3.7). DGASCOST = estimated gasoline cost index for domestic automobiles (*Source:* Table 3.b.1). DCOST = total cost index for domestic automobiles. Computed as .65 (REAL DPRICE) + .35 (DGASCOST). Real FPRICE = hedonic price index for imported automobiles deflated by CPI for all goods and adjusted to make 1974 = 100 (*Source:* Table 3.7). FGASCOST = estimated gasoline cost index for imported automobiles (*Source:* Table 3.B.1). FCOST = Total cost index for imported automobiles. Computed as .65 (Real FPRICE) + .35 (FGASCOST). FDCOST = Relative total cost index of imported to domestic automobiles. Computed as (FCOST/DCOST).

are computed from data on estimated mileage for automobiles of different weight classes developed by Austin and Hellman.[15] For imported automobiles, we used mileage estimates for automobiles weighing 2,000 pounds, while for domestic automobiles we used mileage estimates for automobiles weighing 4,000 pounds. Columns (5) and (6) show estimated indexes of gasoline cost per mile for domestic and imported automobiles respectively, which are computed by dividing the gasoline price in dollars per gallon by the domestic and foreign mileage indexes, respectively, which are measured in miles per gallon.

The computations in the second step are shown in Table 3B.2. The domestic and imported cost indexes are computed as weighted averages of the hedonic price and gasoline cost indexes, using weights of .65 for the price index and .35 for the gasoline cost index. As the separate indexes are computed against a base value of 100 for domestic prices and gasoline costs in 1974, the weights used were chosen to conform to an estimate of the relative proportions to total cost accounted for by initial selling price and gasoline costs for new domestic automobiles in 1974. From data reported in *Automotive News Almanac*, we computed the weighted (by sales) average price of the ten leading domestic models to be $3,815 in 1974. If first-year depreciation is 20 percent, and the interest rate is 5 percent, the annual first-year cost for paying an initial price of $3,815 for a new car is $953.75. Assuming a price of gasoline of $.55 per gallon, and an annual miles driven estimate of 10,000 miles, and using the mileage figure of 11.1 miles per gallon reported by Austin and Hellman as the mileage of 4,000 lb. automobiles in 1974, we computed annual gasoline cost of $495.50, and a total cost of $1,449.25. Dividing fixed cost by total cost, we computed annualized initial selling price to be 65.81 percent of total cost. The weights were then rounded to .65 and .35 in making the computation of the weighted averages.

Columns (4) and (7) show the estimated total cost indexes for domestic and imported automobiles resulting from taking weighted averages of the price indexes and the gasoline cost indexes. The relative import to domestic cost index is shown in Column (8) as the ratio of the import cost index divided by the domestic cost index.

APPENDIX 3.C

Alternate Specifications for Time Series Regressions

In performing the time series regression analysis, we experimented with a number of different specifications of the equations reported in the text of Chapter 3. We also constructed several proxy variables to measure the growth in availability of imported automobiles and to measure the relative market coverage of imported and domestic automobiles. This appendix reviews briefly the statistical results of regressions not reported in the text.

The only form of specification that consistently yielded a stable price coefficient with the theoretically expected sign used the ratio of import-to-domestic new-car sales or the import share as the dependent variable and included the one-year lag term of import to domestic sales ratio and the ratio of imported-to-domestic automobile price as independent variables. We also tested a number of other specifications not reported in the chapter.

• We performed two-stage least-squares estimates of the import share demand equation using an index we constructed of relative unit labor cost of imported cars as an instrument* and the relative import price as a jointly dependent variable. Using two-stage least squares did not improve the results; the constructed instrumental variable performed poorly.

• We tried a number of specifications not using any lag terms, with import share as the dependent variable. All of the estimated equations had positive or statistically insignificant price elasticity estimates.

• We regressed domestic sales per capita on the change in domestic price, the change in the import price, the change in income, and lagged total stock per capita. The equation yielded the theoretically expected positive sign on import price, but the coefficient on domestic price was not significantly different from zero.

• We regressed import sales per capita on the change in the import price, the change in income, the change in domestic price, and the total stock of capital. Both price terms were insignificantly different from zero.

• We regressed total sales per capita on average price, income, and lagged stock. The price variable was constructed as a sales-weighted average of our domestic and imported car price indexes. The estimated equation yielded a positive price elasticity. Use of the BLS new-car price in place of our index did not qualitatively alter the results.

• We estimated a series of equations with domestic sales per capita as the dependent variable and the domestic and foreign price as independent variables. Other variables in the equations included per capita income, the price of gasoline, and lagged automobile stock per capita. The estimated own-price elasticity was positive in all specifications.

• We estimated a series of equations with foreign sales per capita as the dependent variable and the domestic and foreign price as independent variables. Other vari-

---

*To obtain the relative unit labor cost index, we developed, using a number of public sources supplying data on wages, hours, and productivity, indexes of unit labor cost changes in Germany, Japan, and the United States in automobile production. We combined the German and Japanese indexes into an index of foreign labor costs in automobile production by taking a weighted (by relative sales in the United States) average of German and Japanese unit labor costs in automobile production.

ables in the equations included per-capita income, the price of gasoline, and lagged automobile stock per capita. All equations had a positive own-price elasticity and a negative cross-price elasticity.

- We estimated some equations using the small-car share* as an explanatory variable in the import share equation. These specifications did not improve the results.
- We estimated an equation with import sales per capita as the dependent variable and lagged import sales per capita, import price, domestic price, and a dummy for years since the beginning of mass Japanese penetration (1966) as independent variables. We estimated an analogous equation with domestic sales per capita as the dependent variable and lagged domestic sales per capita replacing lagged import sales per capita as an explanatory variable. Some of the own-price elasticities in the import sales equations were negative, but the values were sensitive to changes in specification (that is, using per capita income in place of years since 1966 as an exogenous variable). The domestic equation yielded a positive own-price elasticity for all specifications.
- We regressed import sales per capita on lagged import stock and price terms. This equation yielded the theoretically expected signs, but adding per capita income and the price of gasoline both jointly and separately to the equation made the import price coefficient insignificantly different from zero.

We also added a number of variables to the basic equations explaining the import-to-domestic sales ratio reported in Chapter 3. The variables we added were designed to pick up the underlying trend toward import sales after 1966 by measuring either the availability or market coverage of imported cars. It was hoped that these additional variables would seem more reasonable than the time trend variable *JAPAN* used in the time series regressions reported in the text. However, none of the variables tried, when added to the time series equations as specified in Chapter 3 as substitutes for *JAPAN*, entered with a statistically significant coefficient of the theoretically expected sign. The variables tried in the equation were:

- *BRANDS5*. BRANDS5 was defined as the number of import makes with more than 5 percent of the sales of all imports. This variable was meant as a measure of the variety of imported automobiles available; makes with less than 5 percent of the market were excluded because the proliferation of exotic varieties of imported sports cars, all with trivial total sales, was not expected to affect significantly the import share. The variable *BRANDS5* did not have a statistically significant coefficient in any of the equations.
- *BRANDS10*. BRANDS10 was defined as the number of import makes with more than 10 percent of the sales of all imports. BRANDS10 did not have a statistically significant coefficient in any of the equations.

---

*Small cars were defined as cars with length less than 190 inches. By that definition, all imports in the historical sample were small cars.

- *FDDEALER. FDDEALER* was defined as the ratio of imported-to-domestic new-car dealerships on January 1 of the year for which sales data were recorded. *FDDEALER* had a negative coefficient in some regressions, indicating that relative import sales were lower in years in which more dealerships were available, and a statistically insignificant coefficient in other specifications.
- *RANGE.* The variable *RANGE* was computed to be the ratio of the difference in weight between heavy and light imports and the difference in weight between the heavy and light domestic autos. A heavy auto in each category was defined to be the auto in the 95th percentile of the sales distribution ranked by weight, while a light auto in each category was defined to be the auto in the 5th percen-

TABLE 3C.1

Additional Variables Added to Time Series Regression

Year	BRANDS5	BRANDS10	FDDEALER	RANGE
1960	3	2	.4356	.46
1961	2	2	.4044	.52
1962	2	2	.3796	.54
1963	4	1	.2334	.55
1964	2	1	.1703	.34
1965	1	1	.1908	.43
1966	1	1	.1986	.38
1967	2	1	.2318	.38
1968	3	1	.2576	.59
1969	4	1	.2863	.36
1970	4	2	.2070	.57
1971	4	2	.3774	.36
1972	4	3	.4830	.26
1973	5	3	.5240	.39
1974	5	3	.4436	.37

Variable Definition and Sources: BRANDS5 is number of import makes accounting for over 5 percent of import new-car sales (*Source*: Back issues of *Automotive News Almanac*). BRANDS10 is number of import makes accounting for over 10 percent of import new-car sales (*Source*: Back issues of *Automotive News Almanac*). FDDEALER is ratio of domestic-to-imported dealerships (*Source*: Computed from data in *Automotive News Almanac*). RANGE is ratio of difference in weight between 95th percentile and 5th percentile of sales of imports ranked by weight and difference in weight between 95th percentile and 5th percentile of sales of domestic autos ranked by weight (*Source*: Computed from data in successive issues of *Automotive News Almanac*).

tile of the sales distribution by weight. Thus, in computing *RANGE*, we eliminated models that might have been on the extremes of the weight range for either domestic or imported vehicles and accounted for very few sales. The variable *RANGE*, as defined above, rises when the weight range of popular imports grows, and falls when the weight range of popular domestic autos grows. Thus, introduction of domestic subcompacts tended to lower *RANGE*, while introduction of larger versions of popular imports would tend to increase *RANGE*.

The variable *RANGE* did not have a statistically significant coefficient in any of the regression specifications.

Table 3C.1 lists the values of the variables added. Changes in *BRANDS5* and *BRANDS10* seem to correspond roughly with movements in the import share; the number of popular import makes declined in the early 1960s with the decline in sales of all import makes other than Volkswagen and increased after 1966 with the entry of Japanese autos into the mass market and the increased sales of "captive imports" including Opel and Capri. However, *BRANDS5* and *BRANDS10* do not have a partial positive correlation with the import share when the other variables in the time series regression equations are included. *FDDEALER* also moves roughly with the movement in import shares; it declines in the early 1960s and then rises sharply after 1964. However, fluctuations in *FDDEALER* do not correspond closely to fluctuations in the import-to-domestic sales ratio. Movements in the variable *RANGE* do not seem to follow any clear pattern in relation to movements in the import share; one reason is that *RANGE* is affected not only by increased competitiveness of imports and domestics (that is, increases in the maximum weight of imports available and decreases in the minimum weight of domestics available) but also by accentuations of the extremes of each group (that is, availability of heavier domestic and lighter imported cars).

APPENDIX 3.D

The Hedonic Market Share Model: Theoretical Discussion and Description of Data Base

The first section of this appendix presents a fuller discussion of the theoretical basis of the CRA hedonic market share model used to provide estimates of the effects of changes in imported car prices on market shares.[16] The discussion includes an outline of the algorithm used for the actual computations. The second section of the appendix describes the variables on the database used in the model, including sources, and lists the individual observations of automobile models.

Theoretical Statement of the Hedonic Market Share Model

General Statement of the Problem

The idea that separate economic goods can be thought of as separate bundles (or vectors) of hedonic attributes was first articulated by Court.[17] Recently, the idea has been promoted extensively by Lancaster[18] in theoretical applications and by Ohta and Griliches in empirical research.[19] The similar notion that different consumers could be described by different vectors of taste characteristics is used in this model.

In line with the standard approach to consumer demand analysis, we assume that consumers are utility maximizers. This assumption is translated into our framework in the following statement.

Assumption

Given a particular consumer (as represented by his vector of taste attributes), the good chosen is the one that leads to the highest utility (which is a function of the good's vector of hedonic attributes).

Formally we may write this assumption as

(A1) Good j is chosen by consumer x if and only if

$$u(h_j:x) \geq u(h_i:x) \text{ for all } i \neq j$$

where

h_j is the vector of hedonic attributes of good j and
x is the vector of taste characteristics of the consumer

The utility of a particular good (or vector of hedonic attributes) to a particular consumer (or vector of taste characteristics) can be approximated by a variety of mathematical formulae. For example, using Taylor's formula we can write

$$u(h_j:x) = \alpha_0(x) + \sum_{i=1}^{I} u_i^1(x) f_i(h_j^i)$$

$$+ \tfrac{1}{2} \sum_{i=1}^{I} \sum_{k=1}^{I} u_{i,k}^2(x) f_i(h_j^i) f_k(h_j^k) + R$$

where
h_j^i is the level of the ith hedonic attribute of good j;

I is the number of hedonic attributes; the

u_i^I are $\partial u/\partial f_i$; the

f_i are translations of the characteristics; and

R is the remainder to capture higher order effects.

There is nothing especially important about the form or degree of the approximation presented above. One could just as well have included a set of terms of the type $u_{i,k,n} f_i(h_j^i) \times f_k(h_j^k) \times f_n(h_j^n)$. The inclusion of such terms would increase the closeness between the approximation and the actual utility function, but it would also increase the number of parameters to be estimated. Further, the functions f_i are rather general (for example, $f_i(x) = x$ or $f_i(x) = \ln x$ are certainly possibilities). For the bulk of the remainder of this appendix we use a simple linear approximation as shown below:

$$u(h_j:x) \approx a(x) + \sum_{i=1}^{I} u_i^I(x) \times h_j^i.$$

In the approximation shown above, $u_i^I(x)$ can be interpreted as the marginal utility to consumer x from a unit of hedonic attribute i.

Two further points need to be stressed. First, as we are only comparing the utility between different goods, the utility function could be multiplied by any positive number without any change in the results. Second, our discussion considers the price as just another hedonic attribute of the good. We can normalize the equation so that the coefficient of price is -1. The resulting utility indicator is shown below:*

$$u(h_j:x) = \sum_{i=1}^{I} u_i^I(x) h_j^i - P_j \qquad (3D.0)$$

where

P_j is the price of the jth good.

This type of formulation for the utility indicator will be the basis of much of the remaining analysis.

Consumer Taste Characteristics

Consumers may have different tastes or, alternatively, consumers may have different traits that result in their behaving as though they have different tastes. We show below how consumer taste differences enter the model.

---

*Note that the constant term $a(x)$ has "disappeared." The reason is that since we are interested in only the difference in utility between two goods, a constant term cannot affect this comparison.

The vector x in Equation (3D.0) is meant to represent the taste characteristics of a particular consumer. Differences among consumers (and, hence, differences in their choices) will therefore be felt through differences in the $u_i^1(x)$ s; that is, consumers exhibiting different tastes will exhibit different marginal utilities for one or more hedonic attributes.

Discrete Alternatives

In the automobile market, the hedonic attributes are available in a finite number of discrete goods. We assume that the consumer must choose a single good to maximize his utility.

The assumption that consumers are not able to choose among a "smooth" (or continuously variable) set of alternatives complicates the problem. The lack of smoothness implies that calculus will not be of much value in finding the maximum. (The calculus is concerned with the local conditions for an extremum, and this problem requires a global comparison.)

The formulation of the model embodies three main features: (1) goods are represented by their embodied hedonic attributes; (2) consumers are represented by their taste characteristics; and (3) there are only a finite number of discrete goods available to the consumer. Therefore, it must be the case that at least one good (there may be ties) leads to the attainment of the maximum utility level. Formally, if i is the good being chosen, we have

$$i = S(H,P,x) = \{i \mid u(h_i:x) - P_i \geq u(h_j:x) - P_j, \text{ for all } j\}$$

where

H is the matrix $= (h_1, h_2, \ldots h_n)$; and
h_i is the vector of the level of hedonic attributes embodied in good i;
P is the vector of prices $= (P_1, P_2, \ldots P_n)$ for the goods;
x is the vector representing the taste characteristics of the consumer.

Now, if the set of possible goods and their prices do not change, we can write this just as well as

$$i = S(x).$$

We have indicated above that different consumers may well have different taste characteristics. (Different taste characteristics may be the definition of different consumers choosing, rather than a single consumer choosing repeatedly.) If we don't have observations on choices and the taste characteristics of separate consumers, we need some way to account for the possible difference or variance in tastes. The most appealing solution to this problem is to assume

that taste can be represented as a random variable. In other words, for a consumer drawn at random, we refer to the probability that the consumer exhibits a particular vector of taste characteristics. This probability is written as $f(x)$.

The probability that a consumer (drawn at random from the population) will choose a particular car, call it car i, is equal to the probability that he has a vector of taste characteristics such that car i leads to the maximum utility. Consider the set of all xs such that $i = S(x)$. Formally,

$$\Omega_i = \{x \mid i = S(x)\}.$$

The probability that i is chosen is just the probability that x lies in Ω_i. If we call π_i the probability that car i is chosen, we have

$$\pi_i = Prob\,[x \in \Omega_i] = \int f(x)\,dx.$$

The π_is depend crucially on what the probability distribution for the xs are. We make this dependence explicit by representing the distribution f by a vector α of parameter values. The π_i associated with $f(x:\alpha)$ is written $\pi_i(\alpha)$ and is of paramount importance in the discussion below.

The Shares of Sales

If v is a vector where v_i is the number of occurrences of i, and $\pi_i(\alpha)$ is the probability of occurrence i, then the probability of observing v is

$$Prob\,(v) = \frac{m!}{v_1!\,v_2!\,\ldots\ldots v_n!}\,\pi_1(\alpha)^{v_1}\pi_2(\alpha)^{v_2}\ldots \pi_n(\alpha)^{v_n},$$

where

m is the total number of sales ($m = v_1 + v_2 + \ldots v_n$).[20]

The probability of observing v, given α, is the likelihood of the given sample (v). The log-likelihood is

$$LL\,(v:\alpha) = C + \sum_{ii=1}^{n} v_i \log \pi_i(\alpha)$$

where

$$C = \log m! - \sum_{i=1}^{n} \log v_i!$$

We may also write the log-likelihood function as

$$\frac{LL(v:\alpha)}{m} = \frac{C}{m} + \sum_{i=1}^{n} \frac{v_i}{m} \log \pi_i(\alpha)$$

if we wish to concentrate on the shares of the goods sold ($\frac{v_i}{m}$) rather than total sales.

We seek to choose the αs so that the log-likelihood function is maximized. The αs so chosen will be the maximum likelihood estimates of the parameters of the distribution function on consumer tastes.

If such an α could be chosen, call it α^*, then consumer tastes would be distributed as

$$f(x:\alpha^*).$$

Note that in this formulation of the problem the vector of taste characteristics (the xs) are never observed. We posited the existence of such xs, but they only served to allow the marginal utilities from each hedonic attribute to vary among consumers. We are therefore free to interpret the xs in any convenient fashion. Of course, whatever interpretation is taken, the interpretation of the xs is initimately related to the interpretation of the $u_i^1(x)$s.

We will assume

$$u_i^1(x) = x_i.$$

By so doing, we assume there is a one-to-one relationship between the marginal utilities for each hedonic attribute and a consumer taste characteristic. (Of course, the approach taken to this point does not necessitate this assumption. We make it merely for ease in intepreting the results.) This assumption means that the distribution of the marginal utilities for the population as a whole is just the distribution of the xs (which we have estimated).

Now, suppose we relax our implicit assumption that the hedonic attributes completely describe the good and that the taste characteristics completely describe the consumer. Instead, we assume that "perceived" utility by the consumer is equal to the utility in the observed hedonic attributes plus a stochastic term.

Formally, we have

$$u^*(h_j:x) = \sum_{i=1}^{I} u_i^1(x) h_j^i - P_j + \lambda \epsilon$$

where ϵ is the stochastic term. (We assume that ϵ is distributed independently and identically across all consumers and goods. For the remainder of this book we will often write ϵ to represent $\lambda \epsilon$.)

If we assume the error term is distributed independently of the population taste parameters, the discussion of the probability of choice is altered from the nonstochastic case. Now, the probability of choosing good i given that the consumers tastes are x is equal to the probability that $u^*(h_i:x)$ is at least as large as all other $u^*(h_j:x)$. Thus, we can write:*

Probability that i is chosen, given $x = \pi_i(x)$

$= \text{Prob}(u^*(h_i:x) \geq u^*(h_j:x))$ for all j

$= \text{Prob}\left[\sum_{r=1}^{I} u_r^1(x)(h_i^r - h_j^r) + P_j - P_i \geq (\epsilon_j - \epsilon_i)\right]$ for all j

The probability that good i will be sold (when tastes are allowed to vary over the whole population) is then

$$\pi_i = x\epsilon X \int \pi_i(x) f(x) \, dx.$$

The Estimation Problem

This section outlines the methods used to estimate the parameters of the utility function. Actual estimation requires assumption of functional forms for both the utility function and the distribution function of the taste parameters.

Assume that the utility derived from a certain good is a linear function of the hedonic attributes of the particular good and an additive error. Formally, we write

$$u_j = \sum_{i=1}^{I} e^{\beta_i} h_j^i + \epsilon \qquad (3D.1)$$

where

h_j^i is hedonic attribute i for car j; and
e^{β_i} is the marginal utility of hedonic attribute i.

We also assume that the β_is are independently normally distributed with mean μ_i and standard deviation σ_i. The error term ϵ is assumed to be independently, identically Weibull distributed across all goods and consumers.†

---

*Note that it is at this point that ϵ term vanishes. $\pi_i(x)$ depends on the distribution of ϵ since $\pi_i(x)$ is obtained by integrating ϵ out.
†If ϵ is Weibull, then $Prob\,(\epsilon \leq a) = e^{-e^{-a}}$

RELATIVE PRICES AND DEMAND

$$u_j = \hat{u}_j(\beta) + \epsilon \tag{3D.1a}$$

where

$$\hat{u}_j(\beta) = \sum_{i=1}^{I} e^{\beta_i} h_i^j.$$

McFadden[21] has shown that in this case the probability of choosing good j given β is

$$P_j(\beta) = \frac{e^{\hat{u}_j(\beta)}}{\sum_{k=1}^{K} e^{\hat{u}_k(\beta)}} \tag{3D.2}$$

We account for the fact that β is itself a random variable by integrating over the βs. That is,

$$P_j(\mu,\sigma) = \frac{e^{\hat{u}_j(\beta)}}{\sum_{k=1}^{K} e^{\hat{u}_{jk}(\beta)}} f_N(\beta:\mu,\Sigma)\, d\beta \tag{3.D.3}$$

where

$f_N(\beta:\mu,\Sigma)$ is the density function for a multivariate normal with mean vector μ and variance covariance matrix

$$\Sigma = \begin{bmatrix} \sigma_1^2 & & O \\ & \sigma_2^2 & \\ & & \ddots \\ O & & \sigma_i^2 \end{bmatrix}$$

These probabilities involve a rather complex integral—the order of integration is the same as the number of characteristics. To evaluate the integrals (the $P_j(\mu,\sigma)$) analytically except in the most special cases is virtually impossible. However, we can generally evaluate these integrals numerically.

The numerical evaluation is based on the Monte-Carlo technique. We know that $P_j(\mu,\sigma)$ is the expected value of $P_j(\beta)$. We can approximate $P_j(\mu,\sigma)$ by taking the average of many calculated $P_j(\beta)$, where β is a random vector generated with a normal distribution with mean μ and variance-covariance matrix Σ.

Formally, we have

$$\hat{P}_j(\mu,\sigma) = \frac{1}{m} \sum_{z=1}^{m} P_j(\beta_z)$$

where the estimates of β_z are drawn from independent normal distributions with a vector of nean μ_z and standard deviation σ_z. This technique is employed frequently in the course of our calculations to evaluate such integrals.

The probability of observing a particular sample v (where $v = (v_1, v_2,...v_n)$ and v_j is the number of sales of good j) is

$$\text{Prob}(v \mid \mu,\sigma) = \frac{m!}{\prod_{j=1}^{n} v_j!} \prod_{k=1}^{n} P_k(v,\sigma)^{v_k}$$

We want to choose the vectors μ and σ so as to maximize the probability of the observed sales pattern (v) occurring. Since $\ln(x)$ is a monotonic, increasing function, we maximize $\ln(\text{Prob}(v \mid \mu,\sigma))$ to obtain the same result. That is, we can express the maximand as follows:

$$L(v \mid \mu,\sigma) = \ln(v \mid \mu,\sigma)) = D + \sum_{k=1}^{n} v_k \ln(P_i \mid \mu,\sigma))$$

where

$$D = \ln \left(\frac{m!}{\prod_{i=1}^{n} v_i!} \right)$$

An algorithm to search for the values of μ and σ to maximize $L(v \mid \mu,\sigma)$ was developed. The algorithm is based on

$$\frac{\partial L(v \mid \mu,\sigma)}{\partial \mu_i} \quad \text{and} \quad \frac{\partial L(v \mid \mu,\sigma)}{\partial \sigma_i}$$

We have

$$\frac{\partial L(v \mid \mu,\sigma)}{\partial \mu_i} = \sum_{k=1}^{n} v_k \frac{\frac{\partial P_k}{\partial \mu_i}}{P_k}$$

and (recalling Equations (3.D.1) and (3.D.3):

$$\frac{\partial P_k}{\partial \mu_i} = \int_\beta \frac{\partial P_k(\beta)}{\partial \beta_i} f_N(\eta:0,1) d\eta$$

using

$$\beta_i = \mu_i + \sigma_i \eta_i$$

where

$$\eta_i \sim N(0,1)$$

and, using Equation (3.D.1)

$$\frac{\partial P_k(\beta)}{\partial \beta_i} = \frac{h_k^i e^{\hat{u}_k(\beta)}}{\left[\sum_{j=1}^{n} e^{\hat{u}_j(\beta)}\right]} \times \frac{e^{\hat{u}_k(\beta)}\left[\sum_{j=1}^{n} h_j^i e^{\hat{u}_j(\beta)}\right]}{\left[\sum_{j=1}^{n} e^{\hat{u}_j(\beta)}\right]^2}$$

and

$$\frac{\partial P_k}{\partial \sigma_i} = \int_\beta \frac{\partial P_k(\beta)}{\partial \beta_i} \times \eta_i f_N(\eta:0,1) d\eta_i$$

Each of these integrals is evaluated in the Monte-Carlo method described above for the calculation of such probability integrals.

The algorithm employed to find μ and σ can now be described. Starting with some estimates μ^0 and σ^0, we know how to calculate the likelihood function and its gradient ($\partial L / \partial \mu_i$ and $\partial L / \partial \sigma_i$). Thus, we know what direction to move to increase the likelihood. The algorithm simply moves in that direction by a constant times the gradient. If the likelihood has decreased, some of the $\partial L / \partial \sigma_i$ or $\partial L / \partial \mu_i$ must have changed sign. For those σ_i or μ_i where the gradient changed sign, the average value of the parameter is used in the next integration. For those σ_i or μ_i where the gradient did not change sign, no change is made. This averaging procedure is repeated until a value of the likelihood higher than previously recorded is calculated. As soon as the likelihood is found to increase, we replace μ^0 and σ^0 with the new values and repeat the prodecure.

Notes on Related Research

The case in which it is assumed that there is no error term in the utility indicator is the easiest to analyze. This problem coincides with our description in the beginning of this appendix. Research on this problem was first done by Quandt[22] in 1968.

Quandt analyzes the travel mode split problem for California trips. Quandt posits that consumers choose the mode (either bus, car, or air) that minimizes

the disutility of travel. The disutility of travel is a function of cost and travel time (that is, in our terminology, cost and travel time are the characteristics of the three goods). The weights attached to cost and travel time are assumed to be random. As we noted above, without an error term in the utility indicator, it is possible for some of the goods (in this case, modes) to be dominated. In fact, Quandt observes that buses are dominated. Regardless of the valuation placed on cost or travel time, buses are never the minimum disutility choice.

Quandt assumed that the disutility of both travel time and cost followed independent exponential distributions. Using data on mode choice between 16 pairs of California cities, Quandt empirically estimated parameters for the distributions on the disutility of travel time and cost.

McFadden has developed an empirical approach capable of solving a special case of the general model considered in this appendix.[23] McFadden assumes that utility is a function of the characteristics of goods and a random term. Utility is therefore a random variable. Since we assume that the good exhibiting the highest utility is chosen and since utility is itself random, we see that the choice of a particular good is a probabilistic event. In fact, McFadden shows that if we call u_i the systematic part of the utility of good i (that is, the portion of utility attributable to the observed characteristics of the good) and the additive error in the utility function is Weibull, then

$$P_i = \frac{e^{u_i}}{\sum_{j=1}^{n} e^{u_j}}$$

where

P_i is the probability of choosing good i.

The systematic part of utility (the u_is) can be represented as

$$u_i = \sum_{j=1}^{I} \theta_j \cdot h_i^j$$

where

h_i^j is the level of characteristic j for good i; and

θ_j is marginal utility of characteristic j throughout the population of consumers.

The problem tackled by McFadden is the estimation of the vector θ, given that it is assumed to be constant. The solution is found by maximizing the likelihood function over the range of θ.

Note that both the Quandt and McFadden models have elements of the general model outlined in this appendix. Quandt posits the existence of variable tastes in the population (but no error term in utility) and then estimates the parameters of the distribution of population tastes. McFadden, on the other hand, assumes that utility contains a random component but that tastes are fixed.

Each simplifying assumption is imposed with a severe cost. If we assume there is no error term in utility, then we must ignore all apparently dominated goods even though such goods are chosen in reality. If we assume that population tastes are nonvarying, then we have the problem of independence of irrelevant alternatives—that is, that the ratio of the shares of any two goods is independent of the presence or absence of other goods as alternatives.

A model needs to satisfy three criteria to avoid the above problems. The criteria are as follows:

1. Utility is a function of consumer tastes and the hedonic attributes of the goods and an error term;
2. Consumer tastes are allowed to vary among individuals; and
3. Consumers maximize utility.

The CRA hedonic market share model, as outlined in this appendix, meets these requirements.

Construction of Variables and Observations

The variables in the model correspond to auto characteristics, while the observations represent individual models. Models were chosen as follows. Domestic nameplates used were those whose sales were listed monthly in *Automotive News*. There were two exceptions, Challenger and Barracuda, for which characteristics data could not be found (both had low sales figures). For some nameplates, two submodels were distinguished on the basis of transmission type and number of cylinders. Sales breakdowns were available for each of these parameters, but no joint distribution data exist, according to the manufacturers. Therefore the nameplate was divided along the dimension of the more significant parameter (that is, the one more closely approaching a 50-50 break). The other parameter was taken as uniform. For example, 20 percent of all 1974 Comets were eight-cylinder, but only 8 percent of all Comets were manual. The models chosen were automatic eight (20 percent) and automatic six (80 percent). There were a few exceptions, where the breakdowns for cylinders and transmission seemed parallel. Thus Mustang comprises an automatic six (56 percent) and a manual four (44 percent).

Import models were those with sales figures in *Ward's*. In some cases various similar submodels were amalgamated (see notes on AMALGAM variable). High-priced, low-volume models (Ferrari, Rolls-Royce) were excluded.

Below, a list of variables is presented, with header, units, source, and gloss noted where appropriate. Abbreviations used are: ANA = *Automotive News Almanac;* Ward's = *Ward's Automotive Yearbook.*

ACCEL: Time required to pass a 55-foot vehicle traveling at 50 mph; seconds; DOT, NHSA:[24] Consumer Aid Series, vol. 4, November 1973. Also known as "fast-pass" time.

AMALGAM: This binary flag was set at zero unless the model was used to represent two or more models with different nameplates. This occurred in two situations. Certain domestic models (notably the "flagship" models of GM makes) comprise several models, differing in name, luxury, and price, but not in essential characteristics. For instance, sales for the Chevrolet model include the Bel Air, Impala, and Impala Custom. In these cases, the lowest-priced version was chosen as representative. In addition, some foreign makes were splintered into a profusion of similar models with very low-volume sales (for example, Renault 12, 12TL, 15 17G, 17GC, 17C, 17TL). These were amalgamated on the basis of engine and overall length, with the most popular model chosen as representative.

APRIL: Total U.S. sales for entire model, April 1974; *Automotive News Weekly* for domestic, *Ward's* for foreign. This represents sales for the entire nameplate; sales for the particular model are derived by multiplying SALESSHARE by APRIL.

Ward's gives monthly sales by make and an annual percentage breakdown by model.

Automotive News generally publishes sales figures in the second issue of each month.

AUGUST: See APRIL.

CMPRS: Compression Ratio; ANA '74.

CYLINDERS: Number of cylinders; ANA '74. Engine configuration was not recorded.

DISCOUNT: Proportion of list price represented by dealer's cost; *Consumer Reports*, April 1974, April 1975. Not available for all cars. Assuming a typical 10 percent markup, actual new price for a model may be estimated at 1.1 *DISCOUNT *NEWLIST.

HEADROOM: Headroom, front seat to headliner; inches; ANA '74.

HEIGHT: Overall height; inches; ANA '74.

HP: Net BHP, standard engine; horsepower; ANA '74. Sometimes the model was assigned a slightly more powerful engine for consistency with MPG or ACCEL. If the disparity was too great, the latter were recorded as NA, rather than assigning the car an unreasonably large engine.

JUNE, JULY: See APRIL.

LEGROOM: Legroom, front floor to front seat back; inches; ANA '74.

LENGTH: Overall length; inches; ANA '74.

MAKE: Code for model of car—that is, the observation ID number. See appended code list.

MPG: Estimated mileage per gallon; EPA: *Federal Register* vol. 39, no. 40, part 2.

   The EPA's list was not exhaustive. Where data were missing for some observations, they were fitted by regression techniques. No distinction was made between highway and city driving. In cases where a model was tested both with and without California emissions controls, the non-California figure was recorded.

NEWLIST: List price, representative example, ANA '74. For domestic cars, price includes power disk steering (except Pinto and Vega). Price includes power disk brakes only where standard equipment or where that was the only alternative to nonpower drums. Otherwise, brakes are nonpower disks. The price does not include air conditioning; where air conditioning was standard, the cost of that option on similar models was deducted.

NOPREP: Some domestic models (Valiant, Dart, Maverick, Pinto, Comet) and several imports do not include charges for dealer preparation in the list price. For these models, the dummy NOPREP is set equal to 1. Dealer preparation charges probably run around $50.

NOTSEDAN: Flag = o if model is a four-door sedan, flag = 1 otherwise; ANA '74.

SALESSHARE: Percentage of total sales of model for this submodel; ANA '75 and *Ward's* '75.

TANK: Gas tank capacity; gallons; ANA '74.

TRANS: Transmission type: 1 = automatic, 0 = manual; ANA '74. Imports were taken as manual except for Mercedes.

TURN: Turning diameter; feet; ANA '74.

USEDPRICE: Average retail price, year-old car; dollars; *Red Book* Region A, Oct. 1, 1974. See NEWLIST for option details.

WAGON: Flag = 1 if model available as stationwagon or hatchback, flag = 0 otherwise; ANA '74.

WEIGHT: Curb weight; lbs.; ANA '74.

WIDTH: Overall width; inches; ANA '74.

Model and Make Codes
*Model**

1. Gremlin A6
2. Gremlin M6
3. Hornet A8
4. Hornet A6

---

* A and M refer to transmission (automatic and Manual—Numbers after A and M refer to number of cylinders).

5. Javelin A8
6. Javelin M6
7. Matador A8
8. Matador A6
9. Ambassador A8
10. Valiant, Scamp, Duster
    (Valiant A8)
11. Valiant, Scamp, Duster
    (Valiant A6)
12. Fury and Gran Fury
    (Fury I A8)
13. Satellite A8
14. Chrysler
    (New Yorker A8)
15. Imperial A8
16. Dart A8
17. Dart A6
18. Coronet, Charger
    (Coronet A8)
19. Coronet A6
20. Dodge
    (Monaco A8)
21. Torino A8
22. Ford
    (Galaxie 500 A8)
23. Mustang A6
24. Mustang M4
25. Thunderbird A8
26. Maverick A8
    (two-door)
27. Maverick A6
28. Pinto A4
29. Pinto M4
30. Lincoln A8
31. Mark IV A8
32. Montego A8
33. Mercury
    (Monterey A8)
34. Cougar A8
35. Comet A8
36. Comet A6
37. Buick
    (Le Sabre A8)
38. Riviera A8
39. Century 350 A8
40. Apollo A8
41. Apollo A6
42. Cadillac
    (Calais A8)
43. Eldorado A8
44. Chevelle
    (Malibu A8)
45. Chevelle A6
    (two-door)
46. Nova A8
47. Nova A6
48. Chevrolet
    (Bel Air A8)
49. Corvette A8
50. Corvette M8
51. Camaro A8
52. Camaro M6
53. Monte Carlo A8
54. Vega A4
55. Vega M4
56. Cutlass A8
57. Oldsmobile
    (Delta 88 A8)
58. Toronado A8
59. Omega A8
    (two-door)
60. Omega A6
    (Two-door)
61. Pontiac
    (Bonneville htp A8)
62. LeMans A8
63. Firebird A8
64. Firebird M6
65. Grand Prix A8
66. Ventura A8
67. Ventura A6
    (two-door)
68. Audi 100LS M4
69. Audi Fox M4
70. Marina M4
71. MG
    (MGB – GT M4)
72. Jaguar
    (XJ-6 A6)

RELATIVE PRICES AND DEMAND

73. Triumph
    (TR-6 M6)
74. BMW
    (Bavaria M6)
75. Capri
    (2000 M4)
76. Colt
    (Sedan M4)
77. Datsun B210 M4
78. Datsun 260Z M6
79. Fiat 128 M4
80. Fiat 124
    (Coupe M4)
81. Fiat Xl/9 M4
82. Honda M4
83. Mazda Rx-4 M0
84. Mazda RX-2 & Rx-3
    (RX-2 Sedan M0)
85. Mazda 808 M4
86. Mercedes 280
    (Sedan A6)
87. Mercedes 450
    (450 SL A8)
88. Opel Manta M4
89. Pantera M8
90. Peugeot 504 M4
91. Porsche 914 (1.8) M4
92. Porsche 911
    (911 M6)
93. Renault
    (12 TL M4)
94. Saab
    (99LE M4)
95. Subaru
    (two door M4)
96. Toyota Corolla
    (1600 Sedan M4)
97. Corona
    (Sedan M4)
98. Celica
    (ST M4)
99. Mark II M6
100. VW Beetle M4
101. VW 412 A4
102. Dasher M4
103. Volvo 142, 144, 145
     (144 Sedan M4)
104. Volvo 164 M6
105. Datsun PL 610 M4
106. Datsun PL 710 M4

Make

1. AMC
2. Plymouth
3. Chrysler
4. Dodge
5. Ford
6. Lincoln
7. Mercury
8. Buick
9. Cadillac
10. Chevrolet
11. Oldsmobile
12. Audi
13. Austin
14. MG
15. Jaguar
16. Triumph
17. BMW
18. Capri
19. Colt
20. Datsun
21. Fiat
22. Honda
23. Mazda
24. Mercedes
25. Opel
26. Pantera
27. Peugeot
28. Porsche
29. Renault
30. Saab
31. Toyota
32. Volkswagen
33. Volvo

NOTES

1. For examples, See Gregory C. Chow, "Statistical Demand Functions for Automobiles and Their Use in Forecasting," in *The Demand for Durable Goods*, ed. Arnold C. Harberger (Chicago: University of Chicago Press, 1960); John C. Cragg and Russell S. Uhler, "The Demand for Automobiles," *Canadian Journal of Economics* 3 (August 1970): 386–406; Thomas R. Dyckman, "An Aggregate Demand Model for Automobiles," *Journal of Business* 38 (July 1965):252–56; M. J. Farrell, "The Demand for Motor Cars in the United States," *Journal of the Royal Statistical Society in the United States* 117 (Part 2, 1954): 171–93; Marc Nerlove, "A Note on Long-Run Automobile Demand," *Journal of Marketing* 22 (July 1957): 57–64; Daniel Suits, "Exploring Alternative Formulations of Automobile Demand," *Review of Economics and Statistics* 43 (February 1961): 66–69.

2. For discussion of the problems in computing an automobile price index, see Zvi Griliches, "Hedonic Price Indexes for Automobiles: An Econometric Analysis of Quality Change," in *Price Indexes and Quality Changes: Studies in New Methods of Measurement*, ed. Zvi Griliches (Cambridge: Harvard University Press, 1971), pp. 55–87; Jack E. Triplett, "Determining the Effects of Quality Changes on the CPI," *Monthly Labor Review* 94, 5 (May 1971): 27–32; and Robert J. Gordon, "The Measurement of Durable Goods Prices," unpublished paper (June 1974).

3. See Keith Cowling and J. Cubbin, "Price, Quality and Advertising Competition: An Econometric Investigation of the United Kingdom Car Market," *Economica* (November 1971).

4. See Jack E. Triplett and Keith Cowling, "A Quality-Adjusted Model for Determining Market Shares in Oligopoly," U.S. Department of Labor, Bureau of Labor Statistics, Working Paper, no. 4, (Washington, D.C., December 1971). Lawrence J. White informed us that he also tried to estimate market share changes for U.S. manufacturers as a function of changes in prices and characteristics. White's regressions were not yielding satisfactory results, and he abandoned the project.

5. J. Stuart McMenamin, Jean-Paul Pinard, and R. Robert Russell, "A Multilateral, Multi-Commodity Model of International Trade Flows," unpublished paper. The U.S. Tariff Commission has also performed research on the price elasticity of demand for imports, including automobiles, but their report at the time of this writing had not yet been made available to the public.

6. White reviews the history of list prices and transactions prices of U.S. autos in the early postwar years. See Lawrence J. White, *The U.S. Automobile Industry Since 1945* (Cambridge: Harvard University Press, 1971).

7. Market Facts, Inc., *A Foreign Automobile Impact Study*, report submitted to the U.S. Department of Labor, March 1976.

8. This type of index has been used in previous work. See, for example, Makoto Ohta and Zvi Griliches, "Automobile Prices Revisited: Extensions of the Hedonic Hypothesis," in *Household Production and Consumption*, ed. N. E. Terleckj, Studies in Income and Wealth no. 40, National Bureau of Economic Research (New York: Columbia University Press, 1975), pp. 325–98.

9. This problem is discussed in Gordon, op. cit. It would have been preferable to use performance dimensions directly in the regressions; unfortunately, a reasonably complete set of data on performance dimensions for individual automobile makes, including stopping distance, fuel economy, and acceleration, is only available for years after 1970.

10. For some models, we relied on sales breakdowns supplied in successive issues of *Ward's Automotive Reports Yearbook*.

11. See Thomas C. Austin and Karl H. Hellman, "Passenger Car Fuel Economy: Trends and Influencing Factors," paper presented to National Combined Farm Construction

and Industrial Machinery and Fuels and Lubricants Meetings, Milwaukee, September 10-13, 1973.

12. Appendix 3.D presents a theoretical discussion of the CRA hedonic market share model and describes the data bases used to derive the demand estimates presented in this chapter. The CRA hedonic market share model was first developed in an earlier phase of this study. The model was substantially improved and extended through subsequent work funded by Charles River Associates, the Electric Power Research Institute, and the Bureau of International Labor Affairs, U.S. Department of Labor. A complete statement of the model is presented in Charles River Associates, "Methodology for Predicting the Demand for New Electricity-Using Goods," draft report prepared for Electric Power Research Institute, November 1976.

13. Market Facts, op.cit.

14. See also Appendix 3.B.

15. Austin and Hellman, op. cit.

16. This discussion follows the main lines of the theoretical explanation of the model presented in Charles River Associates, op. cit.

17. L. M. Court, "Enterpreneurial and Consumer Demand Theories for Commodity Spectra," *Econometrica* 9 (April 1941) 135-62.

18. K. L. Lancaster, "A New Approach to Consumer Theory," *Journal of Political Economy* 74 (March-April 1966): 132-57.

19. See, for example, Ohta and Griliches, op. cit.

20. See Emanuel Parzen, *Modern Probability Theory and Its Implications* (Palo Alto, Calif.: Stanford University Press, 1958), p. 108.

21. See Daniel McFadden, "Conditional Logit Analysis of Qualitative Choice Behavior," in *Frontiers in Econometrics*, ed. Paul Zarembka (New York: Academic Press, 1974), pp. 105-39.

22. Richard E. Quandt, "Estimation of Modal Splits," *Transportation Research*, vol. 2, 1968.

23. See McFadden, op. cit.

24. U.S. Department of Transportation, National Highway Safety Administration.

CHAPTER

4

THE IMPACT OF AUTOMOBILE IMPORTS ON DOMESTIC AUTOMOBILE PRICES

Chapter 3 examined the effect of changes in the ratio of imported-to-domestic automobile prices on the import share of new-car sales. Foreign trade policies that change the price of imported autos will change the ratio of imported-to-domestic auto prices by the same proportion only if domestic prices remain constant. If changes in the prices of imported autos caused domestic prices to change, the net effect of a change in the import price on import share depends on a more complex interaction between the elasticity of the import share with respect to the ratio of imported-to-domestic auto prices estimated in Chapter 3 and the effect of changes in the import share on domestic-auto prices.

In this chapter, we present some rough evidence relating domestic-automobile prices to imported-automobile prices and import shares. We estimate alternative specifications of a domestic-auto price-formation equation in which the domestic auto price depends on domestic production costs, capacity utilization, and the amount of import competition. The statistical evidence suggests that increases in imports have a significant downward effect on domestic-auto prices. Further, illustrative computations from the estimated econometric coefficients indicate that the total effect of an increase in the import-to-domestic price ratio on the share of imported new-car sales could be as much as one-third less than the effect implied by the relative demand elasticity estimated in Chapter 3 when the impact of import sales on domestic-auto prices is taken into account.

The estimates presented in this chapter should be interpreted with some caution because all of the econometric results are from single-equation regression equations, which may be subject to simultaneous equations bias. Specifically, variables in the domestic-price-formation equations that are assumed to be exogenous, including import prices and import shares, may themselves be affected by changes in the domestic-auto price. It was not possible to find

suitable instrumental variables to explain movements in imported-auto prices and shares. However, the high explanatory power of the regression, the fact that the equations seem to account correctly for domestic cost changes, and the finding of a strong relationship with the expected coefficient between domestic costs and domestic prices all suggest that the results, though preliminary, provide confirmation of the hypothesis that increased import competition lowers domestic-auto prices.

Changes in the hedonic price of imported automobiles and changes in the import share of new-car sales can both be used as statistical indicators of changes in the competitiveness of imported autos in the U.S. market. If the characteristics mix of available imports relative to available domestic autos and the taste distribution for automobile characteristics among U.S. consumers were unchanging, then changes in the quality-adjusted import price would be the best measure of changes in import competitiveness. However, the impact of import price changes on effective import competition is likely to be small if automobiles produced in foreign countries do not have characteristics that appeal to a large fraction of U.S. buyers. (For example, if all Americans wanted full-size autos with powerful V-8 engines, it would not matter if foreign companies produced subcompacts at a lower quality-adjusted price than the price of full-size cars made in the United States, but import competitiveness would increase if the available range of characteristics of foreign cars became larger.)

Changes in the import share indicate in a rough way whether the popularity of imports is changing and how much domestic manufacturers must consider import competition in setting prices. The weakness of using the import share as a measure of import competition is that the import share is itself partly a function of domestic prices. As we have shown in Chapter 3 that year-to-year changes in the import-to-domestic auto price ratio have not been the principal determinant of year-to-year changes in the import share, it is probably not too unreasonable as a first approximation to use changes in the import share as an exogenous variable measuring changes in import competitiveness in the domestic price equation.

Table 4.1 presents the principal results of domestic price equations that estimate the impact of import share changes on domestic-automobile prices. The dependent variable in Equations (4.1.1) and (4.1.2) is CRA's hedonic price index for domestic automobiles, while in Equations (4.1.3) and (4.1.4) both the hedonic price index for domestic automobiles and an index of the unit production cost of domestic automobiles developed from input price and productivity data are deflated by the Consumer Price Index for all goods and services. The dependent variable in Equations (4.1.5) and (4.1.6) is the ratio of domestic-automobile prices to the domestic-automobile production cost index.

The capacity utilization index ($CUNEW$) included in some of the equations is developed by constructing a ratio between actual automobile production and a trend measure of potential production. (Details of the construction of the

TABLE 4.1

Price Formation Equations: Effect of Import Share Changes on Domestic Auto Prices

Equation (4.1.1)

LOG (UNDPRICE2) = -0.0141 + 1.099 LOG (TOTCOST)
(0.249)   (32.037)

-0.264 LOG (FORSHR)
(4.517)

$S.E.E.$ = .0690 R^2 = .5789 $D.W.$ = 1.723   OBS: 1960-74

Equation (4.1.2)

LOG (UNDPRICE2) = -0.0410 + 1.020 LOG (TOTCOST)
(0.547)   (7.101)

+ 0.0790 LOG (CUNEW) -0.245 LOG (FORSHR)
(0.572)   (3.567)

$S.E.E.$ = 0.710 R^2 = .5911 $D.W.$ = 1.815   OBS: 1960-74

Equation (4.1.3)

LOG (AJDPRICE2) = -0.0337 + 1.093 LOG (TOTCOST2)
(0.568)   (35.816)

-0.241 LOG (FORSHR)
(4.976)

$S.E.E.$ = .0675 R^2 = .7992 $D.W.$ = 1.838   OBS: 1960-74

Equation (4.1.4)

LOG (AJDPRICE2) = -0.0391 + 1.065 LOG (TOTCOST2)
(0.584)   (7.774)

+ 0.0307 LOG (CUNEW) -0.242 LOG (FORSHR)
(0.212)   (4.772)

$S.E.E.$ = .0703 R^2 = .8000 $D.W.$ = 1.844   OBS: 1960-74

(Continued)

IMPORT IMPACT ON DOMESTIC PRICES

Equation (4.1.5)

LOG (DMARKUP) = 0.100 −0.102 LOG (FORSHR)
(1.980) (4.856)

S.E.E. = .0863 R^2 = .4834   *D.W.* = 1.131   OBS: 1960-74

Equation (4.1.6)

LOG (DMARKUP) = −0.0458 −0.239 LOG (FORSHR)
(0.725) (4.912)

+ 0.0972 LOG (CUNEW)
(2.988)

S.E.E. = .0680 R^2 = .7038   *D.W.* = 1.835   OBS: 1960-74

Variable Definitions (and Sources): UNDPRICE2 = undeflated domestic automobile price index (*Source*: CRA hedonic price regressions). TOTCOST = undeflated total cost index of production computed as weighted average of materials price index, labor cost index, and capital cost index (For details of computation and sources, see Table 4.3). FORSHR = Import share of new-car sales (*Source*: Computed from new car registration data in successive issues of *Automotive News Almanac*). CUNEW = Capacity Utilization Index (*Source*: Computed from Federal Reserve Board Index of Production. For details of computation, see Table 7.6, Chapter 7). AJDPRICE2 = Domestic automobile price index deflated by CPI for all goods (*Source*: CRA hedonic regressions). TOTCOST2 = Total cost index of automobile production deflated by CPI for all goods. Computed as TOTCOST/CPI. DMARKUP = Estimated markup on domestic automobiles. Computed as AJDPRICE2/TOTCOST2.

capacity utilization index are provided in Table 7.6.) It is expected that CUNEW might have a positive coefficient, reflecting the fact that prices might rise in the short run when sales are high relative to capacity. A positive and significant coefficient for CUNEW is estimated in Equation (4.1.6), but in other specifications we did not find a statistically significant relationship between capacity utilization and price.

The equations in Table 4.1 show a statistically significant and highly stable negative relationship between the import share and the domestic hedonic price, when domestic costs are held constant. In all the equations except equation (4.1.5), the coefficient of the import share variable is close to −.25. This coefficient implies that a 10 percent increase in the import share would lead to approximately a 2.5 percent reduction in the price of a domestic automobile with a fixed set of characteristics, other things remaining equal. The estimate in

Equation (4.1.5) implies a somewhat smaller effect; a 10 percent increase in the import share would lead to a 1 percent reduction in the domestic price.

(The simultaneous equations bias in the equations in Table 4.1 suggest that we have underestimated the effect of the import share on domestic price because higher domestic prices should lead to a higher import share—that is, the reverse feedback effect would raise the coefficient of FORSHR.

(In addition, the positive effect of import share on domestic price shown in Table 4.1 suggests some simultaneous-equations bias in the time series import share demand equations in Chapter 3. If a higher import share causes domestic prices to fall, then it also is probably causing the import-to-domestic price ratio to rise. This would impart a spurious positive correlation to the variables FDSALE and FDPRICE in Tables 3.3 and 3.4. Thus, the coefficient of FDPRICE in those tables has some upward bias; that is, the absolute size of the short-run— and long run—relative price elasticity could be understated.)

The coefficients attached to TOTCOST and TOTCOST2 in Equations (4.1.1) through (4.1.4) indicate that the elasticity of domestic prices with respect to a change in domestic production costs is close to one—that is, a given percentage change in unit production costs leads to the same percentage change in quality-adjusted price. This result, which would be expected in a long-run equilibrium with profit margins roughly constant, increases confidence in the methods used to construct both the domestic hedonic price index and the production cost index, which were developed independently from different data sources.

(The price index was developed from data on transactions prices and physical characteristics of one-year-old automobiles, while the cost index was developed from price indexes of materials used in automobile production, a construction cost index, and wage and productivity data used in constructing the auto price index. For details of construction of the automobile price index, see Chapter 3, especially Appendix 3.A. For details of construction of the production cost index, see Table 4.3 below.)

Use of the estimated domestic-automobile markup as the dependent variable in Equations (4.1.5) and (4.1.6) does not substantially alter the qualitative nature of the results, partly because the implied assumption of a unit elasticity of price with respect to cost is not far from the elasticity estimated from the data in Equations (4.1.1) to (4.1.4).

Table 4.2 presents alternative specifications of the domestic-auto price formation equation in which the price of imported automobiles is an independent variable. If the price of imported automobiles were determined externally as an exact percentage markup over the sum of foreign production costs, transport costs, and import tariffs, all in dollar terms, then the coefficient of imported-auto prices in Equations (4.1.1) and (4.1.2) would represent a good estimate of the response of domestic-auto prices, all other things the same, to changes in the import price brought about by changes in trade barriers. How-

TABLE 4.2

Price Formation Equations: Relationship Between Import and Domestic Prices

Equation (4.2.1)

$$\text{LOG (UNDPRICE2)} = -0.0432 + 0.100 \text{ LOG (TOTCOST)}$$
$$(0.687) \quad (0.669)$$
$$+ 0.740 \text{ LOG (UNFPRICE2)} + 0.166 \text{ LOG (CUNEW)}$$
$$(4.765) \quad\quad\quad\quad\quad (1.564)$$

S.E.E. = .0595 R^2 = .7122   D.W. = 1.721   OBS: 1961-74

Equation (4.2.2)

$$\text{LOG (UNDPRICE2)} = 0.0246 + 0.176 \text{ LOG (TOTCOST)}$$
$$(0.510) \quad (1.176)$$
$$+ 0.812 \text{ LOG (UNFPRICE2)}$$
$$(5.176)$$

S.E.E. = .0630 R^2 = .6482   D.W. = 1.359   OBS: 1961-74

Equation (4.2.3)

$$\text{LOG (DMARKUP)} = -0.0178 + 0.910 \text{ LOG (FMARKUP)}$$
$$(0.808) \quad (7.465)$$

S.E.E. = .0630 R^2 = .7250   D.W. = 1.482   OBS: 1961-74

Equation (4.2.4)

$$\text{LOG (DMARKUP)} = 0.0211 + 0.835 \text{ LOG (FMARKUP)}$$
$$(0.395) \quad (5.383)$$
$$-0.0105 \text{ LOG (CUNEW)}$$
$$(0.800)$$

S.E.E. = .0639 R^2 = .7389   D.W. = 1.375   OBS: 1961-74

Equation (4.2.5)

$$\text{LOG (AJDPRICE2)} = -0.0263 + 0.534 \text{ LOG (TOTCOST2)}$$
$$(0.571) \quad (2.829)$$
$$+ 0.521 \text{ LOG (AJFPRICE2)} -0.134 \text{ LOG (FORSHR)}$$
$$(2.984) \quad\quad\quad\quad\quad (2.596)$$

S.E.E. = .0524 R^2 = .8890   D.W. = 1.526   OBS: 1961-74

(continued)

Equation (4.2.6)

LOG (DMARKUP) = -0.0361 -0.134 LOG (FORSHR)
                 (0.747) (2.684)
             + 0.0584 LOG (CUNEW) + 0.528 LOG (FMARKUP)
               (2.104)   (3.107)

S.E.E. = .0518 R^2 = .8422   D.W.= 1.628   OBS: 1961-74

Variable Definitions (and Sources): UNDPRICE2, TOTCOST, CUNEW, DMARKUP, AJDPRICE2, FORSHR (See Table 4.1). UNFPRICE2 = Undeflated imported automobile price index (*Source*: CRA hedonic price regressions). AJFPRICE2 = Imported automobile price index deflated by CPI for all goods. FMARKUP = Estimated markup on imported automobiles computes as AJFPRICE2/TOTCOST2.

ever, in the actual process of price formation, foreign manufacturers, in order to remain competitive will tend to alter their prices and profit margins in response to changes in domestic-automobile prices. Thus, the coefficient of UNFPRICE2, the quality-adjusted imported-auto price, in equations (4.2.1) and (4.2.2) is biased upward because of the positive causal link between changes in domestic-auto prices and changes in imported-auto prices.*

The elasticity of domestic price with respect to import price is estimated to be .74 and .81 in Equations (4.2.1) and (4.2.2), respectively. The estimates are much higher than the expected response of domestic prices to changes in auto import prices resulting from tariff or exchange rate changes. Equations (4.2.3) and (4.2.4) show an even higher elasticity of the domestic-car markup

---

*The problem of simultaneous-equations bias in estimating the effect of import price changes on domestic price changes using Equations (4.2.1) and (4.2.2) is aggravated by the fact that we are using one-year-old transactions prices as a proxy variable for new-car transactions prices. Because of arbitrage in the used car market, we would expect both domestic and foreign one-year-old prices to move in the same direction; for example, one-year-old import-car prices would not immediately rise to reflect fully an increase in imported new-car prices because of competition with domestic automobiles, though a reduction in imported new-car sales because of higher prices would eventually rise imported used car prices by reducing the available stock of imported cars.

Evidence that imported new-car prices do not always reflect costs has been found in a recent investigation by the U.S. Treasury Department on dumping of European cars in the United States, though the United States has decided against taking any action against European companies. (See Helen Kahn, "Treasury to Drop Import Dumping Probe," *Automotive News*, May 10, 1976.) European manufacturers were selling automobiles in the United States at prices substantially below the sum of European prices and shipping costs, as a short-run response to competitive pressure.

IMPORT IMPACT ON DOMESTIC PRICES

with respect to the imported-car markup over domestic costs than the estimates of the elasticity of domestic-auto price with respect to imported auto price in Equations (4.2.1) and (4.2.2). A somewhat lower elasticity of domestic price with respect to import price is found by including the import share as an independent variable in Equations (4.2.5) and (4.2.6).

Table 4.3 provides details of the construction of the automobile production cost index. The index was computed as a weighted average of indexes of capital costs, costs of material used in automobile production, and unit labor costs, using as weights the shares of imports from other industries, labor input, and capital input from the 1967 Input-Output Table compiled by the U.S. Department of Commerce, Bureau of Economic Analysis. The capital cost index was constructed by using the GNP deflator for real private domestic fixed investment as a proxy variable for the unit cost of automobile industry plant and equipment. The labor cost index was computed by dividing an index of automobile industry wages by an index of automobile industry output per man-hour. The materials cost index was constructed by taking a weighted average of wholesale price indexes and consumer price indexes of industrial products and consumer goods and services corresponding to the breakdown of sectoral inputs to the automobile industry in the Bureau of Economic Analysis 1967 Input-Output Table for the U.S. economy.

The domestic-auto price formation equations estimated in Tables 4.1 and 4.2, taken as a group, indicate that increased import competitiveness does lead to lower domestic automobile prices. The coefficient of the import share variable in the equations in Table 4.1 are probably much more reliable indicators of the magnitude of the impact of increased imports on domestic-auto prices than the import price coefficient in Table 4.2. The expected arbitrage between substitute goods and spurious correlation casts doubt on an interpretation that the high coefficient on the import price variable in the equations reported in Table 4.2 reflect primarily a causal link from changes in import prices to changes in domestic prices.

The estimates of Table 4.1 can be combined with the estimates of the relative price elasticity of import share demand reported in Chapter 3 to derive predictions of the impact of exogenous changes in imported-auto prices on the import share and domestic-auto prices, which take into account the link between imports and domestic prices.

An increase in the import price caused, for example, by a tariff increase will lead initially to an equal proportional increase in the ratio of imported-to-domestic auto prices. The rise in the relative import price will then lead to a decline in the import share, which will then cause the domestic price to rise. The rise in the domestic price, by reducing the import-to-domestic price ratio, will lead to a rise in the import share, which in turn leads to a reduction in the domestic price. The total effect of the initial import price rise on the import share described by this process can be represented by the equation

TABLE 4.3

Computation of Automobile Production Cost Index

Year	Real Capital Cost Index (1967 = 100)	Real Materials Cost Index (1967 = 100)	Real Unit Labor Cost Index (1967 = 100)	Real Total Cost Index (1967 = 100)
1960	102.6	105.3	112.4	106.4
1961	101.0	103.9	112.2	105.2
1962	100.6	102.5	105.5	102.9
1963	100.2	103.7	104.3	103.4
1964	100.2	101.3	105.6	102.0
1065	99.3	101.0	100.8	100.8
1966	99.2	100.6	100.6	100.4
1967	100.0	100.0	100.0	100.0
1968	99.9	98.8	97.0	98.6
1969	99.4	97.6	99.1	98.1
1970	98.9	97.5	101.4	98.4
1971	100.1	97.5	93.6	97.0
1972	100.6	97.3	94.1	97.1
1973	98.5	96.3	92.5	95.8
1974	99.0	104.2	95.3	101.9

Data Sources and Methods of Computation:

Real capital cost index is an index of the unit costs of real private domestic fixed investment. It is computed by dividing the implicit price deflator for nonresidential private domestic fixed investment (see *Economic Report of the President*, 1976, Table B.3), by the Consumer Price Index.

The materials cost index is computed by taking a weighted average of wholesale price indexes and consumer prices indexes of products and services used as inputs in automobile production, and dividing that average by the CPI for all goods. The products and services included and the weights attached to them were chosen to conform to the percentage distribution of sector inputs to automobile production (excepting the automobile sector) in the 1967 input-output table developed by the Bureau of Economic Analysis of the U.S. Department of Commerce. The consumer and wholesale price indexes used in computation of the material index were taken from U.S. Department of Labor, Bureau of Labor Statistics, *Handbook of Labor Statistics*, for each year. Weights attached to product and service group wholesale and consumer price indexes used in constructing the materials cost index are (1) wholesale prices indexes: industrial commodities .01, textile products .04, fuels and power .02, chemicals .01, rubber and plastics .05, pulp and paper .01, iron and steel .17, primary metals .03, fabricated structural metal .01, machinery and equipment .32, furniture and household durables .02, nonmetal mineral products .03; (2) consumer price indexes: transportation services .08, reading and recreation .01, all commodities .05, all services .04, housing .01; and (3) import deflator .03.

The real unit labor cost index was computed by (1) dividing hourly wages in SIC 3711 by employee output per man-hour in SIC 371 to obtain unit labor costs; (2) dividing unit labor costs by the Consumer Price Index to obtain real unit labor costs; and (3) converting the real unit labor cost series into an index with 1967 = 100 and other years

IMPORT IMPACT ON DOMESTIC PRICES 127

$$E_{S,P_F} = \epsilon_2 + (\epsilon_1\epsilon_2\epsilon_3)\epsilon_2 + (\epsilon_1\epsilon_2\epsilon_3)^2\epsilon_2 + \ldots \quad (4.1)$$

where

E_{S,P_F} = the equilibrium percent change in import share with respect to a change in the import price;
ϵ_1 = the elasticity of domestic price with respect to import share;
ϵ_2 = the elasticity of import share with respect to the import-to-domestic price ratio; and
ϵ_3 = the elasticity of the import-to-domestic price ratio with respect to the domestic price.

If $|\epsilon_1\epsilon_2\epsilon_3| < 1$, the infinite series in Equation (4.1) converges to

$$E_{S,P_F} = \frac{\epsilon_2}{1-\epsilon_1\epsilon_2\epsilon_3} \quad (4.2)$$

Equation (4.2) can be used for illustrative purposes to compute the total impact of an import price change on import shares and domestic prices, using our parameter estimates of a_1 from Table 4.1, and of a_2 from Chapter 3. Suppose that $\epsilon_1 = -.25$ and $\epsilon_2 = -2.0$. Since ϵ_3, the elasticity of the import-to-domestic price ratio with respect to domestic prices, is -1, substituting in Equation (4.2) yields a value of $E_{S,P_F} = (-2/1.5) = -1.33$. The estimated total percentage reduction in the import share with respect to an import price change is reduced by one-third when the feedback effect of higher import shares on domestic prices is taken into consideration. In the absence of the feedback effect, a 10 percent increase in the import-auto price would lead to a 20 percent reduction in the import share. Including the effect of imports on domestic-auto prices, the total predicted effect of a 10 percent increase in the import price is a 13.3 percent reduction in the import share and a 3.325 percent increase in the domestic price. (Note that the implied percentage increase in the domestic price per unit percentage increase in import price from the estimated coefficient on import share in Table 4.1 is much lower than the direct estimate of the elasticity of domestic price with respect to import price reported in Table 4.2. We should expect this

---

equal to 100 × (real unit labor costs/1967 real unit labor costs). Hourly wages in SIC 3711 was from U.S. Department of Labor, Bureau of Labor Statistics, *Employment and Earnings*. The index of employee output per man-hour in SIC 371 was from U.S. Department of Labor, Bureau of Labor Statistics, Bulletin 1827, *Indexes of Output per ManHour: Selected Industries*, 1974 ed.

The real total cost index was computed by the following formula: Total Cost = .70 Materials Cost + .19 Labor Cost + .11 Capital Cost. The 1967 input-output table was used to select the weights assigned to the different components of total cost.

difference between the implied and direct estimates of the response to higher import prices if the import price coefficients in Table 4.2 are biased upward, as discussed above.)

If we combine the lower-bound estimate of the elasticity of domestic price with respect to import share of -.1 reported in some specifications in Tables 4.1 and 4.2 with the relative price elasticity of import share demand of -2 used in the previous example, we find, applying Equation 4.2, that a 10 percent increase in the import price would lead, in equilibrium, to a 16.7 percent reduction in the import share and to a 1.67 percent increase in the domestic price. In general, for lower values of the elasticity of domestic price with respect to import share, the percentage change in import share from an import price change will be closer to the change predicted in the price elasticity estimates from Chapter 3, and the equilibrium change in the domestic-auto price will be smaller.

In conclusion, econometric estimates presented in this chapter show that increased (decreased) import competitiveness is likely to lower (raise) the price of domestically manufactured automobiles. The induced domestic-automobile price changes make the change in the import share corresponding to a change in imported-auto prices smaller than it would be if domestic-auto prices remained constant and reduce the potential employment gain from higher tariffs, as the increased domestic prices will dampen the increase in domestic new-car sales.

CHAPTER

5

THE SHAPE OF AUTOMOBILE COST FUNCTIONS

Previous studies of the automobile industry agree that scale economies are crucial in the production of automobiles. (However, writers disagree both on the annual rate of output required to attain all scale economies, and on the extent to which the current level of concentration in the U.S. automobile industry is mandated by scale economies.)[1] Scale economies both limit the number of firms able to produce at efficient rates within a given country and affect the international location of automobile production. In many countries, demand is not sufficiently great to warrant the existence of local automobile production. However, tariff barriers, if sufficiently high, can outweigh cost disadvantages of small-scale production and encourage investment in subefficient facilities. (Before the 1965 U.S.-Canadian Automotive Agreement eliminating tariffs on finished automobiles between the two countries, inefficient-size production facilities for a number of automobile models were sheltered by Canada's tariff.)[2]

In this chapter we present estimates of the percentage cost penalties from subefficient production volumes of different types of automobiles. The estimates were developed in consultation with Professor Merrill Ebner of Boston University, one of the authors of the Committee on Motor Vehicle Emissions (CMVE) report[3] on the cost of meeting automobile pollution standards. Data on production costs developed for that report[4] were supplemented with information collected separately on the mix of factors used in automobile production and on the division of individual cost components into fixed and variable costs; these revised data were used to compute cost curves for automobile production.

(We were unable to find usable estimates of percentage cost penalties from suboptimal-scale automobile production in previously published literature. Bain gives 300,000 units per year as a "low" estimate of minimum efficient scale, suggesting that some additional efficiencies could be achieved at 600,000 units. For smaller outputs, "costs are 'moderately higher' at 150,000 units,

substantially higher at 60,000 units, and uneconomical at smaller scales." Bain does not give quantitative definitions of the terms "moderate," "substantial," and "uneconomic."[5] White estimates the relative unit cost at 120 percent for 50,000 units, 110-15 percent at 100,000 units, 101-5 percent at 200,000 units, and 100 percent at 400,000 units but does not say how these estimates are achieved.)[6]

There is evidence of scale economies in the retailing and distribution of automobiles as well as in production.[7] In addition, it is likely that scale economies can be found to exist in overall management, marketing, and research and development. While such sources of scale economies are important both for determining the size distribution of firms and for assessing the feasibility of marketing individual firms' products in the United States, we are concerned in this study with a narrower question. Specifically, for models already marketed in the United States, Europe, and Japan, we need to know where production will take place and how production location may be affected by tariff changes. For this purpose, the most relevant information is the percentage cost penalty for suboptimal production rates for different model types. (Location of production also depends on international comparative costs of producing a given output. We present a set of estimates of these cost comparisons in Chapter 6.)

The production scale economy issue is complicated by the fact that automobiles are a highly differentiated good, offered with many different features and options, as well as in different sizes, degrees of luxury, and body styles. Cars with different characteristics can be produced on the same assembly line so long as the differences are not great. For example, a Chevrolet Vega and a Pontiac Astre might be produced together since the main differences between the two cars are in the nameplate and in a small amount of external trim. For purposes of assessing scale economy, it is not sensible to view the Astre as a separate car with a suboptimal level of output; on the other hand, Vegas and Cadillacs clearly cannot be produced on the same line. For less extreme cases, the distinction may be less clear; for some pairs of cars, there are some joint economies of production but not perfect jointness.

We divided cars into four categories: mini, compact, intermediate, and standard-luxury. Within each category, we view cars as perfect substitutes in production in the sense that there are no scale diseconomies from model proliferation. Between categories, we assume no joint economies of production. For compacts, intermediates, and standard-luxury cars, current sales in the United States are more than adequate to enable the three major domestic firms to realize most scale economies; for small cars, U.S. sales, though growing rapidly, were still relatively small in 1974 and were divided into a relatively large number of firms, both domestic and foreign. The foreign firms can realize scale economies from home production; thus, they can supply the U.S. market without incurring scale diseconomies even though U.S. sales are too low to support an optimum production facility by themselves. This shape of the pro-

duction cost curve will determine, in part, how many U.S. companies manufacture subcompacts, the point at which U.S. companies manufacture subcompacts, the point at which U.S. companies begin to manufacture "minis" (GM introduced a "mini," the Chevette, in 1976) and the point at which foreign manufacturers decide that output is sufficiently large to make establishment of production facilities in the United States economical, assuming unit costs are the major relocation consideration. (Foreign manufacturers may be under some political pressure to produce automobiles for export in their home countries. Further, costs of adjustment may delay construction of plants in the United States, even if long-run costs in the United States are lower.)

METHODOLOGY AND RESULTS

In this section, we derive cost functions for producing four types of cars: mini, compact, intermediate, and standard-luxury. While the levels of cost will change over time as input prices rise, the calculations presented here give a reasonable approximation of the shape of cost functions when output is below optimal scale. The estimates can be used to predict the percentage cost penalty associated with suboptimal output.

Following the data in the CMVE report, we have expressed the cost of producing an automobile as the sum of eight "cost elements," or parts of the production process. The cost elements are (1) automotive assembly, (2) body unit (metal stamping), (3) frame (chassis), (4) engine, (5) transmission, (6) tires, (7) body components, and (8) other components. Summing the cost elements, and adding a percentage markup for "corporate costs," we obtain an estimate of the required sticker price.

(The percentage markup includes general and administrative costs, research and development, marketing costs, and dealer markup. The data reported in the CMVE report show a markup for "corporate costs" that varies by type of vehicle produced, reflecting in part the higher markup that has in the past been charged for larger, more luxurious automobiles. We have applied the markup reported by CMVE in our computation as a fixed percentage, which, though varying by car size, does not vary with scale; in effect we are assuming that whatever overhead rate—allocation of general expense plus profit—is viewed as required return for optimal output will be the same for smaller output.

(The assumption of a fixed percentage markup means that we are only considering scale economies in production. If we were attempting to estimate the cost of suboptimal firm size, other potential sources of scale economies—in overall management, in marketing, and in research and development—could not be ignored. However, the main focus here is on how scale economies affect production location choice by optimal-size firms. Optimal-size firms may be limited as to how many separate manufacturing plants they can economically

TABLE 5.1

Unit Costs of Automobile Production at Optimal Scale, 1974 Estimates

	Cost per Automobile (in dollars) Type of Automobile			
Cost Element	Mini	Compact	Intermediate	Standard/Luxury
Automobile assembly	343	343	443	492
Body unit	267	426	487	891
Frame	30	60	70	90
Engine	105	194	253	273
Transmission	25	38	42	111
Tires	25	50	55	110
Body components	112	173	195	400
Other components	277	376	275	828
"Corporate costs"	948	1,671	2,201	4,481
(Mark-up percent)	(80.07)	(101.87)	(120.93)	(140.25)
Sticker price	2,132	3,351	4,021	7,676

Source: Data supplied by Professor Merrill Ebner, Department of Manufacturing Engineering, Boston University, from CMVE report on automobile pollution.

operate for a given type of car by production scale economies. However, other sources of company-wide scale economies should not be a major factor in determining plant location.)

Table 5.1 summarizes from the CMVE data base the unit cost data for each "cost element" for each type of car. The unit costs at optimal scale reported in Table 5.1 are unit costs at optimal scale of production in 1974. The data were developed under contract to CMVE by researchers who conducted numerous interviews and visits at automobile production facilities in the United States.[8]

Table 5.2 gives the optimal scale of production for each type of automobile for each "cost element." We have excluded from Table 5.2 data on tires because they are produced outside the automobile industry and can be purchased at constant cost by manufacturers. Similarly, body and other components are produced by many parts companies, sometimes affiliated with automobile manufacturers and sometimes independent; though scale economies may be important at some level in determining the structure of some sections of the parts industry, it is reasonable to assume that manufacturers can purchase components at constant cost. (For transmission, the data base supplied by Ebner

TABLE 5.2

Minimum Efficient Scale for Automobile Production
(thousands of automobiles per year)

Cost Element	Type of Automobile			
	Mini	Compact	Intermediate	Standard/Luxury
Automotive assembly	400	300	250	200
Body unit	400	300	250	200
Engine	400	400	350	250
Frame	200	200	200	206
Transmission	317	317	317	317

Note: Assumes two-shift, five-day work-week production.

Source: Data supplied by Professor Merrill Ebner, Department of Manufacturing Engineering, Boston University, from CMVE report on automobile pollution.

gave a minimum efficient scale of 1.9 million units. This figure was derived from General Motors' output at its Detroit plant; further discussion with Professor Ebner of Boston University revealed that the plant was actually divided into six sections, which could, if necessary, realize full-scale economies as independent production units. For this reason, we used 317,000 units as minimum efficient scale output.)

The optimal scales reported in Table 5.2 give approximate annual output for two-shift production in a plant large enough to realize all scale economies. Attempts to increase output beyond the level reported in Table 5.2 will, at some point, lead to increasing unit costs of production; in the long run, increasing costs can be avoided by constructing additional plants.

A reasonable approximation of the cost function for each "cost element," for output equal to or less than minimum efficient output, can be expressed as follows:

$$C = A + BX$$

where

C = total cost, X is number of units of output (where a unit is a part for one automobile), A is fixed cost, and B is marginal cost. The data in Tables 5.1 and 5.2 give us X and C at optimal scale for each "cost element."

We estimated A and B from separate data giving the breakdown between fixed and marginal costs for different "cost elements." Two separate sources

TABLE 5.3

Percentage Distribution of Manufacturing Costs

	Cost Element[a]				
	1	2	3	4	5
A. Labor	15	38	25	38	39
B. Labor overhead	5	3	18	9	12
C. Capital overhead	2	11	4	7	5
D. Materials[b]	68	38	43	36	34
E. Profit target	10	10	10	10	10

[a]Cost elements are (1) automotive assembly, (2) body unit, (3) frame, (4) engine, (5) transmission.

[b]Materials number is meant to represent value added at each stage. For automotive assembly, the materials figure is derived from combined data on auto and truck production. Professor Ebner believes that the number greatly overstates the percentage of cost in automotive assembly attributable to materials added at that stage, and that materials probably account for between 30 and 50 percent of the value added in automotive assembly. We performed our calculation using both numbers, and scaling down the other inputs in automotive assembly (except for profit target) proportionately.

Source: Data supplied to Professor Merrill Ebner, of Department of Manufacturing Engineering, of Boston University, by Ford Motor Company.

TABLE 5.4

Percentage Breakdown Between Fixed and Variable Costs for Different Inputs

Input	Fixed Cost	Variable Cost
Labor	17	83
Labor overhead	17	83
Capital overhead	100	0
Materials	0	100
Profit target	100	0

Source: Estimates supplied by Professor Merrill Ebner, Department of Manufacturing Engineering, Boston University, from his knowledge of automobile (and automobile components) assembly line production.

of information were used to derive the cost breakdown: a percentage breakdown of the payments to factors of production and outside firms at minimum efficient scale output for each "cost element" and an estimate of the fixed-variable cost breakdown for each factor. These data are reported in Tables 5.3 and 5.4. Table 5.3 shows the percentage distribution of costs for each cost element, while Table 5.4 indicates the breakdown between fixed and variable cost for each input. The data in Tables 5.3 and 5.4 are then combined with the minimum efficient scale estimates in Table 5.2 to compute the values of A and B for each cost element. A total manufacturing cost function was then derived by taking a weighted sum of the cost functions for each "cost element," using the shares of each of the "cost elements" of total production cost at minimum efficient scale as the weights.

In Table 5.3, profit is expressed as a percentage of total value added for each "cost element." The 10 percent return on value added reported in the table implies a different return on capital for each "cost element." The actual return on capital may be viewed as part of the cost of capital or may be allocated in varying proportions to cost of capital and "economic" profit. (The part allocated to cost of capital is that rate of return required to induce equity owners to supply the funds for the production facilities. "Economic profit" is that part of the rate of return in excess of the cost of capital.)

In computing the unit cost curves, we used two assumptions about the allocation of profits between cost of capital and "economic profit." We performed separate computations for each of the assumptions. In the first case, we assumed all profits were part of the cost of capital; the profit target was included as part of the fixed cost for each "cost element" of the manufacturing process. In the second set of calculations, we assumed that the rate of return on capital in producing the body unit is equal to the cost of capital; the portion of the rate of return above that in other "cost elements" is assumed to be "economic profit." The ratio of capital to output is highest in producing the body unit and the ratio of profit to output is the same for all "cost elements" in Table 5.3. Thus, the ratio of profit to capital overhead is lowest in the body unit stage. From Table 5.3, the ratio of profit to annual capital overhead is 10/11 for cost element no. 2 (body unit). For the other "cost elements," the part of profit target above 10/11 of the capital overhead is eliminated from total cost. The percentages of other inputs are then adjusted upward accordingly to make the total sum to 100 percent.

Table 5.5 shows a sample calculation of the cost curves for minis, assuming that all profits are part of the cost of capital. In Table 5.5, Column (2) gives the percent fixed cost for each cost element. This percentage is computed by taking a weighted average of the fixed and variable cost percentages of each input. Column (3) gives the cost per unit for each "cost element" from Table 5.1, and Column (4) gives the minimum efficient scale for each "cost element" from Table 5.2. Total fixed cost, reported in Column (5), is computed by multi-

TABLE 5.5
Derivation of Cost Curve for Minis (1974 Estimate)

(1) Cost Element	(2) Percent Fixed	(3) Manufacturing Cost per Unit	(4) Number of Units*	(5) Total Fixed Cost	(6) Variable Cost per Unit 0–200,000	(7) Variable Cost per Unit 200,000–317,000	(8) Variable Cost per Unit 317,000–400,000
1 = Car assembly	24.4	$343	400,000	$33,476,800	$259	$259	$259
2 = Body unit	28.0	267	400,000	29,904,000	192	192	192
3 = Frame	21.3	30	200,000	1,278,000	24	30	30
4 = Engine	25.0	105	400,000	10,500,000	79	79	79
5 = Transmission	23.7	25	317,000	1,878,525	19	19	25
6 = Tires	0.0	25	—	0	25	25	25
7 = Body components	0.0	112	—	0	112	112	112
8 = Other components	0.0	277	—	0	277	277	277
Total		1,184		$77,037,025	$987	$993	$999

Markup = 80.07 percent

Cost = [77,037,025 + 987 × D_1 + 993(x − 200,000)D_2 + 999(x − 317,000)D_3] [1.8007]

$$D_1 = \begin{cases} 1, & 0 \leq x \leq 200,000 \\ 200,000/x, & x > 200,000 \end{cases} \quad D_2 = \begin{cases} 0, & 0 \leq x \leq 200,000 \\ 1, & 200,000 \leq x \leq 317,000 \\ 117,000/(x − 200,000), & x > 317,000 \end{cases} \quad D_3 = \begin{cases} 0, & 0 \leq x \leq 317,000 \\ 1, & x > 317,000 \end{cases}$$

*At minimum efficient scale.

Source: Data from Tables 5.1 through 5.4.

plying percent fixed cost (Column (2)) by the cost per unit (Column (3)) by the number of units (Column (4)). The variable cost per unit changes at 200,000 units and at 317,000 units because we are assuming that all parts of the production process are carried out at constant long-run cost at levels of output above minimum efficient scale. For output equal to or less than minimum efficient scale, variable cost per unit is computed as the product of cost per unit and percent variable (one minus percent fixed).

Adding down the columns gives the manufacturing cost per unit, total fixed cost, and variable cost per unit for the sum of all of the "cost elements." To compute total cost of manufacturing for any given output level, we take the sum of unit variable cost multiplied by the number of units and total fixed cost. Manufacturing cost at factory level is multiplied by a constant markup percentage to yield an estimate of retail selling price. (Note that we are interested here in the concept of a retail price using a "normal" markup, not the actual short-term price, which will be affected by demand conditions, and reflected in part by changes in discounts.) The equation for costs reflects the shift between fixed and variable costs when minimum efficient size is reached for one "cost element" (for example, when the frame cost element is at 200,000, or transmission cost element is at 317,000 units), but not for others.

The computation in Table 5.5 is performed under the assumption that materials account for 30 percent of value added in final assembly. The same computation was made under the assumption that materials are 50 percent of

TABLE 5.6

Manufacturing Cost at Below Optimal Scale for Four Types of Automobiles

Number of Units	Production Cost as Percent of Minimum Cost			
	Mini	Compact	Intermediate	Standard
400,000	100.00	100.00	100.00	100.00
350,000	102.20	100.42	100.00	100.00
300,000	105.21	101.01	100.62	100.05
250,000	109.47	104.36	101.54	100.22
200,000	115.90	109.37	106.29	101.03
150,000	126.74	117.96	114.47	106.41
100,000	148.41	135.17	130.86	117.16
50,000	213.51	186.78	179.96	149.43

Note: Materials = 30 percent of cost of automobile assembly. All profit target numbers are assumed to be part of capital cost.
Source: Data from Table 5.5.

TABLE 5.7

Manufacturing Cost at Below Optimal Scale for Four Types of Automobiles

	Production Cost as Percent of Minimum Cost			
Number of Units	Mini	Compact	Intermediate	Standard
400,000	100.00	100.00	100.00	100.00
350,000	102.06	100.42	100.00	100.00
300,000	104.83	100.98	100.62	100.04
250,000	108.77	104.15	101.54	100.22
200,000	114.68	108.89	106.04	101.02
150,000	124.67	117.06	113.78	106.17
100,000	144.70	133.37	129.27	116.50
50,000	204.78	182.31	175.78	147.43

Note: Materials = 50 percent of cost of automobile assembly. All profit target numbers are assumed to be part of capital cost.
Source: Data from Table 5.5.

TABLE 5.8

Manufacturing Cost at Below Optimal Scale for Four Types of Automobiles

	Production Cost as Percent of Minimum Cost			
Number of Units	Mini	Compact	Intermediate	Standard
400,000	100.00	100.00	100.00	100.00
350,000	102.02	100.39	100.00	100.00
300,000	104.74	100.89	100.55	100.04
250,000	108.54	103.97	101.37	100.18
200,000	114.31	108.53	105.69	100.87
150,000	124.02	116.34	113.08	105.80
100,000	143.43	131.93	127.82	115.63
50,000	201.78	178.74	172.13	145.14

Note: Profit rates equal to or less than return on capital for body unit assumed to be part of capital cost; other profit excluded from cost computation. Materials cost assumed to be 30 percent of final assembly cost.
Source: Data from Table 5.5.

THE SHAPE OF AUTOMOBILE COST FUNCTIONS 139

value added. Under that assumption, percent fixed cost in assembly is 20.1 percent instead of 24.4 percent.

From the computation in Table 5.5, we can derive the per-unit cost for different scales of automobile production and the ratio of costs at any given output to costs at optimal scale. Tables 5.6 and 5.7 summarize the results of these computations for the four types of automobiles with materials costs of 30 and 50 percent of final assembly cost, respectively, with all profits treated as part of the cost (fixed) of capital. Table 5.8 shows the results of the same computations with profit rates on capital above the targeted profit for body unit production assumed to be pure "economic profit."

It can be seen from Tables 5.6, 5.7, and 5.8 that unit costs eventually rise sharply at lower levels of output. Optimal scale is higher for minis and compacts than for standards and intermediates. The percentage cost penalty for large cars is small as long as annual output is at least 200,000 units; however, for small cars (minis), the percentage cost penalty for 200,000 units is on the order of 15 percent.

The results of our computations are not particularly senstitive either to the choice among alternative assumptions about materials costs in automotive assembly or to the proper way to allocate the profit target figure.

(On the other hand, the results are sensitive to variations in the estimate of minimum efficient scale. In particular, the finding that the relative cost penalty for low volumes is higher in small car production than in large car production follows in great part from the estimates in Table 5.2, which show that minimum efficient scale in major production processes is higher for small cars than for larger ones.)

(One way of explaining the difference in minimum efficient scale among different types of cars is to view a given investment in tooling as producing a roughly similar value of output for different types of cars. The types of operations and tools used in the production of both small cars and big cars are the same, but big cars require more operations—and more stations in the factory for a given output—because they have more parts. Thus, the same number of workers with the same amount of capital can produce fewer big cars than small cars. For example, to make eight-cylinder engines requires twice as many operations as it does to make an equal number of four-cylinder engines but does not require proportionately more tooling. Thus, for a given investment in tooling, a higher volume of output—though not necessarily value—of minicars is possible, or, conversely, more minicar output than big-car output is required before the average fixed cost curve begins to flatten out.)

SOME PROBLEMS AND QUALIFICATIONS

This section discusses some problems with the methodology used to compute the shape of cost curves, noting the possible biases in our procedure.

A major determinant of the optimal scale of production of automobiles is the high cost and long durability of dies used in the body-stamping process. Experts in the industry have differing views on the extent of the resulting scale economies in body stamping.[9] McGee believes there are infinite economies of scale in automobile production because of the high cost of dies and the advantages in variety for different body types and parts.[10] McGee claims that the durability of dies can be increased without a proportionate increase in cost. Since dies represent a large fixed investment, it is economical to realize the return, namely finished automobiles, as soon as possible. Thus, increasing annual output reduces unit costs for all ranges of output. According to White, the maximum output from a set of dies is 400,000 units;[11] White's current view is that McGee is right in principle but that the cost savings to be realized by expanding output beyond 500,000 units is trivial.[12] In White's view, Ebner's estimates of minimum efficient output in stamping are somewhat low.

Ebner's estimates are based on actual plant sizes chosen by manufacturers producing enough output to have several stamping plants. Thus, while the Ebner data may be correct for single plant operation, they ignore multiplant economies from increased durability of dies; these economies can be realized by rotating dies among plants. There may be some advantage to having the different plants within some proximity, at least on the same continent. Thus, while Ebner's estimates are probably good for determining the optimal size of a single plant, they may not account for all economies of scale in producing more automobiles within a given country.

On the other side, our estimates of the percentage cost penalty exaggerate to some degree the loss from operating below optimal scale. It is reasonable to assume capital is fixed in the short run, but in the long run plants can be built with less capital if planned output is to be lower. This is particularly true for dies used in the stamping process; where retooling is done every year, or even every three years, there can be some savings from using less durable dies if annual output is to be reduced. We do not account for these potential savings in our computations, which treat all capital costs as fixed. (Ebner does not believe this source of bias is big. In his view, the cost savings from redesigning a plant for smaller output, provided assembly line methods are still used, are at most 5 percent and possibly smaller.)

Figure 5.1 compares the cost curve we have estimated with a "true" cost curve. In general qualitative terms, we have probably overstated unit costs both below and above "minimum efficient scale" output, failing to account for potential scale economies beyond existing plant sizes, and not considering potential ways of reducing the capital stock when output is planned to be lower.

FIGURE 5.1

Qualitative Comparison of Our Cost Curve Estimates with "True" Long-Run Cost Curve

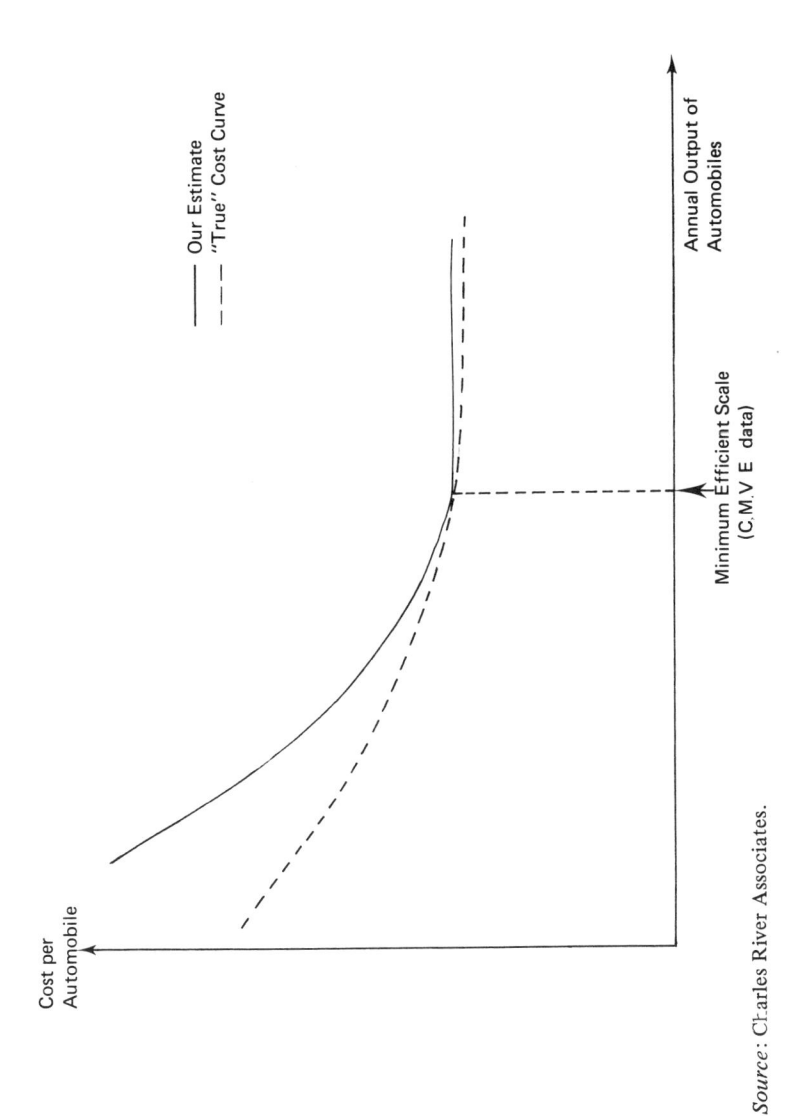

Source: Charles River Associates.

CONCLUSIONS AND IMPLICATIONS

Scale economies are very important in the production of automobiles. Per-unit cost penalties of producing below optimal scale are fairly steep, especially below 200,000 units. Optimal scale is higher for small cars than for larger cars, and in addition, the percentage cost penalty from producing 300,000 or fewer units per year is much greater for small-car, especially minicar, production than for large-car production. The greater importance of scale economies in small-car production provides an incentive to locate production where sales are greatest, and to export extra units to relatively smaller markets.

Foreign manufacturers are more likely to realize cost savings by producing automobiles in the United States as sales approach 400,000 units. Following current trends, it is likely that Datsun and Toyota will reach that level in a few years. Volkswagen has already decided to establish an assembly plant in the United States. A successful domestic entry into the small-car field may delay or permanently prevent investment in local production facilities by some foreign-owned firms.

Tariffs would make it economical for Toyota and Datsun to produce cars for the U.S. market in the United States, if they were at optimal scale. Below optimal scale outputs, foreign producers would have to choose between paying a fixed percentage tariff on units produced abroad or absorbing a percent unit cost penalty if those units were produced in the United States. The tariff, by increasing the price, would reduce the level of sales for all currently imported autos whatever choices manufacturers made. (If one foreign manufacturer could minimize the cost increase by shifting production location while others do not, that manufacturer could gain a net increase in sales at the expense of the other foreign firms. Thus, it is not clear how a tariff would affect the relative shares of imports among firms or the total sales of any individual firm.) The outcome depends on the elasticity of the production cost curve, the elasticity of demand for the manufacturer's autos, the comparative cost of manufacturing at a given scale in different locations, and unit transport costs.

In Chapter 6, we use available data on wages, productivity, exchange rates, and materials prices to compare costs of producing automobiles in different major producing countries. These production cost comparisons are then combined with our scale economy estimates and our demand elasticity estimates from Chapter 3 to make some rough illustrative computations about potential effect of tariffs on production location.

NOTES

1. See Lawrence J. White, *The Automobile Industry Since 1945* (Cambridge: Harvard University Press, 1971); Joe S. Bain, *Barriers to New Competition* (Cambridge: Harvard University Press, 1956); John S. McGee, "Economies of Size in Auto Body Manufacture," *Journal of Law and Economics* 16 (October 1973): 239-74.

THE SHAPE OF AUTOMOBILE COST FUNCTIONS

2. See P. Wonnacott and R. J. Wannacott, *Free Trade Between the United States and Canada: The Potential Economic Effects* (Cambridge: Harvard University Press, 1967).

3. *Manufacturability and Costs of Proposed Low-Emissions Automotive Engine Systems*, Consultant Report to the Committee on Motor Vehicle Emissions, Commission on Sociotechnical Systems (CMVE report) (Washington, D.C.: National Research Council, September 1974).

4. The production cost data used in the CMVE report were developed in numerous visits to U.S. automobile and parts plants by LeRoy H. Lindgren, Merrill Ebner, and other members of the CMVE panel of consultants on manufacturability and costs. See Appendix A, Schedule of Panel of Consultants on Manufacturability and Cost, CMVE report, pp. 93-97.

While we have no independent verification on the accuracy of the CMVE data, the implications of the data for the shape of production cost curves do not appear unreasonable to experts whom we have consulted, and the results, taken together with the findings from the international production cost comparisons in Chapter 6, appear to be consistent with recent trends in automobile production location. Though a more thoroughly documented source would be desirable, the CMVE data were used because the author found no alternative way to obtain the same type of information.

5. See Bain, op. cit., p. 245.

6. See White, op. cit., p. 39.

7. See Bedros Peter Pashigian, *The Distribution of Automobiles, An Economic Analysis of the Franchise System* (Englewood Cliffs, N.J.: Prentice-Hall, 1961).

8. The data are reported in the CMVE report, op. cit. Note that it is the relative costs for different "cost elements" and not the absolute costs, that determine the shape of production cost curves. Even if total costs of production are biased downward in the CMVE estimates, the implication of those estimates may still be adequate for the purposes of this chapter if any errors that may be in the data all point in the same direction.

9. White believes that "it is impossible to get a straight story on dies." Personal conversation with Lawrence J. White, May 9, 1975.

10. McGee, op. cit.

11. White, *Automobile Industry*, op. cit.

12. Personal conversation with White, May 9, 1975.

CHAPTER

6

INTERNATIONAL COMPARISON OF PRODUCTION COSTS

In this chapter, we estimate the comparative cost of producing automotive industry output in the United States, West Germany, and Japan. We then combine our estimates from Chapter 3 and the cost curve estimates from Chapter 5 to develop hypothetical scenarios illustrating the potential effects of tariff changes on the location of production of small cars for sale in the United States.

If trade barriers are eliminated, and if consumption patterns of automobiles in the major producing nations become more uniform,* then international differences in production costs and intercountry transport cost of automobiles will determine the location of automobile production and the flow of trade in automobiles. If transport costs exceed the difference in production costs between major consuming regions, then each region will produce most of its own automobiles; if not, then automobiles will be produced in the region(s) with the lowest production costs and exported to the other region(s) (except for some specialty cars and luxury cars. We do not expect, for example, that Mercedes-Benz sales in the United States will fall to zero if unit production costs in West Germany are higher than unit production costs in the United States.).

The cost comparisons presented in this chapter are developed from data on comparative wages, productivity, and materials prices of inputs used in the

---

*Rising fuel costs may eventually lead Americans to purchase more of the type of cars bought by Europeans and Japanese. If this occurs, and if the U.S. demand will support several companies producing small cars at minimum efficient scale, the comparison of U.S. unit cost at scale with the sum of European (Japanese) unit costs at scale and unit transport costs from Europe (Japan) will determine the location of production for sales in the United States.

production of automobiles. We aggregate this input cost information using weights from a U.S. input-output table. The results can be interpreted as rough estimates of the comparative costs of producing automobile industry products when each country is producing at or above minimum efficient scale.

An alternative approach to cost comparison would be to compare prices of equivalent products sold in each region.* Such a comparison, if it could be made, would yield a composite of the effects of cost differences at optimal scale, differences in domestic market structure (if any), effects of tariff protection, and cost differences due to differences in degree of realization of scale economies. Our method compares hypothetical costs at efficient scale production levels by comparing unit input costs, adjusted for productivity differences. While our procedure is admittedly only a rough approximation, it yields an answer more in line with the purpose of the investigation than would a straight output-price comparison. (It would be preferable to obtain cost estimates directly from international automobile companies that must make these production location decisions. Data from this source were not available to us.)

Our computations for a recent year (1974) show Japanese unit costs at about 83.2 percent of U.S. unit costs and German unit costs at about 109.3 percent of U.S. unit costs. When transport costs are added to the computation, Japanese delivered unit costs in the United States are estimated to be 3.6 percent greater than domestic unit costs of production of the same automobiles, while German delivered unit costs are estimated to be 15.1 percent greater than U.S. unit costs. Product differentiation enables imports to have large sales in the United States even with a unit cost disadvantage. Auto production in Europe and Japan is feasible because most foreign manufacturers' output for the U.S. market is still below minimum efficient scale.

(Our computations suggest that Volkswagen costs in 1974 would have been lower had they been produced in the United States. However, straight cost

---

*To do this properly for automobiles is no small problem because of the need to adjust for different mixes of characteristics in different countries' automobiles and also because the actual value added in the automobile industry may differ. For example, is a car assembled in Brazil using a U.S.-produced engine a U.S. car, and what does a difference between the price of that car and the price of a car made in Detroit indicate about relative costs of production in the United States and Brazil?

Some comparisons of quality-adjusted prices of automobiles in different countries are presented in a recent volume by Irving Kravis et al. (see Irving B. Kravis, Zoltan Kenessey, Alan Heston, and Robert Summers, *A System of International Comparisons of Gross Product and Purchasing Power*, United Nations International Comparison Project: Phase One [Washington, D.C.: 1975], chap. 8.) The findings by Kravis et al. are reviewed briefly in Appendix 6-C.

considerations are not the only factor in production location decisions of multinational corporations. In addition, the international comparative advantage in automobile production may have changed greatly to Germany's disadvantage just prior to 1974 because of the revaluation of the mark in 1969 and again in 1971. The recent decision by Volkswagen to begin production in the United States is consistent with the implications of our analysis.)

Our estimates only give a snapshot at one point in time. International comparative advantage changes as exchange rates, relative domestic price levels, relative labor costs, and relative productivities in different countries change. However, the big disequilibrium resulting from the pegging of other currencies to the U.S. dollar prior to 1971 has been eliminated. It is possible that future changes in relative costs of production will be more gradual; thus our estimates for 1974 may be reasonably indicative of international cost differences in automobile production through the mid-1970s.

APPROACH TO COST COMPARISON COMPUTATION

Comparing the costs of manufacturing requires information about the proper weights to assign to different factor and material inputs. The data used for developing the weights are supplied in published input-output tables, which give interindustry flows in value terms.

We developed formulas for aggregating relative input prices into a relative cost of production index, using two alternative assumptions about the form of the production function relating factor and material inputs to output: a fixed proportions production function and a Cobb-Douglas production function. In the former, it is assumed that the physical shares remain constant and the value shares change in inverse proportion to changes in relative input prices. The fixed proportion function assumes a zero elasticity of substitution between factor and material inputs, while the Cobb-Douglas function assumes a unitary elasticity of substitution. (Both production functions exhibit constant returns to scale. It is reasonable to assume constant returns to scale for production levels above minimum efficient scale—that is, to assume that doubling output by having two efficient scale plants instead of one would double production cost. For discussion of the shape of cost curves below minimum efficient scale, see Chapter 5.)

Using the fixed proportions function, we express the cost of manufacturing ratio between the United States and Europe as follows:

$$\frac{C_e}{C_a} = \frac{1}{1 - f_a{}^a} \sum_{i=2}^{n} \left[\left(\frac{P_e{}^i}{P_a{}^i}\right) f_a{}^i \right] \qquad (6.1)$$

where

C_a = the U.S. average cost of production,

C_e = the European average cost of production,

$f_a{}^a$ = the automobile industry's value share of inputs to automobile production in the U.S. input-output table,

$P_a{}^i$ = the unit price in the U.S. of the ith input,

$P_e{}^i$ = the unit price in Europe of the ith input, and

$f_a{}^i$ = the ith input's value share in the input-output table from all sectors other than the automobile industry. (See Appendix 6.A for details of the derivation.)

In deriving Equation 6.1, we assumed that (1) all factors and materials are purchased in competitive markets (the factor and material supply curves are horizontal to the automobile industry), and (2) the same technology prevails in all economies, specifically, that the production functions in all countries have the same parameters.* Differences in unit costs of producing automobiles are thus assumed to be caused by differences in factor and material prices and also by differences in the efficiency of labor. (Labor efficiency differences are entered into the model by assuming a difference in the physical number of labor-hours required to produce one "efficiency unit" of labor input. The production function is defined in "efficiency units" of labor. In practice, we estimate an adjusted labor input price by combining estimates of wage rates and labor productivity.)

The estimated costs are independent of the scale of production. Thus, the estimates are meaningful only for levels of output greater than minimum efficient scale, or less than minimum efficient scale by the same proportion in each region.

For the Cobb-Douglas case, we express the relative costs of production as

$$\frac{C_e}{C_a} = \prod_{i=2}^{n} \left[\left(\frac{P_e{}^i}{P_e{}^i}\right)^{\left(\frac{f_a{}^i}{1-f_a{}^a}\right)} \right] \qquad (6.2)$$

---

*This assumption was necessitated by lack of any empirical evidence on international differences in automobile industry production functions. Because of this omission, the differences in costs reported here are based solely on estimated differences in factor prices and labor productivity.

It should be noted that the principal qualitative result of the calculations—that the United States has a net advantage over Europe and Japan in producing automobiles, at efficient scale volumes, for sale in the United States—does not rest on the assumption of similar production functions so long as (1) U.S. technology is at least as progressive as foreign technology and (2) U.S. automobile production methods are not more labor-intensive than foreign production methods.

where the notation is the same as in Equation 6.1. Equation 6.2 is derived using the same competitive and equal technology assumptions used in deriving Equation 6.1, the fixed proportions equation.

The term $1/(1 - f_a^a)$ in Equations 6.1 and 6.2 accounts for the fact that automobile sector products are an input in automobile sector production in the input-output table.

Equations 6.1 and 6.2 are solutions of the function implied by the input-output table, which expresses costs as a function of the prices of all inputs other than automobile. (See Appendix 6.A for details of the derivations.)

SOURCES OF DATA AND DATA PROBLEMS

The comparative cost relationships in Equations 6.1 and 6.2 are expressed as functions of relative factor and materials prices, and also of the U.S. value shares for each input from the input-output table. The value shares, f_a^i, are provided by the direct requirements input-output table developed by the Bureau of Economic Analysis of the U.S. Department of Commerce for the 1967 U.S. economy. This table is available at the 83-sector level of aggregation and at the 367-sector level. The sectors in the table can be aggregated to conform to the breakdown of available relative price data.

Value shares for all inputs for 1974 are computed directly from the 1967 table for the Cobb-Douglas case since the production function assumes value shares are constant. In the fixed proportions case, input prices are constant, but value shares change between 1967 and 1974 in proportion to changes in relative prices of inputs in that time interval. Price changes are available for 450 product classes in the Bureau of Labor Statistics' monthly Publication *Wholesale Prices and Price Indexes*; 1972 data were used to update the value shares according to the following equation:

$$f_{1972}^i = \frac{R^i f_{1967}^i}{\Sigma R^i f_{1967}^i} \tag{6.3}$$

where

f_{1967}^i = 1967 value share of ith input,
f_{1972}^i = 1972 value share of ith input, and

$R^i = \dfrac{P_{1972}^i}{P_{1967}^i}$ = price of ith input in 1972 relative to 1967 price.

Relative price data for material inputs are constructed from unit value statistics in the United Nations' *World Trade Annual* on imports to and exports

from every nation, broken down by the UN's Standard Industrial Trade Classification (SITC). We used a weighted average on import and export prices for SITC sectors comparable to the sector breakdown used in the Bureau of Economic Analysis input-output table.

Labor accounted for 19 percent of the value of all materials and factors used in automobile production in the United States in 1967. We constructed indexes of unit labor costs using estimated relative hourly compensation for the motor vehicle industry supplied by the U.S. Department of Labor, Bureau of Labor Statistics, Office of Productivity and Technology. The indexes were adjusted by labor productivity figures for automobile production supplied to us by Jack Baranson, an expert on the international automobile industry. The Baranson data gave estimates of value added per man-hour in the motor vehicle industries of the United States, Japan, and Germany for the years 1973 and 1974. (The method used by Baranson to derive his index, and the primary sources of data used, are detailed in Appendix 6.B.)

Relative, "quality-adjusted" labor prices are estimated using the following equation:

$$\frac{P_e L}{P_a L} = \left(\frac{W_e L}{W_a L}\right) / Q_e L \tag{6.4}$$

where

$P_e L$ = unit cost of labor in Europe,

$P_a L$ = unit cost of labor in the United States,

$W_a L$ = hourly labor compensation in the United States (in dollars),

$W_e L$ = hourly labor compensation in Europe (in dollars), and

$Q_e L$ = index of European labor productivity relative to U.S. labor productivity in the motor vehicle sector.

We assumed that capital was internationally mobile and that unit "capital costs" were the same in all regions in 1974.

The data used in the computation were the best we could obtain for the purpose of estimating international comparative advantage; still, it is worth noting that shortcomings in the data make the estimates somewhat imprecise. There are four major data problems: an inconsistency between the measures of value added and the measures of input prices used in the cost functions, differences between BLS production data and production data from the UN's SITC, problems in using the labor productivity data, and problems caused by missing prices for some input sectors. The problems that these limitations in the data present are discussed briefly below.

1. The value shares for material inputs are defined for sectors in the input-output table, while the available materials price data are for specific commodities. Where possible, we chose representative goods or sets of goods to obtain a relative price measure for each sector in the input-output table. The sector prices we used are inaccurate to the extent that the international relative prices of the goods chosen as representative of the sector differ from a weighted average of the international relative prices of the actual mix of within-sector commodities used in producing automobiles.

2. The BLS product definitions for which price change data between 1967 and 1972 are available do not correspond exactly to the product definitions from the UN's SITC. We chose closely comparable BLS product definitions to estimate changes in the prices of SITC commodities; there is nevertheless some inaccuracy because the products compared are not exactly the same. (In the computations shown below, which assume a Cobb-Douglas function, the shares do not change between 1967 and 1972 or 1974.)

3. The labor productivity data were developed using value added per man-hour figures from 1967, and updating them by changes in output per man-hour in the United States, West Germany, and Japan. Thus, the relative productivity figures are inaccurate to the extent that the ratio of value of output to value added in the automobile industries of the United States, Japan, and Germany changed relative to each other between 1967 and 1974.

4. We do not have commodity prices corresponding to each sector in the input-output table. For the missing sectors, we assumed that the relative sector prices were the same as the weighted average of the prices computed for all the included sectors. This may lead to a bias if the included commodities are not representative of all the commodities.

The inaccuracies in the data described above suggest that the computations in this chapter should be regarded as first approximations only. The implications of the results presented below, however, are consistent with observed patterns of production and trade in the world automobile industry.

RESULTS AND IMPLICATIONS

Table 6.1 summarizes the results of the international cost comparisons. Column (5) shows that, compared to the United States, unit costs of producing final automobiles are about 17 percent lower in Japan and 9 percent higher in West Germany. Both West Germany and Japan have lower unit labor costs and higher materials prices than the United States. Table 6.2 summarizes the steps in computing the relative labor cost index. Hourly compensation for workers in both Japan and West Germany is lower in comparison to the United States than labor productivity. Both hourly compensation and productivity are higher in West Germany than in Japan.

TABLE 6.1

Summary of Automobile Industry Unit Cost Comparisons Index (U.S. Cost = 1.000)

Country	Unit Labor Cost	Unit Cost: Other Value Added	Unit Cost: Inputs from Other Sectors	Unit Cost: Weighted Average
Japan	.423	1.000	1.089	0.832
West Germany	.812	1.000	1.288	1.093

Source: Figures computed using Equation (6.2).

TABLE 6.2

Summary of Relative Unit Labor Cost Computations, 1974

Country	Local Compensation per Hour in U.S. Dollars	U.S. Compensation per Hour in U.S. Dollars	Relative Hourly Compensation	Relative Productivity Index	Relative Labor Cost
Japan	$3.10	$8.34	.372	.880	.423
West Germany	$6.70	$8.34	.803	.989	.812

Relative Labor Cost = $\left(\dfrac{\text{Relative Hourly Compensation}}{\text{Relative Productivity Index}}\right)$

Source: Hourly Compensation Data from U.S. Department of Labor, Bureau of Labor Statistics, Office of Productivity and Technology. Relative Productivity Index from Jack Baranson. For Baranson's sources, see Appendix 6B.

Relative costs of supplying to the United States automobiles produced in different locations depend on production costs in the United States, production costs in alternative locations, and transport costs between the alternative location(s) and the United States. We estimated transport costs between Japan and the United States and between West Germany and the United States using data supplied by Massport Authority on international freight rates between east coast ports, Tokyo and Bremerhaven. Table 6.3 presents our calculations of transport costs between Japanese and West German ports and the United States for selected Japanese and European imports. (Quoted rates from Le Havre, Amsterdam, Southhampton, Bremerhaven, and Gothenberg, Sweden, to East Coast ports are all $0.54 per cubic foot. It is possible that foreign firms can ship at a lower cost than the quoted rates if they use their own ships; Volkswagen, for example, uses its own ship, which is specially designed to carry Volkswagens efficiently. Thus our estimates of the cost of supplying foreign-made automobiles to the United States may be biased upward.)

Table 6.3 shows that freight charges on Japanese imports to the United States are much higher than freight charges on European imports. Freight on the low-cost Datsun (the 1200) is more than three times the freight on the low-cost Volkswagen. Freight charges as a percentage of U.S. price minus international freight are much lower on luxury cars. The freight charge is based on volume; thus, improvement in the interior luxuriousness, handling, and engine performance of a car raises its price much more than it raises the freight charge. The Datsun 240Z, for example, has only a slightly higher shipping cost than the Datsun 1200, though its price is over twice as high. These figures suggest that it is likely that foreign cars will be most competitive in the high-quality segment of the market for any size class. The Japanese, especially, are likely to specialize in high-quality small cars since production costs in Japan are low relative to U.S. production costs, and shipping costs are high (around 20-25 percent for the most popular Datsuns and Toyotas) relative to the price.

We estimated the transport cost of a "typical" Japanese car to the United States as a percentage of its cost of production by averaging the percent transport cost figures in Column (5) of Table 6.3 for the Datsun 610, the Datsun 1200, the Toyota Corona two-door hardtop, and the Toyota Corona four-door sedan; for the German cars, we averaged the transport cost percent of the Volkswagen Super-Beetle and the Ford Capri. The results of these computations are shown in Table 6.4. Our best estimate is that the supply cost to the U.S. market of "typical" German imports would have been 15 percent lower in 1974 had they been produced in the United States at volumes sufficiently large to attain minimum efficient scale in production, while the corresponding supply cost for Japanese autos produced in the United States at scale would have been only about 3 percent lower. Our estimates imply that, in 1974, it would have been cheaper to produce Volkswagens for U.S. sale in the United States. The estimated Datsun and Toyota supply costs are lower in Japan for 1973 sales

TABLE 6.3

International Transport Costs: Selected Imported Cars

Model	Freight per Cubic Ft.[a]	Cubic Feet	Total Freight	U.S. List Price ('75)	Percent Transport Cost[b]
Datsun 240Z	$2.23	299	$667	$6,284[c]	11.87%
Datsun 610, 4 dr. sedan	$2.23	330	$736	$4,029	22.35%
Datsun 1200, sedan	$2.23	271	$604	$2,849[c]	26.90%
Toyota Corona, 2-dr. hardtop	$2.23	356	$794	$4,379	22.15%
Toyota Corona, 4-dr. sedan	$2.23	358	$798	$3,789	26.68%
Ford Capri	$ .54	320	$173	$4,117	4.39%
Mercedes 280, 4-dr. sedan	$ .54	415	$224	$12,576	1.81%
VW Super Beetle	$ .54	339	$183	$2,895	6.75%
Volvo 142	$ .54	391	$211	$5,625	3.90%

[a]From Japan and Western Europe ports to east coast (U.S.) ports for autos from Japan and Europe, respectively.
[b]Percent transport cost is expressed as a markup over the foreign price. Percent transport cost = (Total Freight)/(U.S. List Price − Total Freight)
[c]Price of Datsun B-210, the successor to the Datsun 1200, and price of Datsun 280-Z, the successor to the 240-Z.
Sources: Freight data supplied by Massport Authority, list prices from *Automotive News Almanac*, 1975.

TABLE 6.4

Estimated Relative Supply Cost Index to United States of "Typical Imports" at Minimum Efficient Scale, 1973

Country	Foreign Production Cost / U.S. Production Cost	Transport Cost Percent Markup	Foreign Production Cost / U.S. Supply Cost
West Germany	1.093	5.57%	1.154
Japan	0.832	24.52%	1.036

Source: Data in Tables 6.1 and 6.3

volumes. (We have used 1973 rather than 1974 sales volumes for the comparisons because the 1974 recession and energy crisis made sales volumes for both domestic and imported autos abnormally low.)

Table 6.5 presents the comparison between hypothetical foreign and domestic production costs for different output levels in 1973. (These estimates assume no U.S. tariff. The 3 percent tariff makes foreign supply costs a bit higher than the Table 6.5 data show.) Production in foreign countries is above minimum efficient scale because sales of Toyotas, Datsuns, and Volkswagens in their respective domestic markets exceeds 400,000 units. (The discussion below treats Datsuns, Toyotas, and Volkswagens as if they are each one model. In effect, it is assumed that different models of each make are sufficiently similar to achieve joint economies of scale in production. See discussion in Chapter 5 above.) Columns (2) and (3) give the units of supply (production plus transport) to the United States for automobiles produced in Japan and West Germany, respectively, relative to unit costs of minimum efficient scale production in the United States. Column (4) gives the unit cost in the United States for selected outputs relative to unit cost in the United States at minimum efficient scale. The numbers in Column (4) are from Table 5.8 in Chapter 5; they are estimated from our study of the shape of cost curves. (See Chapter 5 for a full discussion of the estimation of the shape of automobile industry production cost curves. Other estimates made with slightly different assumptions are of the same order of magnitude.)

In 1973, sales in the United States of the leading imports were Volkswagen 469,000, Toyota 275,000, and Datsun 228,000. Comparing Columns (3) and (4) at 400,000 units, we can see that long-run Volkswagen production costs would have been lower in the United States than they were in West Germany, by our estimate. (It should be noted that our estimate does not account for short-run costs of establishing a new plant in a foreign country. As German costs rose

TABLE 6.5

Estimates of Relative Supply Costs to United States from U.S. and Domestic Production of Popular Imports at Different Annual Sales Levels in United States

Case 1 = no tariff on imported automobiles

(Index—U.S. at 400,000 units = 1.000)

Annual U.S. Sales	Cost in Japan	Cost in West Germany	Cost in U.S.	Minimum Cost Location U.S. v. Japan	Minimum Cost Location U.S. v. West Germany
400,000	1.036	1.154	1.000	U.S.	U.S.
350,000	1.036	1.154	1.021	U.S.	U.S.
300,000	1.036	1.154	1.048	Japan	U.S.
250,000	1.036	1.154	1.088	Japan	U.S.
200,000	1.036	1.154	1.147	Japan	U.S.
150,000	1.036	1.154	1.247	Japan	Germany

Note: At annual output levels below 150,000, Japan and West Germany have cost advantages over the United States.

Source: Data in Table 6.4. Figures in column 4 from Table 5.7, column 2.

TABLE 6.6

Estimates of Relative Supply Costs to United States from U.S. and Domestic Production of Popular Imports at Different Annual Sales Levels in United States

Case 2: Tariff that raises supply price of imported automobiles by 10 percent
(Index—U.S. at 400,000 units = 1.000)

Annual U.S. Sales	Cost in Japan	Cost in West Germany	Cost in U.S.	Minimum Cost Location U.S. v. Japan	Minimum Cost Location U.S. v. West Germany
400,000	1.140	1.269	1.000	U.S.	U.S.
350,000	1.140	1.269	1.021	U.S.	U.S.
300,000	1.140	1.269	1.048	U.S.	U.S.
250,000	1.140	1.269	1.088	U.S.	U.S.
200,000	1.140	1.269	1.147	Japan	U.S.
150,000	1.140	1.269	1.247	Japan	U.S.

Note: At lower outputs, Japan and West Germany have cost advantage over the United States.
Source: Charles River Associates.

relative to U.S. costs after 1969, it is quite likely that long-run Volkswagen production costs had just recently become lower in the United States; thus, it is not surprising that Volkswagen did not immediately establish a U.S. plant. Volkswagen sales in the United States declined between 1970 and 1975; this trend may be caused in part by the increased relative cost of producing autos in Europe. In deciding to establish a plant in the United States, Volkswagen may be acting in the belief that the sales decline could be halted or reversed by the resultant lowering of supply costs.)

Comparing Columns 2 and 4 at 300,000 and 250,000 units, it can be seen that Toyota and Datsun supply costs would have been higher if produced in the United States. Both Toyota and Datsun sales in the United States declined in 1974 and then recovered to some degree in the early months of 1975. If international cost comparisons remain roughly stable, it might become less expensive, ignoring start-up costs, to produce most Toyotas and Datsuns in the United States by the late 1970s. This suggests that Japanese firms are likely to consider building production plants in the United States in the late 1970s. (We expect that specialty cars, such as the Datsun 280-Z, will continue to be produced in Japan if they require separate production facilities. A *Wall Street Journal* story on Volkswagen's decision to establish a plant in the United States notes that officials of local communities seeking to influence Volkswagen's choice of a plant location expect Japanese companies to follow Volkswagen's decision within the next few years.)[1]

Table 6.6 presents a similar cost comparison assuming a 10 percent tariff on imported cars. The 10 percent tariff reduces the level of output for which production in the United States remains the least cost solution. However, simulation of the marginal effect of the tariff on the production location decision is slightly more complicated than that depicted in Table 6.6 because the increase in the supply price of foreign cars reduces the volume of sales. Thus, the appropriate sales volume at which the cost comparison decision would have been made is not the actual sales volume for 1973.

For Volkswagen, with 469,000 sales, production in the United States remains the least-cost long-run solution, as it was in the example with no tariffs (subject to the same qualifications noted above for the no-tariff case).

For Toyota, sales in 1973 were 273,000 cars. Applying linear interpolation to the unit cost estimate of U.S. production between 250,000 and 300,000 units reported in Table 5.7, we find unit cost at that output level to be approximately 6.75 percent greater than unit cost in the United States at minimum efficient scale. Since production in 1974 actually occurred in Japan, where cost was about 3.6 percent greater than U.S. cost at minimum efficient scale, the price increase for Toyota brought about by the tariff is estimated to be about 3 percent if Toyotas were produced in the United States. If the demand elasticity for imports were equal to −2 and the tariff caused all import sales to decline proportionately, Toyota sales would decline by 6 percent to about 256,600

units.* The reduction in sales would raise unit cost still further, which would lead to another rise in price. The solution converges to equilibrium at 244,000 units, an output at which U.S. supply price, though 9.2 percent higher than the supply price at minimum efficient scale, is still lower than the sum of Japanese supply price and the tariff. As Japanese costs are 3.6 percent higher than U.S. costs at minimum efficient scale, a tariff equal to 10 percent of the retail price, by this estimate, would switch Toyota production to the United States and would increase the cost of a Toyota to U.S. consumers by 5.4 percent (1.092/-1.036).

Use of a higher demand elasticity in the above simulation could reverse the above conclusion because, if the tariff-induced price increase leads to too great a reduction in annual sales, unit costs of domestic production would become higher than the foreign supply price.

For Datsun, 1973 sales were about 225,000 units. Applying linear interpolation to the data in Table 6.6, we find that the supply price of a Datsun, if produced in the United States at 225,000 units annual output, would have been approximately 11.4 percent above U.S. minimum efficient scale price in 1973. This would represent an increase of approximately 7.5 percent (111.4/103.6) above the price of Datsuns made in Japan. Using a demand elasticity of −2, a 7.5 percent price increase reduces Datsun sales to 191,000 units. At that level of output, unit costs would be lower if Datsun were produced in Japan. Thus, the prediction of our sample simulation is that a 10 percent tariff would not shift Datsun production to the United States at 1973 levels of demand.

The trend growth of sales of Japanese cars in recent years suggests, however, that it will be economical to manufacture both Toyota and Datsun in the United States, even without a tariff, if the trends continue.

In conclusion, our simulations indicate that significant increases in tariff rates may cause production of some foreign car models to become more economical in the United States. The extent of economic incentive for foreign firms (and U.S. firms producing cars abroad) to shift production of small cars to the United States depends on the initial volume of sales for the firm's small car line, the level of the tariff, and the price elasticity of demand for the specific model(s). Higher tariffs may give foreign firms a greater incentive to form cooperative ventures in the United States in order to avoid the tariff by producing at or near efficient scale in the United States. As the demand for small cars grows, how-

---

*The demand elasticity of −2 is consistent with several independent methods of estimation, and we consider it more reliable than other estimates we obtained which were higher. See Chapter 3.

If the tariff caused Toyota to shift production to the United States, but Japanese manufacturers with smaller U.S. sales continued producing in Japan, at the 10 percent higher price caused by the increased tariff, Toyota's share of U.S. imports from Japan would increase. In that event, the fall in Toyota sales, and the increase in the supply price of a Toyota in the United States, would both be smaller than the amount computed in the illustrative simulation. The same point applies to Datsun.

ever, the likelihood that individual foreign manufacturers will find it economical to build plants in the United States on their own will increase, even in the absence of trade barriers.

APPENDIX 6.A
DERIVATION OF COST OF MANUFACTURING COMPARISON RATIOS

The Fixed-Proportions Production Function

The fixed-proportions production function, characterized by zero elasticity of substitution among the inputs, is represented by L-shaped isoquants. The production function yields constant returns to scale. We assume there is perfect competition in factor markets and that the same technology is prevalent in each economy considered. Cost differences are caused only by differences in relative factor prices. (The price of labor is defined in efficiency units. Thus, if one worker in the United States is equivalent to two workers in Europe, and U.S. wages are twice as high as European wages, the price of labor is the same in both regions.)

The general form of the fixed proportions production function is

$$Q = \min k^i q^i \qquad (6A.1)$$

where

Q = output;
q^i = quantity of ith input; and
k^i = output per unit of ith input.

In the input-output table, the output sector is also an input into the production function. We will denote by q^a the total physical units of automobile industry inputs used in the production of automobiles and let k^a equal the output of the automobile industry sector per unit of automobile industry input.

The cost function may be written

$$C(Q) = \sum_{i=1}^{n} p^i q^i \qquad (6A.2)$$

where

$C(Q)$ = total cost of producing Q units of output, and
p^i = unit price of the ith input.

We may alternately express $C(Q)$ as

$$C(Q) = q^a p^a + \sum_{i=2}^{n} q^i p^i \qquad (6A.3)$$

where

q^a = physical input of the automobile sector required to produce Q units of automobile sector output, and

p^a = unit price of the input of the automobile sector.

Since the price of an input is equal to its unit cost of production under competition, we can write

$$p_a = \frac{C(Q)}{Q} \tag{6A.4}$$

Substituting Equation 6A.4 into Equation 6A.3, we obtain

$$C(Q) = \frac{C(Q)}{Q} q^a + \sum_{i=2}^{n} q^i p^i \tag{6A.5}$$

Transposing Equation 6A.5, rearranging terms, and using the relationship $f^a = \frac{q^a}{Q}$, where f^a is the share of automobile sector input cost in the total cost of automobile sector output, we obtain a new expression for automobile production costs:

$$C(Q) = \frac{1}{(1-f^a)} \sum_{i=2}^{n} q^i p^i \tag{6A.6}$$

From Equation 6A.6, the relative cost of producing Q units of output in two regions, for example the United States or Europe, can be expressed as

$$\frac{C_e(Q)}{C_a(Q)} = \frac{\frac{1}{1-f^a} \sum_{i=2}^{n} p_e^i q_e^i}{\frac{1}{1-f^a} \sum_{i=2}^{n} p_a^i q_a^i} \tag{6A.7}$$

where

$C_a(Q)$ = cost of producing Q units of output in the United States;
$C_e(Q)$ = cost of producing Q units of output in Europe;
p_e^i = unit price of the ith input in Europe;
p_a^i = unit price of the ith input in the United States;
q_e^i = quantity of ith input used in Europe; and
q_a^i = quantity of ith input used in the United States.

The assumption of equal technologies in both regions implies that f^a, the number of automobile industry units of input needed to produce an automobile industry unit of output, is the same in both regions.

The same technology assumptions also imply that

INTERNATIONAL COMPARISON OF PRODUCTION COSTS

$$k_e^i = k_a^i = k^i \qquad (6A.8)$$

and

$$q_a^i = q_c^i = q^i \qquad (6A.9)$$

for equal units of output in the two regions. Thus,

$$\frac{C_e(Q)}{C_a(Q)} = \frac{\frac{1}{1-f^a} \sum_{i=2}^{n} p_e^i q^i}{C_a(Q)} \qquad (6A.10)$$

The value share of the ith input, f^i (f_a^i in the United States and f_e^i in the other country) is defined as follows:

$$f^i = \frac{p^i q^i}{C(Q)} \qquad (6A.11a)$$

$$f_a^i = \frac{P_a^i q_a^i}{C_a(Q)} \qquad (6A.11b)$$

$$f_e^i = \frac{p_e^i q_e^i}{C_e(Q)} \qquad (6A.11c)$$

Combining Equations (6.A.11a) and (6.A.9), we obtain

$$q^i = \frac{f_a^i C_a(Q)}{p_a^i} \qquad (6A.12)$$

Thus,

$$\frac{C_e(Q)}{C_a(Q)} = \frac{\frac{1}{1-f^a} \sum_{i=2}^{n} p_e^i \cdot \frac{f_a^i C_a(Q)}{p_a^i}}{C_a(Q)} = \frac{1}{1-f^a} \sum_{i=2}^{n} \frac{p_e^i}{p_a^i} f_a^i \qquad (6A.13)$$

The ratio of European production costs to U.S. production costs, Equation (6A.13), is simply the product of $(1/1 - f_a)$ and the weighted sum of rel-

ative input prices, with the weights being the sector shares in the input-output table.

The only data required for the international cost comparison are the (internationally) relative nonautomotive input prices and the U.S. value shares of the inputs.*

THE COBB-DOUGLAS PRODUCTION FUNCTION

The Cobb-Douglas function has unitary elasticity of substitution and constant returns to scale. We again assume competition in factor markets and equal technology in both regions.

The Cobb-Douglas function can be written

$$Q = k \prod_{i=1}^{n} (q^i)^{e^i} \tag{6A.14}$$

where

Q = output;
k = a scale constant;
q^i = quantity of ith input; and
e^i = elasticity of output with respect to ith input.

Constant returns to scale imply that

$$\Sigma e^i = 1. \tag{6A.15}$$

Further, $e^i = \dfrac{p^i q^i}{C(Q)}$ is the value share of the input in the total cost of output.

The same technology assumptions give the relation

$$\epsilon_a^i = \epsilon_e^i \tag{6A.16}$$

which implies that

$$f_a^i = f_e^i = f^i = e^i \tag{6A.17}$$

Equation (6A.17) expresses the familiar property of the Cobb-Douglas function, namely that value shares are constant, regardless of differences in input prices.

---

*As noted above, comparative wages of labor must be adjusted by comparative labor productivities to obtain the price of labor in efficiency units.

INTERNATIONAL COMPARISON OF PRODUCTION COSTS 163

The cost function is again expressed as

$$C(Q) = \Sigma p^i q^i. \tag{6A.18}$$

Let $C(Q_e)$ equal the total cost of producing Q_e units of output in some European country, and let $C(Q_a)$ be the cost of producing Q_a units in the United States. Then, the average production costs are

$$C_a = \frac{C(Q_a)}{Q_a}, \quad C_e = \frac{C(Q_e)}{Q_e} \tag{6A.19}$$

and the cost in Europe relative to that in the United States is expressed as

$$\frac{C_e}{C_a} = \frac{C(Q_e)/Q_e}{C(Q_a)/Q_a} \tag{6A.20}$$

For equal levels of total input cost in both regions, $(C(Q_e) = C(Q_a))$, the unit cost ratio can be written

$$\frac{C_e}{C_a} = \frac{Q_a}{Q_e} \tag{6A.21}$$

The relative unit cost of production is inversely proportional to the relative level of output attainable with a fixed level of expenditure.

Substituting Equation 6A.14 into Equation 6A.21, and recalling that $e^i = f^i$, we obtain

$$\frac{Q_a}{Q_e} = \frac{\prod_{i=1}^{n}(q_a^i)^{f^i}}{\prod_{i=1}^{n}(q_e^i)^{f^i}} \tag{6A.22}$$

Recall that

$$f^i = \frac{p^i q^i}{C(Q)} = \frac{p_a^i q_a^i}{C(Q_a)} = \frac{p_e^i q_e^i}{C(Q_e)}$$

This implies that

$$q_a^i = \frac{f^i C(Q_a)}{p_a^i}$$

$$q_e^i = \frac{f^i C(Q_e)}{p_e^i} \tag{6A.23}$$

Substituting Equation (6A.23) into Equation (6A.22), we obtain

$$\frac{Q_a}{Q_e} = \frac{\prod\limits_{i=1}^{n}\left[\frac{f^i C(Q_a)}{p_a^i}\right]^{f^i}}{\prod\limits_{i=1}^{n}\left[\frac{f^i C(Q_e)}{p_e^i}\right]^{f^i}} = \prod\limits_{i=1}^{n}\left(\frac{p_e^i}{p_a^i}\right)^{f^i} \qquad (6A.24)$$

when $C(Q_a)$ is equal to $C(Q_e)$.

To eliminate the automotive input, we rewrite Equation (6A.24) as

$$\frac{Q_a}{Q_e} = \frac{\frac{C(Q_e)}{Q_e}}{\frac{C(Q_a)}{Q_a}} = \left(\frac{p_e^a}{p_a^a}\right)^{fa} \prod\limits_{i=2}^{n}\left(\frac{p_e^i}{p_a^i}\right)^{f^i} \qquad (6A.25)$$

From the constant returns to scale and competitive input pricing assumptions

$$p_e^a = C(Q_e)/Q_e$$

and (6A.26)

$$p_a^a = C(Q_a)/Q_a.$$

Therefore

$$\frac{\frac{C(Q_e)}{Q_e}}{\frac{C(Q_a)}{Q_a}} = \left[\frac{\frac{C(Q_e)}{Q_e}}{\frac{C(Q_a)}{Q_a}}\right]^{fa} \times \prod\limits_{i=2}^{n}\left(\frac{p_e^i}{p_a^i}\right)^{f^i} \qquad (6A.27)$$

Transposing and eliminating the first term on the right, we obtain

$$\frac{\frac{C(Q_e)}{Q_e}}{\frac{C(Q_a)}{Q_a}} = \frac{C_e}{C_a} = \prod\limits_{i=2}^{n}\left(\frac{p_e^i}{p_a^i}\right)^{\left(\frac{f^i}{1-f^a}\right)} \qquad (6A.28)$$

Equation (6A.28) can be used to compute relative costs with the fixed value shares production function. As in the fixed proportions case, the only data needed are the relative input prices and the shares of the input in the input-output table.

APPENDIX 6.B

Sources for Labor Productivity Index

The labor productivity index used in the derivation of the comparative cost of production labor for the automobile industry is developed from estimates of value added, in dollars, per man-hour in the automobile industry of Germany, Japan, and the United States. The data were made available to us by Jack Baranson, an expert on the world automobile industry.[2]

Baranson obtained estimates of automobile industry value added in each country's currency for 1973 and 1974. Conversion to U.S. dollars was made using first quarter 1974 conversion rates obtained from the International Financial Statistics of the International Monetary Fund (IMF).

The Japanese output data were obtained in factor prices, whereas the U.S. and German output values were in market prices. Market price output includes subsidies and taxes. Factor prices in Japan were assumed to be 15 percent less than market price.

$$Q_k = (Q_{1970}) * (I_k / I_{1970}) \tag{6B.1}$$

where

Q_k = output per man-hour in year k (1973 and 1974);
Q_{1970} = output per man-hour in 1970;
I_k = index of output per man-hour in year k; and
I_{1970} = index of output per man-hour in year 1970.

The index of output per man-hour was obtained from the following sources: the U.S. index was from Division of Foreign Labor Statistics, Bureau of Labor Statistics, U.S. Department of Labor; the Japanese index was from *Quarterly Journal of Productivity Statistics*, Productivity Research Institute, Japan; and the German index was from Division of Foreign Labor Statistics, Bureau of Labor Statistics, U.S. Department of Labor, and from *Wirtschaft und Statistik*, Statistics Bundesampt Wiesbaden.

The value added data for 1970 for the United States, Japan, and Germany were obtained from the following sources: United States: Bureau of Domestic Productivity, U.S. Department of Labor; Japan: Japanese Census of Manufacturers and Division of Foreign Labor Statistics, Bureau of Labor Statistics, U.S. Department of Labor; and Germany: computed by the formula

$$V_{1970} = (V_{1967}) * (O_{1970} / O_{1967}) \tag{6B.2}$$

where

V_{1970} = value added in 1970;
V_{1967} = value added in 1967;
O_{1970} = output index in 1970; and
O_{1967} = output index in 1967.

The source for the value-added data and output index was the Division of Foreign Labor Statistics, Bureau of Labor Statistics, U.S. Department of Labor.

Output per man-hour in 1970 was computed by dividing the 1970 value added estimates by data on aggregate manhours in the automotive industry of the three countries. The sources for the man-hours data were for the United States, the Bureau of Domestic Productivity, U.S. Department of Labor; for Japan, the Bureau of Labor Statistics, U.S. Department of Labor; and, for Germany, the Division of Foreign Labor Statistics, Bureau of Labor Statistics, U.S. Department of Labor.

APPENDIX 6.C

International Comparisons of Production Costs from Hedonic Price Regressions

An alternative way of estimating comparative international costs to the method used in this chapter is to examine the differences in automobile prices, adjusted for automobile characteristics differences, among countries. If automobile manufacturing is fully integrated in all countries, and if markups over production cost are the same everywhere, then relative prices should closely approximate relative production costs.

A comparison of automobile prices among major producing countries for 1969 has been made in a recent study for the United Nations by Irving Kravis et al.[3] Kravis et al. estimated hedonic price regressions for separate cross-sections of new 1969 automobiles sold in France, West Germany, Hungary, Italy, Japan, the United Kingdom, and the United States. The price data used were list prices in the respective countries. Imports and domestically manufactured automobiles were included together in each regression for each country. Thus, the regressions were designed to compare characteristics-adjusted prices of automobiles sold rather than of automobiles produced, in each country.

(Thus, for example, a Volkswagen sold in the United States would be in the U.S. price equation, while a Volkswagen sold in West Germany would be in the German price equation. For our purposes, it would have been better to classify automobiles by country of origin rather than by country of sale, though the latter method is obviously more useful for comparing consumer prices and living standards. To the extent that imports are a minor fraction of automobile sales, and thus a minor determinant of the coefficients of the price equations in

each country, the equations are reasonably close estimates of the prices of domestic autos.)

In all of the estimated price equations for automobiles, the variance in measured characteristics explains a large fraction (over 94 percent in the United States, West Germany, and Japan) of the variance in list price. Characteristics that are important in explaining price differences within major markets include horsepower, engine revolutions per minute, weight, and engine displacement. Coefficients for the individual characteristics differ among countries.

The coefficients of the price equations can be used to compute predicted prices for an automobile with any given set of characteristics in each of the countries studied. Table 6C.1 summarizes the price comparisons reported by Kravis et al. using this technique.

Column (2) of Table 6C.1 compares the prices in the seven countries studied of an automobile with typical U.S. characteristics, while Column (3) compares the prices among the countries (relative to the U.S. price) of automobiles with characteristics typical for each other country. Comparison of the two columns shows that the price in the United States is relatively lower for automobiles with U.S.-type characteristics. In effect, smaller (larger) automobiles seem to be relatively more (less) expensive in the United States. (A recent study with 1975 data shows, in a similar manner, that characteristics-adjusted

TABLE 6C.1

Comparison of Fitted Automobile Prices, 1969

Country	Price Index Using U.S. Weights (U.S. Price = 100)	Price Index Using Own Weights (U.S. Price = 100)	Price Index Using Own Weights Plus Est. Transport Costs (U.S. Price = 100)*
France	140	101	107
West Germany	163	93	98
Hungary	186	177	187
Italy	120	85	90
Japan	111	89	111
United Kingdom	184	104	110
United States	100	100	100

*Computed from transport cost estimates in Table 6.4. Transport cost markup = 24.52 percent for Japanese cars and 5.57 percent for all Euorpean cars.

Sources: Irving B. Kravis, Zoltan Kenessey, Alan Heston, and Robert Summers, *A System of International Comparisons of Gross Product and Purchasing Power*, United Nations International Comparison Project, Phase One (Washington, D.C.: International Bank for Reconstruction and Development, 1975), chap. 8.

prices of light trucks are about the same in the United States and West Germany, while adjusted prices of heavy trucks are much lower in the United States.)[4] For U.S.-characteristics, automobiles are less expensive in the United States than in all other countries. Using "own-country" characteristics, automobiles are relatively less expensive in West Germany, Italy, and Japan than in the United States, and only slightly more expensive in France and the United Kingdom.

Column (4) of Table 6C.1 adds CRA's estimates of transport costs to the relative "own-country" prices reported in Column (3) to derive an estimated comparative delivered price in the United States of automobiles sold in foreign countries. The resulting estimates show both Italian and West German automobiles less expensive than automobiles sold in the United States; these estimates were made, however, before the decline in European competitiveness following the devaluation of the U.S. dollar and successive revaluations of the West German mark. (The value of the West German mark in terms of U.S. dollars rose from .25491 in 1969 to .38723 in 1974, an increase of 52 percent. Because some of the increase in the value of the mark may reflect relative improvements in West German productivity and different relative inflation rates in West Germany and the United States, the relative cost of West German goods need not have increased by the full amount of the increase in currency price.)[5] The comparison with Japan shows only a slightly greater relative price disadvantage at efficient scale for Japanese automobiles than is shown in CRA's comparison reported in Table 6.4. (Though the Kravis comparisons are of actual prices, rather than of prices of autos produced at efficient scale, we can interpret the estimated U.S. price of autos with "Japanese characteristics" as a price at efficient scale because it is extrapolated from a trend line of automobiles [including imports] that are produced at efficient scale.)

NOTES

1. See Terry F. Brown, "As VW Nears Decision on a Plant in the U.S., Bidders Become Eager," *Wall Street Journal*, April 22, 1976.

2. Baranson's past research includes several works on the automobile industry in developing countries. See Jack Baranson, *Automobile industries in Developing Countries*, World Bank Staff Occasional Papers no. 8 (Baltimore: John Hopkins Press, 1969); and Jack Baranson, *International Transfer of Automotive Technology to Developing Countries*, UNITAR (United Nations Institute for Training and Research) Research Reports no. 8 (New York: UNITAR, 1971).

3. Irving B. Kravis, Zoltan Kenessey, Alan Heston, and Robert Summers, *A System of International Comparisons of Gross Product and Purchasing Power*, United Nations International Comparison Project: Phase One (Washington, D.C.: International Bank for Reconstruction and Development, 1975), chap. 8.

4. See Charles River Associates, *Analysis of the Effects of Trade Policy Changes on the U.S. Truck Industry* (final report submitted to U.S. Motor Vehicle Manufacturers' Association Inc., April 1976).

5. See successive issues of the *Federal Reserve Bulletin*.

CHAPTER 7

THE EFFECT OF OUTPUT CHANGES ON DEMAND FOR LABOR IN THE U.S. AUTOMOBILE INDUSTRY

This chapter presents the results of our estimation of the relationship between automobile industry output and the derived demand for factors of production, particularly employment production workers. The estimated relationship between output and employment provides the link between the effect of trade policy changes on domestic-auto production and the labor market impact of output change in terms of employment.

The statistical relationships that have been estimated provide two pieces of information about the labor adjustment process in the automobile industry.

1. The long-run elasticity of production worker employment with respect to output is an estimate of the number of required total labor displacements (or additions to the labor force) as output changes. Both the time series and cross-section samples indicate that, for the purpose of analyzing labor adjustment effects, it is reasonable to assume a unitary long-run output elasticity of employment.

2. The pattern of labor adjustment to output change, measured by the percentage of long-run adjustment occurring within a specified period of time, can be derived from the distributed lag structure implicit in the estimated time series relationship. Estimates reported here indicate a rapid adjustment for production worker employment; approximately 40 percent of the total adjustment occurs in the first quarter following a once-and-for-all change in the level of output, and a little over 80 percent of the total effect will have been felt within the first year.

The rapid adjustment process suggests that the ability of local labor markets to absorb a given total number of displaced workers will be taxed more severely than would be the case if the adjustment process were slower. The

disequilibrium in labor markets will be greater in geographic areas in which the industry employs a large share of the local labor force. A rapid adjustment process decreases the share of total employment displacement that the normal work force turnover can be expected to absorb. A given output decline would thus tend to affect higher tenure and wage levels, and older employees with relatively poor alternative employment opportunities. In the next section we review the basic institutional facts of the automobile industry labor market and describe the composition of the automobile industry work force and its geographic dispersion. Likely effects of unions and seniority rules on the incidence and composition of unemployment are briefly discussed. In the following sections we outline a theoretical framework for estimating the effect on employment in the U.S. automobile industry of changes in the demand for U.S. automobiles, and results of econometric estimates using time series and cross-section data are presented. We then comment briefly on the likely geographic distribution of employment changes. In the final section, we review the empirical findings and outline the implications for assessing the welfare impact of trade policy changes.

THE AUTOMOBILE LABOR MARKET: INSTITUTIONAL BACKGROUND

The Motor Vehicle and Motor Vehicle Equipment Industry (Standard Industrial Classification [SIC] #371) provides 4 percent of U.S. manufacturing employment. Most of the motor vehicle industry employment is concentrated in the Great Lakes area, particularly in Michigan. Of the 797,300 workers employed in SIC 371 in 1970, there were 44.1 percent in Motor Vehicle Parts and Accessories (SIC 3714), 42.2 percent in Motor Vehicles (SIC 3711), 5.8 percent in Car Bodies (SIC 3712), 4.8 percent in Truck and Bus Bodies (SIC 3713), and 3.2 percent in Truck Trailers (SIC 3715).

The labor force employed in Motor Vehicles includes a larger fraction of males than the labor force and the manufacturing labor force as a whole. The average level of education for the motor vehicle labor force is about the same as the average for all workers, and higher than the average for workers in manufacturing. The industry employs a larger percentage of minority group members than is characteristic of the general U.S. labor force, reflecting the industry's concentration in areas with large minority populations, especially Detroit.

Employment in the industry is heavily in production job slots, more so than in manufacturing in general; nearly 50 percent of employees are operatives. The largest single job category is assemblers; most of the remainder are craftsmen.

Table 7.1 summarizes the demographic characteristics, hours worked, and earnings of the motor vehicle labor force compared both to the manufacturing labor force and to the U.S. labor force as a whole. Motor vehicle employ-

ees are very well paid relative to the entire U.S. labor force and to the manufacturing labor force. The areas in which they work are in general high-wage areas. In addition, the motor vehicle industry has an attractive program of fringe benefits, which are essentially the same across firms. Among these is the supplemental unemployment benefits (SUB) plan, which provides almost full take-home pay for up to a year to laidoff workers. This plan, which was intended to serve as guaranteed annual income plan in a cyclical industry, provides an incentive to laid-off auto workers to wait until benefits expire before beginning serious search for alternative employment.

Tables 7.1 and 7.2 show that earnings in SIC 371 have been far above the manufacturing average. Average weekly earnings in 1970 in SIC 371 were $170.07; average hourly earnings were $4.22. Earnings in the motor vehicle industry have consistently exceeded manufacturing earnings, with the premium rising from 14 percent in 1947 to 42 percent in 1974. The relative growth rates of real earnings of the U.S., manufacturing, and motor vehicle labor forces were 1.6 percent, 1.9 percent, and 2.6 percent per year, respectively, for the 1947-72 period.

Motor vehicle employment is concentrated in the Great Lakes area, although plants making vehicles or parts are scattered throughout the country. Table 7.3 presents the geographic distribution of motor vehicle industry production workers by region. Table 7.3 shows that, within the east north central region, employment was predominantly located in Michigan and Ohio.

The motor vehicle industry provides a significant fraction of total employment in a number of metropolitan areas. Locations where the motor vehicle and equipment industry provides at least 10 percent of total employment are Ann Arbor, Detroit, Flint, Jackson, Lansing, and Saginaw in Michigan, and Kenosha, Wisconsin. (SIC 371 data are unavailable for Flint, Kenosha, and Lansing; for those localities, data from SIC 37, Transportation Equipment, were used. Most employment in SIC 37 in the localities included in Table 7.4 is accounted for by motor vehicles and parts.) In these areas, earnings and hours worked are roughly the same for motor vehicle industry workers as for the local labor force as a whole. In other areas, such as Cleveland and St. Louis, where significant motor vehicle employment exists but accounts for only a small fraction of total employment, earnings for motor vehicle industry workers are higher than earnings for the labor force as a whole. The data on relative earnings and hours worked of motor vehicle industry employees in localities with high motor vehicle industry employment are summarized in Table 7.4.

Conditions of employment—wages, fringe benefits, work rules, seniority provisions—for the majority of employees in SIC 371, or 90 percent of hourly rated employees, are determined in collective bargaining between the UAW and the management of the major automobile companies.. The respective national bargaining units agree on general questions relating to wage schedules, benefit levels, seniority provisions, and grievance procedures. Specifics on all

TABLE 7.1

Characteristics of Motor Vehicle and Equipment Labor Force in 1970

Item	U.S. Labor Force[a]	Manu-facturing Labor Force	SIC 371	SIC 3711	SIC 3712	SIC 3713	SIC 3714	SIC 3715
Total number (thousands)	82,715	19,393	797.3	336.3	45.9	38.3	351.3	25.6
Race								
White	88.9%	90.1%	86.2%			Not available		
Other	11.1%	9.9%	13.8%					
Sex								
Female	38.1%	28.1%	8.9%	6.9%	3.5%	6.8%	12.0%	5.1%
Male	61.9%	71.9%	91.1%	93.1%	96.5%	93.2%	88.0%	94.9%
Age								
16–24 years	21.6%	16.4%	13.8%			Not available		
25–54 years	60.9%	67.7%	72.8%					
55 and over	17.5%	16.0%	13.4%					
Median	40.3	39.9	39.1					
Education[b]								
Elementary school	17.5%	21.8%	19.5%			Not available		
High school	56.3%	57.0%	65.9%					
College	26.2%	21.2%	14.6%					
Median years	12.4	12.2	12.1					
Occupation[c]								
"White collar"[d]	64.0%	27.5%	24.2%	28.7%	21.3%	19.8%	20.7%	25.8%
"Blue collar"	36.0%	72.5%	75.8%	71.3%	78.7%	80.2%	79.3%	74.2%
Farmers, service	14.6%	2.3%	2.8%			Not available		

Prof., tech., mgt.	24.0%	15.3%	10.7%			
Clerical, sales	23.5%	15.2%	10.6%			
Operatives, etc.	37.8%	67.3%	75.8%			
Average weekly hours[e]	37.2	39.8	40.3	39.8	39.7	39.9	40.9	39.1
Average weekly earnings ($)[e]	120.16	133.73	170.07	174.32	186.59	138.45	170.55	127.86

[a]Total civilian labor force, aged 16 years and over.
[b]Highest level reached; "elementary school" includes through eighth grade.
[c]For U.S. applies to experienced civilian labor force (excludes unemployed persons who have never worked).
[d]"Blue collar" = production workers; "white collar" = all others.
[e]Of production workers.

Note: Percentage totals may not add to 100 due to rounding.

Sources: U.S. labor force: All items from U.S. Department of Labor, Bureau of Labor Statistics, *Handbook of Labor Statistics 1971* (Washington, D.C.: Government Printing Office, 1971).

Total number	Table 1
Race, Sex, Age	Table 4
Education	Table 12
Occupation	
Hours	Table 76
Earnings	Table 93

except median age: from U.S. Bureau of the Census, 1970 Census of Population Subject Report PC(2)-7B, *Industrial Characteristics*, Table 3.

Manufacturing Labor Force:

U.S. Department of Labor, Bureau of Labor Statistics, *Handbook of Labor Statistics 1971* (Washington, D.C.: Government Printing Office, 1971).

Total number	Table 39
Sex	Table 43
Occupation (white collar/blue collar)	Table 39

U.S. Bureau of the Census, 1970 Census of Population Subject Report PC(2)-7B, *Industrial Characteristics*.

Race	Table 33
Age	Table 34
Education	Table 3

(continued)

(TABLE 7.1, continued)

U.S. Bureau of the Census, 1970 Census of Population Subject Report PC(2)-7C, *Occupation by Industry*.
    Occupation   Table 1
U.S. Department of Labor, *Employment and Earnings United States 1909-72*. Bulletin 1312-9.
    Hours
    Earnings
Industry Labor Forces:
U.S. Department of Labor, *Employment and Earnings United States 1909-72*, Bulletin 1312-9.
    Total number
    Sex
    Occupation (blue/white collar)
    Hours
    Earnings
U.S. Bureau of the Census, 1970 Census of Population Subject Report PC(2)-7B, *Industrial Characteristics*.
    Race   Table 33
    Age   Table 34
    Education Table 3
U.S. Bureau of the Census, Census of Population Subject Report PC(2)-7C, *Occupation by Industry*.
    Occupation   Table 1

Census Definition: SIC 371 = Motor Vehicles and Equipment

TABLE 7.2

Comparative Real Average Weekly Earnings and Growth of Earnings in Motor Vehicle Industry (1967 dollars)

Year	U.S.	Manu-facturing	371	3711	3712	3713	3714	3715
1947	68.13	73.50	87.64	—	—	—	—	—
1950	73.69	80.89	103.81	—	—	—	—	—
1951	74.37	81.41	99.18	—	—	81.75	—	—
1955	84.44	94.39	124.49	—	—	96.98	—	—
1958	86.70	95.51	116.91	120.10	133.31	98.57	113.78	—
1960	90.95	101.15	129.89	113.27	140.77	108.94	127.58	—
1964	98.31	110.84	148.58	154.99	153.18	115.19	148.34	111.37
1965	100.59	113.79	156.22	163.45	158.23	118.57	155.76	118.14
1970	102.72	114.99	146.23	149.89	160.44	119.05	146.65	109.91
1971	101.28	113.36	155.20	159.42	174.30	118.75	154.45	110.30
1972	102.01	116.22	164.70	170.67	175.66	129.70	165.42	112.58
			Annual Growth Rates (Nominal Earnings (%))					
1947–72	4.5	4.7	5.4	—	—	—	—	—
1958–72	4.3	4.6	5.7	5.7	5.2	5.2	5.9	—
1964–72	5.1	5.2	6.0	5.9	6.4	6.2	6.0	4.7
1970–71	6.2	6.2	14.3	14.6	17.0	7.5	13.5	8.1
1971–72	7.0	8.9	12.7	13.7	7.1	16.0	13.8	8.4

(continued)

175

(TABLE 7.2, continued)

Year	U.S.	Manu-facturing	371	3711	3712	3713	3714	3715
			Annual Growth Rates					
			Real Earnings					
1947–72	1.6	1.9	2.6					
1958–72	1.2	1.4	2.5	2.5	2.0	2.0	2.7	
1965–72	0.5	0.6	1.3	1.2	1.7	1.5	1.4	0.3
1970–71	−1.4	−1.4	6.1	6.4	8.6	−0.3	5.3	0.4
1971–72	0.7	2.5	6.1	7.1	0.8	9.2	7.1	2.1

Sources: Nominal Earnings: 1947–71–U.S. Department of Labor, Bureau of Labor Statistics, *Employment and Earnings United States, 1909–72*, Bulletin 1312-9 (Washington, D.C.: Government Printing Office, 1973). U.S. Department of Labor, Bureau of Labor Statistics, *Employment and Earnings*, vol. 19, no. 9 (March 1973), Table C.2. (Washington, D.C.: Government Printing Office). Consumer Price Index: Bureau of Labor Statistics, *Handbook of Labor Statistics 1971* (Washington, D.C.: Government Printing Office, 1971), Table 112; "Consumer Price Index: All Items and Major Groups, U.S. City Average, 1935–70."

TABLE 7.3

Distribution of Production Workers, SIC 371

	Percent of U.S. SIC 371 Employment	Percent of Regional Production Workers	Percent of State Production Workers
By Census Region			
Northeast	1.1	–	–
Middle Atlantic	10.2	–	–
East North Central	66.2	–	–
West North Central	7.4	–	–
South Atlantic	6.0	–	–
East South Central	3.0	–	–
West South Central	1.6	–	–
Pacific	4.6	–	–
By State			
Illinois	–	4.9	2.0
Indiana	–	11.8	8.7
Michigan	–	54.8	28.6
Ohio	–	23.0	8.9
Wisconsin	–	5.8	6.1

Source: Derived from Chapter 9, various Tables 3, *Annual Survey of Manufacturers, 1970-1971* (Washington, D.C.: U.S. Department of Commerce, Bureau of the Census, September 1973).

of these issues except benefit levels and, in some cases, wage levels are determined through supplemental negotiations between local union and management units.[1]

The UAW has traditionally been interested in good pay, job security, a compressed wage structure, and obtaining essentially the same conditions of employment for its members wherever they are employed. The motor vehicle industry is characterized by a more compressed wage structure than is typical of other equally mechanized industries. For production jobs, there is one wage rate per classification, with provisional employees starting out at $.10 per hour less than regular employees, attaining full pay after 90 days. A larger wage spread exists in skilled trade classifications. Recent years have seen the development of a bimodal wage structure—of a gap between production and skilled worker wage scales—under pressure from the skilled membership.

The UAW has been successful in obtaining contractual agreements for wage equality across plants with all the automobile companies except General Motors and has recently achieved wage parity across the Canadian border.

TABLE 7.4

Employment Characteristics of Motor Vehicle Workers Relative to Local Labor Forces

Location	Relevant SIC	Number in SIC Labor Force (thousands)	SIC as Percent of Total Local Labor Force	Average Weekly Hours[a] SIC (hours)	As Percent of Local	Average Weekly Earnings[a] SIC ($)	As Percent of Local
Ann Arbor, Mich.	371	13.3	13.2	41.4	99.5	183.57	103.8
Atlanta, Ga.	37	35.2	5.7	38.0	97.4	162.64	124.1
Baltimore, Md.	37	17.4	2.2	39.4	98.0	164.69	116.4
Boston, Mass.	37	20.2	1.6	38.2	97.2	158.15	111.8
Chicago, Ill.	371	11.9	0.4	39.1	97.3	142.94	96.3
Cincinnati, Ohio	371	12.7	2.5	41.4	101.5	185.06	125.6
Cleveland, Ohio	371	26.5	3.1	40.7	101.0	181.93	117.3
Detroit, Mich.	371	211.4	14.1	41.8	101.0	184.67	102.0
Flint, Mich.	37	49.2	31.4	40.4	100.0	187.13	99.4
Indianapolis, Ind.[b]	371	17.3	4.1	41.0	101.7	177.12	117.5
Jackson, Mich.[b]	371	5.8	12.6	38.3	99.0	155.84	99.0
Kansas City, Mo.	371	12.0	2.4	39.9	100.0	163.19	124.7
Kenosha, Wis.	37	9.4	26.3	\multicolumn{2}{c}{Not available}		
Lansing, Mich.	37	22.4	17.2	40.6	100.3	184.49	105.0
Los Angeles, Cal.	371	21.1	0.7	38.8	97.7	155.59	107.1
Louisville, Ky.	37	7.7	2.3	41.9	106.1	168.02	115.6
Milwaukee, Wis.[b]	371	10.2	1.8	40.7	101.2	180.71	114.5
Minneapolis-St. Paul, Minn.	37	5.1	0.7	42.0	105.0	169.37	113.7

New York City[b]	371	3.3	0.1	41.2	110.5	142.55	112.4
Newark, N.J.	37	8.3	1.1	39.8	99.8	167.96	121.3
Paterson-Clifton Passaic, N.J.	37	11.7	2.3	38.6	98.2	159.42	117.6
Rockford, Ill.	37	10.3	9.5	40.1	98.8	161.20	111.1
Saginaw, Mich.	371	10.1	14.4		Not available		
St. Louis, Mo.	371	23.3	2.6	38.1	96.0	161.54	106.8
San Francisco-Oakland, Cal.	371	8.3	0.7	38.4	98.7	164.42	99.5
San Jose, Cal.	37	4.5	1.2		Not available		
Toledo, Ohio	371	17.7	5.2	40.7	99.5	172.98	106.3
Westchester Co., N.Y.	37	4.3	1.4	38.6	99.5	182.96	139.5
Wilmington, Del.				Not available			
Youngstown-Warren, Ohio	37	10.7	5.5	42.1	105.8	180.19	112.6

Note: 52.2 percent of U.S. SIC 371 labor force in locations "denoted" SIC 371.

[a]Of production workers.

[b]Hours and earnings data apply to SIC 37.

General Note: "SIC" columns denote characteristics of automotive or transportation workers (as specified in "Relevant SIC" column) within each local labor force. "As Percent of Local" columns relate local SIC characteristics to characteristics of local total/manufacturing labor forces.

Source: U.S. Department of Labor, *Employment and Earnings States and Areas 1939-71* (Washington, D.C.: Government Printing Office, 1973), Table 5.

Fringe benefit programs among the companies and plants are essentially the same, although slight differences in seniority determination across firms could affect the potential total amount of benefits a company might have to pay.

The impact of output changes on the initial magnitude, distribution, and duration of unemployment is influenced by seniority provisions in union contracts and by guaranteed income plans won by the UAW in recent years. The typical SUB plan pays up to 95 percent of a laid-off employee's after-tax pay, less a small amount for work-related expenses not incurred. The amount to be paid is determined by the extent of funding of the plan and an individual's seniority. At full funding levels, any senior employee would be eligible for a year of benefits.[2] Short-week benefits are also available under the plan to ensure income equality between laid-off workers and the typically more senior employees who continue to work. There has been pressure from more senior employees for reverse-seniority provisions in some cases, allowing the senior employees to take lay-off first.

A major possible impact of the SUB plan is suggested by the experience of employees laid off beginning in the winter of 1974. Many reportedly postponed job search, waiting for recall until their SUB benefits were near expiration. The continued slump in auto production in the winter of 1974-75 was exacerbated by the general recession, which increased lay-offs in the auto industry (encompassing some senior employees) and reduced other employment opportunities at the same time that laid-off workers from the previous winter were beginning to search for employment.[3]

The distribution of employment among workers in the automobile industry is affected by seniority rules. "Bumping" provisions within seniority units result in the more recently hired being laid off first. Seniority units are groups of similar job classifications, perhaps including jobs of increasing complexity. Seniority units are determined at the local level and differ in breadth, with the result that lay-offs are not always made strictly on the criterion of length of service.

The breadth of seniority units varies across plants and across firms. Broadly defined seniority units, combined with liberal bumping provisions, can result in the inefficient utilization of labor; management generally bargains for narrowly defined units.[4] On the other hand, the traditional interest of the UAW membership in the use of seniority rules to provide job security is well informed in light of the difficulty experienced by older, and particularly older semi-skilled, workers in finding new jobs.[5] This general problem is exacerbated in the automobile industry by the fact that older, high-seniority workers typically are not out of work except during periods of high unemployment, especially high local unemployment due to the concentration of the industry near the Great Lakes.

In the motor vehicle industry, employment change resulting from an output reduction may potentially have high social costs. Employment is concen-

trated geographically and, in some areas, represents a high fraction of local manufacturing employment; other employment opportunities may be scarce during a period of heavy layoffs in the industry. Employees in the industry, being highly paid, are likely to wait at least some time to regain their old jobs. While seniority provisions shifting the burden of unemployment to more mobile younger workers may speed up the adjustment to layoffs, generous unemployment benefits encourage slower adjustment.

The short-run and long-run effects of output changes on total employment in the industry depend on the coefficient of the automobile industry production function and on costs of changing the level of employment. A theoretical framework for estimating the effects of output changes on employment is outlined below.

THEORETICAL FRAMEWORK: TIME SERIES ESTIMATION

We have estimated the derived demand for production worker employment in the automobile industry as one of a set of factor demand equations. The particular formulation adopted allows for interaction between the utilization levels of the various factors of production, in the context of a model of partial adjustment toward optimum long-run levels of factor inputs. The model is developed in Nadiri and Rosen.[6]

Letting Y_i^* represent the optimum long-run input level for factor Y_i, the approach to long-run equilibrium in the face of adjustment costs can be estimated as

$$Y_{i,t} - Y_{i,t-1} = \sum_{j=1}^{n} \beta_{i,j} [Y_j^* - Y_{j,t-1}] + \epsilon_{i,t}, \quad i = 1, \ldots, n \qquad (7.1)$$

where n is the number of factors of production and $\epsilon_{i,t}$ are random disturbance terms. This formulation implies that the speed of adjustment of factor i toward its equilibrium level may depend on the degree to which utilization of factor i and other factors depart from their long-run equilibrium levels.

Factor i might depart from its optimum level because of transactions costs that, in addition to direct rental charges, are involved in changing the level of usage of a factor. Nadiri and Rosen enumerate search, hiring, training, and layoff costs and morale problems among workers associated with changing the level of employment as transactions costs. Costs of search, waiting, and installation are associated with purchases of new capital goods. Poorly organized capital goods secondary markets may impose further costs. The existence of transactions costs provides an explanation of observed hoarding of input stocks when demand declines.

Deriving the long-run optimum levels of factor demand, Y_j^*, as the solution to the firm's dynamic optimization problem in the context of adjustment costs, we can express the factor demand equations as functions of relative factor prices, R, and the long-run equilibrium level of output, X^* [7], as

$$Y_j^* = f(R, X^*). \tag{7.2}$$

The nonlinear derived demand relationships can be linearized in the neighborhood of current output levels so that X^* is replaced by X_t in Equation (7.2). Substituting Equation (7.2) into Equation (7.1) and rearranging terms we have, in matrix notation, the relationship to be estimated

$$Y_t = AX_t + BR_t + CY_{t-1} + \epsilon_t \tag{7.3}$$

where A is an $n \times 1$ vector of output coefficients, B is an $n \times (m-1)$ matrix of relative factor price coefficients (where m is the number of factors of production), and C is an $n \times n$ matrix of own and cross adjustment coefficients equal to $(I - \beta)$, where β is the matrix of partial adjustment coefficients in Equation (7.1), the behavioral equation.*

The derivation of the factor demand equations in Equation (7.3) is shown in Appendix 7A. We note here that the $\beta_{i,j}$ of Equation (7.1) are the focus of our interest; they are the partial adjustment coefficients describing the speed at which factor inputs approach their long-run equilibrium levels.

When a particular empirical specification of Equation (7.3 is estimated, the $\beta_{i,j}$ can be derived from the estimates of the elements of the C matrix.† Estimates of own adjustment coefficients—$\beta_{i,i}$—are calculated as $(1 - C_{i,i})$; cross-adjustment estimates, $\beta_{i,j}$—are calculated as $-\hat{c}_{i,j}$. The βs thus estimated are coefficients on the $[Y_j^* - Y_{j,t-1}]$ terms in behavioral Equation (7.1). A statistically significant coefficient on a $Y_{j,t-1}$ term in an equation of the form of Equation (7.3) for $Y_{i,t}$ thus indicates that departure of Y_j from its long-run equilibrium level affects the speed with which Y_i adjusts to its own equilibrium level. A positive $\beta_{i,j}$ would imply that if the desired level of Y_j exceeds the actual level, Y_i would increase more rapidly, other things being equal.

---

*If $X = X^* + \epsilon$ where ϵ is a random error uncorrelated with X^*, it can be shown that the coefficients of X in Equation (7.3) will be biased downward.

†The individual elements of $(I - \beta)$ included in a particular derived factor demand equation are given by the relevant row of the $(I - \beta)$ matrix, which is equal to the C matrix, element by element.

$$\begin{pmatrix} 1-\beta_{11} & -\beta_{12} & \cdots & -\beta_{1n} \\ -\beta_{21} & 1-\beta_{22} & \cdots & -\beta_{2n} \\ -\beta_{n1} & -\beta_{n2} & \cdots & 1-\beta_{nn} \end{pmatrix} = \begin{pmatrix} C_{11} & C_{12} & \cdots & C_{1n} \\ C_{21} & C_{22} & \cdots & C_{2n} \\ C_{n1} & C_{n2} & \cdots & C_{nn} \end{pmatrix}$$

Estimation of Factor Demand from Time Series Data

The relationship we estimate is an empirical representation of the factor demand functions implied by the conceptual Cobb-Douglas production function.

$$X_t \leqslant A \prod_{i=1}^{4} (Y_{it})^{ai} \qquad (7.4)$$

where X is output, Y_1 is the stock of labor, Y_2 is the rate of labor services per unit of the labor stock (average weekly hours per workers), Y_3 is the rate of utilization of capital services, Y_4 is capital stock, and A is an exogenous technological shift parameter. Following Nadiri and Rosen, we allow for separate effects of both the stock and flow dimensions of input, rather than restricting the production function inputs to total flows of labor and capital services. This formulation permits the estimation of cross-adjustment effects between stocks and flows.

In the previous section, transactions costs were suggested as an explanation for the firm's frequently observed failure to adjust factor inputs to their equilibrium levels instantaneously. The hypothesis of partial adjustment due to transactions costs leads us to expect that own adjustment coefficients will be positive and less than unity, since so long as factor i is below its equilibrium level it is growing, other things being equal. The estimated equation is not constrained to eliminate negative own adjustment coefficients. Also, individual cross-effects could be positive or negative as long as their weighted sum across equations is approximately zero.[8]

Large transactions costs associated with adjustment in stocks relative to adjustment in utilization rates suggest that costs, including transactions costs, could be minimized by adjusting utilization rates in the short run and stocks in the long run. The inclusion of lagged values of the factor inputs, other than the dependent variable in the equations, makes it possible to estimate initial overshooting of utilization of an input level past its long-run equilibrium.

We do not estimate a regression equation for the capital stock because no capital stock series is available for the automobile industry. Therefore, in the equations, lagged values of capital stock are not among the independent variables for the other factors of production.

The failure to include the theoretically relevant capital stock variable in the estimated relationship may well introduce biases into the estimated coefficients. We are particularly interested in the biases on estimates of the coefficients of output and lagged employment in the employment equation, since it is from these estimates that long-run output elasticity and the distributed lag weights of the effects on employment of a once-and-for-all change in output are computed. If the coefficient of lagged capital stock in the equation for employment is positive, the coefficients of output and lagged employment

are biased upward (downward), respectively, if the lagged capital stock variable is positively (negatively) correlated with output and lagged employment, respectively, holding other independent variables in Equation (7.3) constant. In general, it is not possible a priori to determine the direction or magnitude of the bias.

The empirical relationship that we estimate is

$$Y_{i,t} = a_0 + a_1 X_t + a_2 R_t + \sum_{j=1}^{3} a_{i,j} Y_{j,t-1} + \epsilon_{i,t} \qquad (7.5)$$

$$i = 1, \ldots, 3$$

where

Y_1 = number of production workers;
Y_2 = average weekly hours worked;
Y_3 = index of capacity utilization for Motor Vehicles and Parts; and
X = total production of autos and trucks; and
R = ratio of wage rate to estimated real interest rate.

The model is estimated by ordinary least squares for SIC 371 (Motor Vehicles and Equipment) for the period 1950:I to 1973:IV. The estimates are presented in Table 7.5.

Estimates of Structural Coefficients

The estimated coefficients are generally of the sign that would be expected from a consideration of the effects of costs of adjustment on adjustment in factor demands toward their long-run equilibrium levels. The coefficients on output are positive and significant in the regression equation for each factor. The own adjustment coefficients show average hours adjusting rapidly in the short run (1 - .22 = .78). Capital utilization responds less rapidly (1 - .65 = .35) than hours worked, but slightly more rapidly than the stock of labor (employment), which has the slowest adjustment (1.0 - .67 = .33). As expected from a consideration of transactions costs, the stocks of labor appear to adjust more slowly than the labor utilization rate.

Turning to the cross-adjustment coefficients between employment and average hours per worker implied by the estimated coefficients,* we find no significant cross-adjustment effect in the regression for employment. Evidently disequilibrium in average hours per worker does not affect the adjustment process for employment.

---

*Note that cross-adjustment effects are calculated as minus one times the coefficient on the lagged input term.

TABLE 7.5

Estimated Structural Equations and Implied Long-Run Output Elasticities (SIC 371)

	Dependent Variables		
Independent Variables	Average Employment	Weekly Hours per Worker	Capacity Utilization
Output	0.102	0.002	0.011
	(10.259)	(6.628)	(6.614)
Relative cost of labor	-67.062	-1.125	-4.161
to capital	(-5.174)	(-2.922)	(-1.991)
Average employment	0.633	-0.007	-0.029
lagged one quarter	(10.187)	(-3.941)	(-2.893)
Hours/Worker lagged	0.472	0.221	0.045
one quarter	(0.140)	(2.210)	(0.082)
Capacity utilization	-0.690	0.025	0.651
lagged one quarter	(-1.202)	(1.468)	(7.027)
Constant	265.310	34.315	36.833
	(2.086)	(9.088)	(1.797)
$\bar{R}^2$	0.799	0.506	0.741
	Implied Long-Run Output Elasticities		
	0.89	0.03	0.26

Note: The structural equations are estimated from quarterly data over the period 1950:1 to 1973:4. *t*-statistics are in parentheses. $\bar{R}^2$ is the coefficient of determination corrected for degrees of freedom.

Variable Definitions and Sources

Average Employment = quarterly average number of production workers (in thousands). *Sources*: U.S. Department of Labor, *Employment and Earnings for the U.S., 1909-72* (Washington, D.C.: Government Printing Office, 1973), and issues of *Employment and Earnings* from March 1972 through March 1974.

Hours/worker = average weekly hours per production worker. *Sources*: same as for employment.

Capacity Utilization = quarterly index of capacity utilization for Motor Vehicles and Parts. *Source*: See Table 7.6.

Output = total quarterly production of autos and trucks (in thousands). *Source: Automotive News*, Almanac Issues, 1952-75.

Relative Cost of Labor to Capital = the ratio of the real average hourly wage rate of production workers to the inflation (percentage change in CPI)–adjusted Moody's AAA bond rate plus one. *Sources*: same as for employment and for Moody's AAA bond rate, U.S. Department of Commerce, *Business Statistics 1973* for data for 1950-68; and *Survey of Current Business*, March 1970-March 1974 for data for 1969-73.

In the equation for average hours per worker, disequilibrium in employment has a significant, small positive implied adjustment coefficient, suggesting that when desired employment exceeds actual employment the utilization rate for labor may itself adjust somewhat more rapidly. The change in hours substitutes, in the short run, for an increase in the number of employees in providing the desired change in labor input.

Implied Long-Run Output Elasticities

The long-run elasticities with respect to output are presented in Table 7.5. We are primarily interested in the output elasticity of employment. The elasticities, calculated at the point of means, are computed from the stationary solutions to the entire system of equations. Their calculation is discussed more extensively in Appendix 7.B.

Our estimate of the long-run output elasticity of employment is 0.89. The possible positive bias in this elasticity was discussed above. Another potential source of bias is the possibility of autocorrelation of the error terms in the presence of lagged values of the dependent variable. This source of inconsistency, particularly in the coefficient on the lagged dependent variable, is always possible due to specification error.[9] The Durbin-Watson statistic, a standard test for the presence of autocorrelation, is not applicable to an equation containing lagged values of the dependent variable, although a large sample test developed by Durbin can be used to test for autocorrelation in these circumstances. The statistic, which is tested as a standard normal deviate, is

$$h = r \sqrt{\frac{n}{1 - n\hat{V}(b_1)}}$$

where r is approximately $1 - \frac{d}{2}$, d is the Durbin-Watson statistic, $\hat{V}(b_1)$ is the estimate of the sampling variance of b_1 in the least-squares regression, and n is the number of observations. Values of h calculated for the SIC 371 results fail to reject the hypothesis of no autocorrelation at the 95 percent confidence level.[10] Therefore we have no evidence that serial correlation is causing other biased or inconsistent estimates.

Estimates of long-run output elasticities of employment from time series data are frequently well under unity, implying significantly increasing returns to the stock of labor alone. (An estimated long-run output elasticity of employment greater than unity automatically would imply increasing returns to scale, as long as the underlying production function is homogeneous. This would be inconsistent with our assumption of an underlying Cobb-Douglas production function.) Our estimated output elasticity of employment of 0.89 implies very slightly increasing returns to employment (1/0.89 = 1.12).

TABLE 7.6

Capacity Utilization Series for Automotive Products

Year	Quarter I	II	III	IV
1950	82.1	95.4	100.0	97.7
1951	90.3	82.3	70.5	68.2
1952	66.9	68.3	58.3	77.5
1953	84.8	87.7	83.0	74.8
1954	72.4	76.9	72.5	97.3
1955	94.0	97.9	100.0	94.5
1956	81.6	75.5	72.4	76.6
1957	82.0	78.2	79.8	74.1
1958	61.0	56.8	54.6	67.3
1959	76.2	79.7	76.5	65.0
1960	87.1	84.7	81.2	78.2
1961	62.9	74.8	75.7	82.8
1962	82.8	86.6	90.1	89.9
1963	90.7	92.8	93.9	95.9
1964	96.0	100.0	97.1	84.6
1965	101.7	100.0	99.6	100.1
1966	100.0	96.1	86.7	95.2
1967	83.2	86.9	86.8	87.5
1968	94.6	100.0	98.7	100.0
1969	98.6	96.7	99.3	93.1
1970	84.5	91.8	86.1	69.3
1971	94.5	97.5	100.0	97.1
1972	94.3	100.0	94.8	99.3
1973	98.5	100.0	77.9	83.6

Note: The capacity utilization series is a derived series using the maximum-attained-output concept of capacity. The derivation proceeds as follows: (1) peak values are identified in the quarterly (average of seasonally adjusted monthly values) FRB index of industrial production for automotive products, 1967 = 100 base; (2) capacity output by linear interpolation are derived between peaks and for quarters beyond most recent peak, extrapolated linearly; and (3) actual output, given by the index, is divided by the derived capacity output to obtain the capacity utilization rate.

This approach to derivation of a capacity utilization series is similar in methodology to that used by Wharton Econometric Forecasting Associates. That approach and others that differ in methodology are described in M. P. Hertzberg, A. I. Jacobs, and J. E. Trevathan, "The Utilization of Manufacturing Capacity, 1965-1973," *Survey of Current Business* 54, 7 (July 1974): 57.

Source: Charles River Associates.

Long-run output elasticity of average weekly hours is as expected, very small; it is in fact almost zero. The output elasticity of capital utilization is also quite small but not as close to zero as it should be, an indication of our inability to measure capital inputs correctly. (Both labor and capital utilization rates should be relatively insensitive to output in the long run; these are presumably set at optimum levels initially and will depart from the long-run optimum termpoarily to compensate for disequilibrium in labor and capital stocks.)

Our overall results for the utilization of labor services are consistent with our prior belief in a long-run unit elasticity of demand for labor services with respect to output. The estimates indicate that in the long run employment maintains a roughly stable relationship to output. Average weekly hours per worker are more volatile in the short run than is employment, indicating that temporary shortfalls in output can be made up with minimal cost by overtime utilization of the stock of labor. Over the long run, adjustment to a change in output is taken up mostly by employment.

Distributed Lag Relationships

Estimates of the speed of adjustment to a once-and-for-all unit output change are indicated by the implied distributed lag weights derived from the estimated factor demand equations. In Table 7.7, we present the distributed lag weights, percentage of total long-run response, and cumulative percentage response of employment for the quarter in which the change occurs and for several quarters thereafter.

The information presented in Table 7.7 is derived from the system of equations in Table 7.5. Since there are no significant coefficients on lagged inputs other than employment in the regression for employment, our estimated lag is similar to a Koyck distributed lag.

As mentioned in the discussion of anticipated adjustment coefficients, the inclusion of interaction effects in the factor demand equations allows for a more flexible lag structure than would otherwise be the case. If lagged values of factor inputs other than the lagged dependent variable were excluded from each equation of the form of Equation (7.3), we would be estimating a Koyck distributed lag in each case.

For employment, Y_1, our estimates are close to those of a one-period Koyck lag because there are no significant coefficients on lagged values of factors other than employment. The simplest structure that was more flexible and that would allow initially rising weights would include output lagged once among the independent variables. A regression that included lagged output also predicted steadily declining lag weights. The results reported in Table 7.7 suggest that employment adjustment is a little over 80 percent completed within a year and essentially fully completed within three years.

TABLE 7.7

Distributed Lag Relationship
Derived Demand for Employment (Y₁)

Lag Quarter	Lag Weight*	Normalized Lag Weight*	Percent of Total Effect*	Cumulative Percentage
0	.102	1.000	39.23	39.23
1	.058	.569	22.31	61.76
2	.034	.333	13.08	74.84
3	.021	.206	8.08	82.92
4	.013	.127	5.00	87.92
5	.009	.088	3.46	91.38
6	.006	.059	2.31	93.69
7	.004	.039	1.54	95.23
8	.003	.029	1.15	96.38
9	.002	.020	0.77	97.15
10	.002	.020	0.77	97.92
11	.002	.020	0.77	98.69
12	.001	.010	0.38	99.07

*Lag weights reported here and total long-run effect are derived from the coefficients in the first column of Table 7.5. Normalized lag weights are derived from normalization on the zero-th lag.

Source: Data from Table 7.5.

Regression equations for average hours per worker and for capacity utilization do include statistically significant coefficients on lagged input variables other than the lagged dependent variable. Calculation of the distributed lag relationships in these cases is discussed in Appendix 7.C; our results are presented there. Both hours and capacity utilization exhibit initial overshooting of their long-run equilibrium levels. Average hours per worker rise immediately to well above the equilibrium level and then adjust downward. Capacity utilization rises more slowly, exceeding the equilibrium level in the first quarter after the change in output, and then rising through the second quarter before starting to decline toward equilibrium. These results are consistent with lower transactions costs being associated with the levels of utilization relative to the stock of labor.

ESTIMATION OF FACTOR DEMAND FROM CROSS-SECTION DATA

As a check on our time series results, we estimate two cross-sections—one for states and one for SMSAs—on 1967 data for SIC 371. Use of a cross-

TABLE 7.8

Cross-Section Estimation
SIC 371

Dependent Variable: SIC 371 Production Workers (in thousands)

Independent Variable	SMSAs	States
Constant	−2.50	−2.06
	(5.59)	(3.35)
Value added (in SIC 371)	0.92	0.98
	(36.54)	(22.55)
Percent establishments with 20+ workers	0.12	0.01
(in SIC 371)	(1.19)	(0.09)
Average hourly wage	−0.47	−0.74
(in SIC 371)	(1.95)	(2.22)
$\bar{R}^2$	.990	.990
N	28	21

Note: t-statistics in parentheses. $\bar{R}^2$ is the coefficient of determination corrected for degrees of freedom.

Source: U.S. Department of Commerce, *1967 Census of Manufactures* (Washington, D.C.: Government Printing Office, 1967).

section relationship avoids most problems associated with technological change and some of the problems associated with capital stock measurement. Capacity utilization is not at issue since 1967 was a very good year for the auto industry.

The available cross-section data do not distinguish areas by the age of the capital stock in place or by the mix of subindustries within SIC 371. If the labor-output relationship varies among subindustries, the implied output elasticity from the cross-section equation will be biased. The percent of establishments employing 20 or more workers is included as a proxy for a concentration of the large units that are typical of assembly facilities; however, this variable does not perform well.

Our cross-section results are presented in Table 7.8. The relationship that we estimate is

$$y_i = \beta_0 + \beta_1 q_i + \beta_2 z_i + \beta_3 w_i + \epsilon_i \tag{7.6}$$
$$i = 1, \ldots, n$$

where y is production worker employment, q is value added, z is the percentage of establishments with 20 or more employees, w is the average hourly

wage rate, n is the number of observations, and all variables are measured as natural logarithms.

The coefficient on value added is an estimate of the long-run output elasticity of employment. Estimates for both state and SMSA samples are close to unity, tending to lend credence to our earlier time series estimate of an elasticity of 0.89 for SIC 371.

GEOGRAPHIC DISTRIBUTION OF EMPLOYMENT CHANGES

We have noted above that motor vehicle industry employment is concentrated in the Great Lakes region, especially Michigan and Ohio. However, automobile assembly plants are scattered throughout the United States and Canada.

A decline in the demand for motor vehicles will reduce demand for labor at all stages of the production process including final assembly, engine assembly, body stamping, transmission, and production of numerous smaller parts and supplies. Body, engine, and transmission plants are located mostly in Michigan; assembly production is decentralized. Parts factories are spread throughout the country, but are mostly found in the Great Lakes region.

Decline in demand for special types of vehicles, or failure of an automobile producing company, can lead to permanent or long-term plant closings in the industry. There have been very few long-term plant closings in the past

TABLE 7.9

Shutdowns of Auto Assembly Facilities

Year	Company	Plant Location[b]
1962-63	G.M.	Oakland, Calif.
1963-64[a]	Studebaker	South Bend, Ind. (engine production)
1963-64[a]	Ford	Metuchen, N.J. (reopened for 1966 modeling)
1967-69[a]	G.M.	Bloomfield, N.J. (i.e., Newark)
1967-69[a]	Ford	Dallas, Texas
1970-71[a]	Chrysler	Los Angeles, Calif.
1971-72	Chrysler	Warren, Michigan (reopened for 1972 model year)

[a]Apparently permanent closing.

[b]The plant is listed if it appeared in the list of plants in one annual issue of the source and not in the following annual issue. A year indicated 1962-63 thus suggests the plant ceased operations sometime between roughly September 1962 and September 1963 (that is, it did not produce during the 1963 model year).

Source: Through the 1965 model year: *Automotive News Almanacs*; thereafter, *Ward's Automotive Reports Yearbooks*.

decade. Table 7.9 provides a list of closings of automobile assembly facilities, compiled by comparing lists of operating plants in successive issues of *Automotive News Almanac* and *Ward's Automotive Reports*.

Short term plant closings are more common; the usual procedure during a period of declining demand is for a company temporarily to close assembly plants producing cars for which demand is slack and inventories are excessively high. These temporary closures create unemployment in the locations where the shutdowns occur; as the shutdowns are frequently for short periods, it is likely that most employees wait for the plant to reopen instead of seeking alternative employment.

Many assembly plants were closed for varying periods of time during the 1974-75 slump in the U.S. automobile industry. For example, on February 1, 1975, eleven assembly plants in the United States and three assembly plants in Canada were temporarily out of operation. The U.S. plants were located in Hamtramck and Dearborn, Michigan; Newark, Delaware; Chicago; Kansas City and Leeds, Missouri; Mahwah and Metuchen, New Jersey; Belvedere, Illinois; and South Gate and Van Nuys, California. Actual employment declines in the industry are much more heavily concentrated in Michigan because of the location of body-stamping, engine, and transmission plants there.

SUMMARY OF FINDINGS

The econometric evidence reported in this chapter shows that employment in the motor vehicle industry changes in proportion to changes in total long-run output. An estimate of long-run elasticity of labor demand in the neighborhood of unity is found in both the time series and cross-section estimates. The distributed lag estimates from the time-series equation indicate a rapid adjustment of employment to changes in output, which in turn indicates that short-term unemployment problems resulting from a decline in domestic automobile production brought about by a trade policy change are potentially severe and merit close examination. The effect on U.S. unemployment of a reduction in domestic demand for "domestically made" automobiles is likely to be mitigated by the fact that some assembly plants producing autos that are likely to be impacted by the fall in demand are located in Canada.

The automobile industry is a high-wage industry with a strong union that has negotiated generous benefits for unemployed workers. These facts suggest that laid-off workers in the motor vehicle industry may be likely to move more slowly to jobs in other industries when motor vehicle demand falls than would typical unemployed workers. The fact that many motor vehicle industry workers are located in areas where the industry accounts for a large fraction of unemployment may further contribute to extended unemployment.

APPENDIX 7.A

Derivation of Factor Demand Equations

Consider as an example the case of two factors of production. Equation 7.1 in the text becomes

$$Y_{1,t} - Y_{1,t-1} = \beta_{11}[Y_1^* - Y_{1,t-1}] + \beta_{12}[Y_2^* - Y_{2,t-1}] + \epsilon_{1,t} \tag{7A.1}$$

$$Y_{2,t} - Y_{2,t-1} = \beta_{21}[Y_1^* - Y_{1,t-1}] + \beta_{22}[Y_2^* - Y_{2,t-1}] + \epsilon_{2,t} \tag{7A.1'}$$

Equilibrium levels of Y_1 and Y_2 (Y_1^* and Y_2^*) are assumed to be functions, although not necessarily the same function, of equilibrium output X^* and relative factor prices, about which we assume static expectations. Thus equilibrium output and expected prices are approximated by their current levels.

$$Y_1^* = f(X^*,R) = f(X,R) \tag{7A.2}$$

$$Y_2^* = g(X^*,R) = g(X,R) \tag{7A.2'}$$

For purposes of exposition, assume f and g are linear functions of X and R.

$$f(X,R) = f_0 + f_1 X + f_2 R \tag{7A.3}$$

$$g(X,R) = g_0 + g_1 X + g_2 R \tag{7A.3'}$$

Then, substituting Equation (7A.3) into Equation (7A.1) and collecting terms in $Y_{1,t-1}$:

$$Y_{1,t} = c_{10} + c_{11} X_t + c_{12} R_t + c_{13} Y_{1,t-1} + c_{14} Y_{2,t-1} + \epsilon_{1,t} \tag{7A.4}$$

where

$c_{10} = (f_0 \beta_{11} + g_0 \beta_{12})$

$c_{11} = (f_1 \beta_{11} + g_1 \beta_{12})$

$c_{12} = (f_2 \beta_{11} + g_2 \beta_{12})$

$c_{13} = 1 - \beta_{11}$

$c_{14} = -\beta_{12}$

Therefore:

$$\beta_{11} = 1 - c_{13}$$

$$\beta_{12} = -c_{14}$$

These are the partial adjustment coefficients measuring the effects of departure from equilibrium of factors 1 and 2 on the current level of Y_1. They are the βs of Equation (7A.1), the behavioral equation.

Looking at the c_{11} term, we see that the effect of current output on $y_{1,t}$ is a weighted average of the effects output has on equilibrium levels Y_1^* and Y_2^* (that is, the coefficients f_1 and g_1 in Equation [7A.3]) with the weights being the partial adjustment coefficients of Equation (7A.1). A parallel interpretation applies to the coefficient on R, c_{13}.

Proceeding similarly, we can derive from Equation (7A.1') and Equations (7A.2) and (7A.3) the partial adjustment coefficients β_{21} and β_{22} in Equation (7A.1').

APPENDIX 7.B

Calculating Long-Run Output Elasticities

We derive long-run output elasticities from the coefficients on output and lagged inputs in the regression equations. Implied long-run elasticities allowing for interrelated dynamic factor adjustment are derived from the stationary solutions to the entire system of equations. (In the new steady state, levels of output and factor inputs will not change from period to period. Thus, time subscripts are superfluous and have been omitted.)

$$Y_1 = .102X + .633Y_1 + .472Y_2 - .690Y_3 \qquad (7B.1)$$

$$Y_2 = .002X - .007Y_1 + .221Y_2 + .025Y_3 \qquad (7B.2)$$

$$Y_3 = .011X - .029Y_1 + .045Y_2 + .651Y_3 \qquad (7B.3)$$

The stationary solutions to the above system of equations are

$$Y_1 = .26X$$

$$Y_2 = .0006X$$

$$Y_3 = .011X$$

OUTPUT CHANGES AND LABOR DEMAND

The coefficient on X in any one of these three equations is the implied long-run impact of a unit increase in the level of output of autos and trucks on the level of the respective factors of production. To calculate the elasticity of a particular factor of production with respect to output, we multiply the coefficient on X in the relevant equation by the ratio of the mean level of output to factor input.

Thus, the long-run output elasticity of employment (Y_1) calculated at the point of means is

$$.260 \frac{\bar{X}}{\bar{Y}_1} = (.260)\left(\frac{2139}{624.4}\right) = 0.89 \tag{7B.4}$$

Similarly, the long-run output elasticity of average hours per worker (Y_2) is

$$.0006 \frac{\bar{X}}{\bar{Y}_2} = (.0006)\left(\frac{2139}{41.79}\right) = 0.03 \tag{7B.5}$$

and of capacity utilization (Y_3) is

$$.011 \frac{\bar{X}}{\bar{Y}_3} = (.011)\left(\frac{2139}{36}\right) = 0.26 \tag{7B.6}$$

APPENDIX 7.C

Distributed Lag Relationships

Distributed lag relationships in which interrelated dynamic factor adjustment is allowed must be calculated from the system of equations. Estimation of the lag weights is accomplished by successive substitution of previously calculated one-period lag values into the factor demand equations.

For example, the lag weights for average employment, Y_1, following a unit change in the level of output, X, are calculated as follows.*

$$\text{lag} \quad Y_{1,t} = .102 X_t + .633 Y_{1,t-1} + .472 Y_{2,t-1} - .690 Y_{3,t-1} \tag{7C.1}$$

0	.102 =	.102 (1)
1	.058 =	.633 (.102) + .472 (.002) − .69 (.011)
2	.034 =	.633 (.058) + .472 (.000003) − .69 (.0043)
3	.021 =	.633 (.034) + .472 (−.0003) − .69 (.0011),
etc.		

*The lagged values of $Y_{2,t}$ and $Y_{3,t}$ substituted into this equation are calculated in similar equations.

TABLE 7C.1

Distributed Lag Relationships for Average Hours per Worker and Capacity Utilization

	Hours/Worker		Capacity Utilization	
Lag	Lag Weight	Cumulative Percentage Effect	Lag Weight	Cumulative Percentage Effect
0	.002	333	.011	100
1	.0000	333	.0043	139
2	-.0003	283	.0011	149
3	-.0002	250	-.0003	146
4	-.0002	217	-.0008	139
5	-.0002	184	-.0009	131
6	-.0001	167	-.0009	123
.				
.				
.				
n	.0006	100	.011	100

Source: CRA factor Demand Regressions.

The implied long-run impacts of a unit change in the level of output of autos and trucks on the levels of the factors of production have been calculated from the system of stationary equations as a step in the calculation of long-run output elasticities in Appendix 7.B. They are 0.26 for average employment, 0.0006 for average hours per worker, and 0.011 for capacity utilization. The percentage of the long-run impact achieved in each quarter following a unit change in the level of output is calculated for a particular factor of production by dividing the lag weight for the quarter by the implied long-run impact. The cumulative percentage of the effect experienced by a particular quarter following the change in the level of output is the sum of the percentage impacts achieved in that and all preceding quarters.

Distributed lag weights, percentage of total impact achieved, and cumulative percentage of total impact achieved by quarter are presented for the case of average employment in Table 7.6 of the text. Distributed lag weights and the cumulative percentage response for average hours per worker and capacity utilization are presented in Table 7C.1.

NOTES

1. The institutional environment in the automobile industry labor market is discussed in Robert M. McDonald, *Collective Bargaining in the Automobile Industry* (New Haven, Conn.: Yale University Press, 1963); Lawrence J. White, *The U.S. Automobile Industry Since 1945* (Cambridge: Harvard University Press, 1971) and R. J. Wonnacott and P. Wonnacott, *Free Trade Between the United States and Canada: The Potential Economic Effects* (Cambridge: Harvard University Press, 1967). Basic union demands in various collective bargaining rounds are discussed in the *Labor Regulations Yearbook* of the Bureau of National Affairs, Inc., Washington, D.C., which also reports contract provisions by company.

2. Detailed provisions of contracts are outlined in the *Labor Relations Yearbook*, op. cit., and in individual UAW-company agreements.

3. See "Layoff Lament," *Wall Street Journal*, October 29, 1974.

4. See McDonald, op. cit.

5. For evidence of the effect of age on the probability of finding employment, see J. W. Dorsey "The Mack Case: A Study in Unemployment," in O. Eckstein, ed., *Studies in the Economics of Income Maintenance*, (Washington, D.C.: Brookings Institution, 1967) pp. 175-248; Stuart J. Faber, Louis Ferman, and Harold Sheppard, *Too Old to Work— Too Young to Retire: A Case Study of a Permanent Plant Shutdown*, Institute of Labor and Industrial Relations, University of Michigan, Wayne State, December 21, 1959; M. S. Gordon and A. McCorry, "Plant Relocation and Job Security," *Industrial and Labor Relations Review*, 11 (October 1957): 13-36.

6. See M. I. Nadiri and S. Rosen, "Interrelated Factor Demand Functions," *American Economic Review*, 59, 4 (September 1969): 457-71. See also R. E. Lucas Jr., "Adjustment Costs and the Theory of Supply," *Journal of Political Economy*, 75, 4, Part I (August 1967): 321-34, for an exposition of the basic approach to modeling economic behavior in the context of adjustment costs, and A. Katz, "Factor Demand Model: Preliminary Results," in James Jondrow et al., *Removing Restrictions on Imports of Steel*, PRI 75-2, Public Research Institute, Arlington, Va., Center for Naval Analysis, May 1975, for an application of the methodology developed in Nadiri and Rosen.

7. See Nadiri and Rosen, op. cit.

8. Ibid, p. 465.

9. For a discussion of the consequences of autocorrelation in the presence of lagged dependent variables see H. Theil, *Principles of Econometrics* (New York: Wiley, 1971), pp. 261-62; and Zvi Griliches, "Distributed Lags: A Survey," *Econometrica* 35, 1 (January 1967): pp. 33-44.

10. The h statistic for our results is 0.37, and the critical value is approximately 1.65. The test is discussed in J. Johnston, *Econometric Methods*, 2d ed. (New York: McGraw-Hill, 1972).

CHAPTER

8

WELFARE EFFECTS OF TRADE POLICY CHANGES AFFECTING THE U.S. AUTOMOBILE MARKET

In this chapter, we present estimates of the economic gains and losses to society as a whole from changes in trade policy affecting the U.S. automobile industry. We compare the quantitative magnitude of decreases in the efficiency of resource allocation in product markets brought about by tariffs on imported automobiles to estimates of the increase in output from the reduction in unemployment of U.S. auto workers.

If we view a "foreign car" as a distinct product with a different bundle of utility-producing characteristics than a "domestic car," then we can define conceptually, and measure, the net reduction in the value of output from tariffs that raise the price of a "foreign car," at any given level of aggregate demand. Imposition of a tariff on imported automobiles leads to a misallocation of resources between "foreign cars" and "domestic cars," and also between "foreign cars" and other goods, including goods and services complementary to ownership of used "domestic" and "foreign" cars. From the standpoint of static economic efficiency, too many resources are allocated to the production of domestic automobiles and other goods and services, and too few resources to the production of exports and/or substitutes for other imports. This loss in the efficiency of resource allocation can be compared to the increase in total output that would result if the tariff accelerates the reemployment of previously displaced automobile workers. We will use the term "product market welfare loss" to denote the resource allocation cost of tariffs, and the term "net welfare loss" to denote the difference between the "product market welfare loss" and the reduction in labor adjustment cost.

Higher tariffs may make it economical for foreign manufacturers to establish production facilities in the United States that they either would not have built had there not been a tariff or would have built at a later time. If a shift to production in the United States becomes economical because of

tariffs, then the unit cost of production will not have risen by the full amount of the tax. However, costs will still be higher than in the nontariff equilibrium, where production cost abroad is lower than production cost in the United States.

As we showed in Chapter 6, there is some possibility that higher tariffs will make it economical for foreign manufacturers to establish production facilities in the United States. These production shifts, however, may occur in the future even in the absence of tariffs if growth in demand for "foreign cars" in the United States makes it possible for several firms to establish minimum efficient scale production facilities serving the U.S. market alone. (Alternatively, foreign firms may set up combined operations in the United States, or a major U.S. company may begin production of automobiles with the same characteristics mix as a "foreign car.")

As the production location decision depends on many factors we have not measured, such as political considerations in foreign countries and interrelationships among foreign firms, and on factories we have measured imprecisely, such as international production cost comparisons and transport costs, it is difficult to forecast with any precision the marginal effect of a given tariff change on location. In this chapter, we estimate the product market welfare loss from a tariff change, assuming the tariff does not affect the location of production of specific models of automobiles, and also assuming that the supply of foreign manufactured automobiles to the United States is perfectly elastic. In that case, a given percentage tariff increase applied in the final sale price will add the same percentage to the supply cost of a "foreign car" in the United States.

The product market welfare loss from an increase in the price of foreign cars is an annual flow that persists through time; it may be measured either as the loss per year, or as the present discounted value of all future losses. On the other hand, the labor adjustment cost depends on the rate of change of domestic automobile output caused by a trade policy change, and not on the difference between two long-run equilibrium output levels. (In the long run, the level of employment in the domestic-automobile industry would be higher in the presence of a higher auto import tariff. The computations below assume that the additional auto industry employment, in the long run, will be drawn from employment in other industries. This assumption is based on the view that the entire package of monetary, fiscal, and exchange rate policies determines the aggregate demand for labor in the economy as a whole, not policies that affect relative prices in individual industries.)

The estimated product market welfare loss is sensitive to the choice among estimated demand elasticity parameters that show the effect of changes in relative foreign-to-domestic auto prices on relative foreign-to-domestic new-car sales. For higher values of the substitution elasticies estimated in Chapter 3, the product market welfare loss is generally greater. Using sales data from 1974 and assuming pure competition and constant long-run supply curves in the

domestic market,* our estimates of the annual product market welfare loss from a 10 percent increase in foreign-car prices brought about by an increase in the auto import tariff range from $36.7 million per year to $198.6 million per year, or from $4.42 per new car sold to $14.40 per new car sold. (These estimates represent the deadweight loss from the tariff. The total welfare loss to consumers, which includes the tariffs paid to the U.S. government, is much greater.) The estimated gains from removing the current 3 percent tariff are much smaller; the estimates range from $4.07 million per year ($.47 per car) to $22.07 million per year ($2.54 per car). Small changes in the tariff rate on imported automobiles will not have a monumental impact on national welfare; the welfare effect is even smaller as a fraction of current spending on automobiles. However, we find that the present discounted value of the product market welfare loss (gain) from higher (lower) tariffs is probably at least as great as the present discounted value of the reduction (increase in labor adjustment cost from higher (lower) tariffs for all estimated values of the demand elasticity.

Estimation of the product market welfare loss is more complicated if we drop the assumption that the domestic automobile industry is perfectly competitive. (Our research has not assessed the competitiveness of the U.S. automobile industry, and we make no judgment on this issue.) The net product market welfare loss from a small increase in the import tariff will be lower if automobile companies have some power over price than if the domestic market is in pure competition; the welfare loss may even be negative, because the loss from the distortion in the foreign-car price is counterbalanced by welfare gains from increased sales of domestic automobiles. (If domestic companies have some power over price, the price of a car will be greater than marginal cost. Thus, marginal social gains brought about by an increase in domestic sales in response to a rise in the foreign-car price will be greater than the marginal social cost of additional domestic production. This welfare gain may to some extent be dampened if the demand shift makes it profitable for domestic companies to raise prices. See the fourth section of this chapter, beginning on page 212, for a fuller explanation.) However, under imperfect competition, all the net welfare gains from more domestic car sales brought about by a tariff will accrue to factors in the domestic-automobile industry; in addition there will be a large income transfer from consumers of automobiles to factors of production in the domestic industry. (We have not attempted to assess the extent to which such gains would be divided between stockholders of automobile companies and unionized workers.) We analyze the impact of an import tariff on welfare in the absence of perfect competition in the domestic industry in more detail in the fourth section of this chapter.

---

*These assumptions imply that, in the long-run, changes in the price of imports do not affect the price of domestic automobiles.

PRODUCT MARKET WELFARE LOSS: METHODOLOGY

Imposition of a tariff on imported automobiles imposes a welfare loss on U.S. residents by diverting scarce resources from their most productive use. A reasonable approximate measure of this product market welfare loss can be quantified using standard consumer surplus analysis. In this section, we present estimates of the product market welfare loss from assumed changes in the import tariff, using as input data estimates of the price elasticity of demand from Chapter 3, and assuming the U.S. automobile industry is competitive. We also assume that the supply curve of foreign cars to the U.S. market is totally elastic; most high-volume imports, accounting for the major fraction of imports purchased by U.S. buyers, are produced at volumes far in excess of minimum efficient scale for local consumption.

Figure 8.1 depicts the product market welfare loss from imposition of a tariff on imported automobiles, assuming pure competition and elastic supply in the domestic automobile industry. In Figure 8.1, we approximate the demand for foreign cars, using a linear demand curve. $P_{F2}AC$ is the demand curve for foreign cars; $P_{F0}BC$ is the supply curve. Imposition of a tariff rate equal to t/P_{F1} raises the supply curve to the U.S. market to $P_{F1}A$. In the absence of the tariff, the price of a foreign car is P_{F0} and sales are OF_0 units per year; the tariff raises the price to P_{F1}', and reduces sales to OF_1 units per year.

The loss to domestic consumers from the tariff is equal to the area P_{F1}-$P_{F0}BCA$. $P_{F1}P_{F0}BA$ represents the additional dollar cost to consumers purchasing imports after the price increase while ABC represents an approximation of the dollar value of the utility loss to buyers diverted by the higher price to purchase of what had previously been lower-utility goods. The area ABC represents the difference between what consumers are willing to spend on imported cars, and what they would have had to spend at the lower price. The area P_{F1}-$P_{F0}BA$ represents an income transfer from foreign-car buyers to taxpayers,* while the area ABC represents the deadweight loss, or the net product market welfare loss.

The area ABC in Figure 8.1 is equal to $\frac{1}{2}(P_{F0} - P_{F1})(F_0 - F_1)$ = $\frac{1}{2}a_2(P_{F0} - P_{F1})^2$, where a_2 is equal to the partial derivative of F with respect to P_F—that is, the reciprocal of the slope of the foreign-car demand curve. Thus, the product market welfare loss is proportional to the square of the price change brought about by the tariff increase.

---

*Enumeration of the characteristics of the individuals who gain and lose from this income transfer requires an assumption about what the government would do with the extra tax revenue. Alternative possibilities include increased expenditures on a wide range of public programs and reduction in any of a variety of federal taxes (income taxes, corporate profits taxes, federal excises, and others).

FIGURE 8.1
Product Market Loss from Tariff on Imported Automobiles

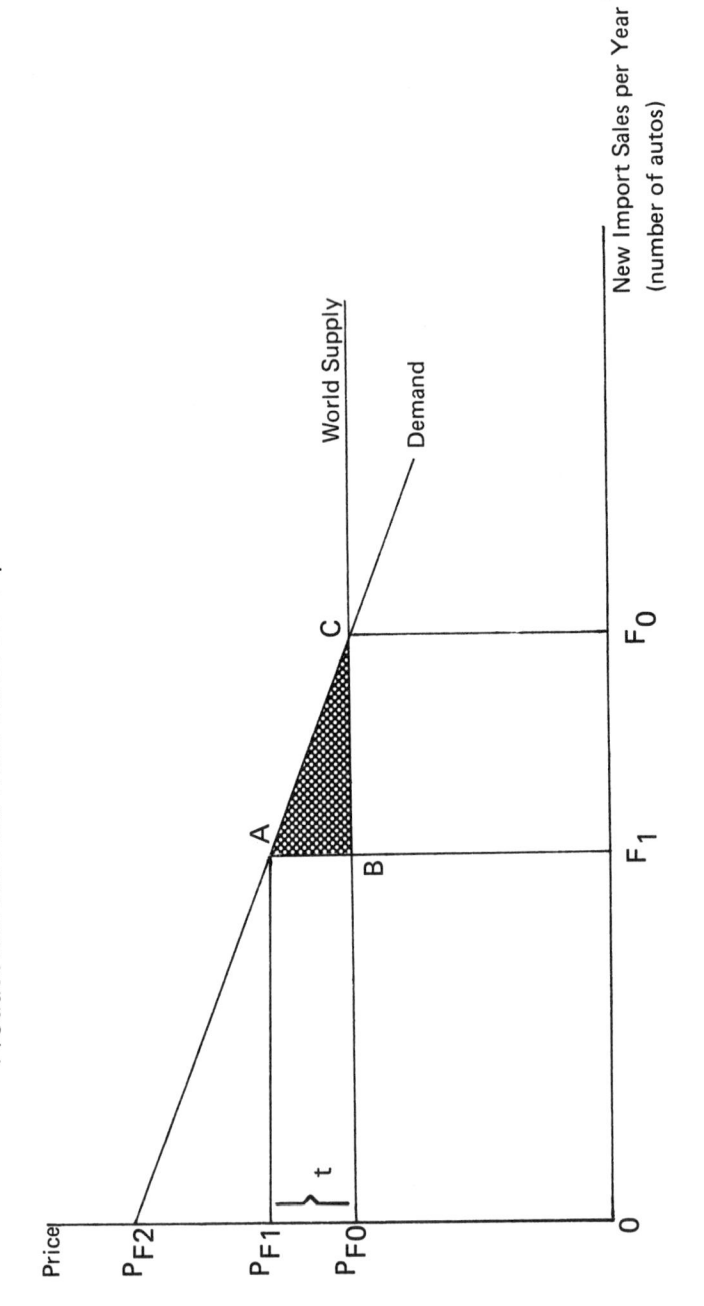

Source: Charles River Associates.

WELFARE EFFECTS OF TRADE POLICY CHANGES

While the simple consumer surplus analysis used here has some theoretical and empirical shortcomings and qualifications, it still provides a reasonable approximation of the net social gains, or losses, in long-run equilibrium from changes in trade restrictions.[1] The major quantitative problem with the use of the welfare loss derived by this method is that the magnitude of the loss is extremely sensitive to the choice of the estimated slope of the foreign car demand curve. We computed this parameter using linear conversions of estimates of the relative price elasticity of foreign-car shares and the price elasticity of total new-car demand. The slope of the foreign-car demand curve is highly sensitive to changes in the magnitude of the share elasticity coefficient; to derive a range of plausible estimates we computed the product market welfare loss both for the extreme values and for an intermediate value of our estimated share elasticities from Chapter 3.

The area ABC in Figure 8.1 gives the annual product market welfare loss for any one year; the present value of the future stream of losses is computed by taking the discounted sum of estimates of the adjustment rate of foreign share demand to its final equilibrium (from Chapter 3) to derive values of the estimated slope that reflect the cumulative adjustment that would take place as of each time period after the tariff change. The present discounted value of the future stream of product market welfare losses is greater the faster the adjustment to final equilibrium is.

Estimation of the Linear Demand Curve Parameters

To facilitate computation of a reasonable approximation of the welfare loss from a tariff on foreign cars, we sought estimates of the parameters of the equations

$$F = a_0 + a_1 P_F + a_2 P_D \tag{8.1a}$$

$$D = b_0 + b_1 P_F + b_2 P_D \tag{8.1b}$$

where F is foreign new-car sales, D is domestic new-car sales, P_F is foreign new-car price, and P_D is domestic new-car sales.

In chapter 3, we estimated econometrically the equation

$$\log(\frac{F}{D}) = A_0 + A_1 \log(\frac{P_F}{P_D}) + A_2 X \tag{8.2}$$

where X is a vector of exogenous variables. Equation (8.2) can be written as

$$\log F - \log D = A_0 + A_1 [\log P_F - \log P_D] + A_2 X. \tag{8.2a}$$

A general constant elasticity formulation of a system of demand curves for domestic and foreign cars can be written

$$\log F = b \log P_F + c \log P_D \tag{8.3a}$$

$$\log D = g \log P_F + h \log P_D . \tag{8.3b}$$

If $\frac{F}{D}$, the ratio of foreign-to-domestic sales, depends only on P_F/P_D, the ratio of foreign-to-domestic car price—that is, if the effect on the foreign-to-domestic car sales ratio of an x percent rise in foreign-car prices is the same as the effect of an x percent fall in domestic-car prices, then we can write

$$A = b - g = h - c. \tag{8.4}$$

Let us further assume that $\frac{\partial F}{\partial P_D} = \frac{\partial D}{\partial P_F}$ —that is, that the rate of change in foreign-car sales with respect to a one-unit change in domestic-car prices is the same as the rate of change in domestic sales with respect to a one-unit change in foreign-car prices.

Then, converting elasticities into slopes at current prices and outputs, we obtain

$$c = g \frac{D^0 P_D^0}{F^0 P_F^0} \tag{8.5}$$

where D^0 is current domestic sales, P^0 is average current domestic price, F^0 is current import sales, and P_F^0 is average current import price, since

$$\frac{\partial F}{\partial P_D} = \frac{cF^0}{P_D^0} \quad \text{and} \quad \frac{\partial D}{\partial P_F} = \frac{gD^0}{P_F^0}$$

at the points F^0, P_D^0, D^0, P_F^0.

Then, combining Equations (8.4) and (8.5), we obtain

$$b - g = h - g \frac{D^0 P_D^0}{F^0 P_F^0}, \text{ or}$$

$$b = h + g(1 - \frac{D^0 P_D^0}{F^0 P_F^0})$$

We have estimated

WELFARE EFFECTS OF TRADE POLICY CHANGES

$$A_1 = b - g = h - c = h - g\frac{D^0 P_D^0}{F^0 P_F^0} \tag{8.6}$$

To obtain all four parameters of the system of equations, we need one more equation in h and g. We can obtain this extra equation by using the value of the total market elasticity of demand for automobiles from previous published research. The results center around an estimated price elasticity of -1.[2]

If we let $\epsilon_T = -1$, we can express $\dfrac{d(F+D)}{dP}$, the change in total new-car sales with respect to a given change in average new-car price, at the point F^0, D^0, P_F^0, P_D^0 as

$$\frac{d(F+D)}{dP} = \frac{dF}{dP} + \frac{dD}{dP} = \frac{F^0 + D^0}{P^0} \epsilon_T = -\frac{F^0 + D^0}{P^0}$$

Linearizing Equations (8.3a) and (8.3b) at the values of F^0, D^0, P_F^0, P_D^0 we obtain

$$F = K_0 + [(h + g - g\frac{D^0 P_D^0}{F^0 P_F^0}) \cdot \frac{F^0}{P_F^0}] \cdot P_F + (g\frac{D^0 P_D^0}{F^0 P_F^0})(\frac{F^0}{P_D^0}) \cdot P_D \tag{8.7a}$$

and

$$D = K_1 + g(\frac{D^0}{P_F^0})P_F + h(\frac{D^0}{P_D^0})P_D \tag{8.7b}$$

Adding Equations (8.7a) and (8.7b) and rearranging terms yields

$$(F + D) = (K_0 + K_1) + [h\frac{F^0}{P_F^0} + g[\frac{(F^0 + D^0)}{P_F^0} - \frac{D^0 P_D^0}{(P_F^0)^2}]]P_F$$

$$+ D^0 \left[\frac{g}{P_F^0} + \frac{h}{P_D^0}\right] P_D \tag{8.8}$$

For an equal change in both P_F and P_D

$$\frac{d(F+D)}{dP_F} + \frac{d(F+D)}{dP_D} = \frac{d(F+D)}{dP} = \frac{-(F^0+D^0)}{P^0} \tag{8.9}$$

Combining Equations (8.8) and (8.9) into Equation (8.10), and recalling Equation (8.6), we have two equations in the unknowns g and h.

$$\frac{hF^0}{P_F^0} + g\left[\frac{(F^0+D^0)}{P_F^0} - \frac{D_0 P_D^0}{P_F^{0\,2}}\right] + D^0\left[\frac{g}{P_F^0} + \frac{h}{P_D^0}\right] = \frac{-(F^0+D^0)}{P^0} \tag{8.10}$$

$$h = A_1 + g\frac{D^0 P_D^0}{F^0 P_F^0} \tag{8.6}$$

Substituting Equation (8.6) into Equation (8.10), and rearranging terms, we obtain

$$g = \frac{\left(\dfrac{-F^0+D^0}{P^0}\right) - A_1\left[\dfrac{F^0}{P^0} + \dfrac{D^0}{P^0}\right]}{\left(\dfrac{F^0+2D^0}{P_F^0}\right) + \dfrac{(D^0)^2}{F^0 P_F^0}} \tag{8.11}$$

Substituting back into Equations (8.7) and (8.1), we obtain, as estimates of the slopes of the demand curves, in terms of g and h

$$\begin{aligned}
a_1 &= \frac{\partial F}{\partial P_F} = \left[h + g\left(1 - \frac{D^0 P_D^0}{F^0 P_F^0}\right)\right] \cdot \frac{F^0}{P_F^0} \\
a_2 &= \frac{\partial F}{\partial P_D} = g\left(\frac{D^0}{P_F^0}\right) \\
b_1 &= \frac{\partial D}{\partial P_F} = g\left(\frac{D^0}{P_F^0}\right) \\
b_2 &= \frac{\partial D}{\partial P_D} = h\left(\frac{D^0}{P_D^0}\right)
\end{aligned} \tag{8.12}$$

Using 1974 data, we let $D^0 = 7{,}329{,}000$, $F^0 = 1{,}369{,}000$, $P_F^0 = 2{,}874$, and $P_D^0 = 3{,}815$.

The average prices are computed by taking sales weighted averages of the list prices of the 10 domestic and imported cars with the most new-car sales in 1974.

WELFARE EFFECTS OF TRADE POLICY CHANGES

Substituting the 1974 values of D^0, F^0, P_F^0, and P_D^0 into equations for g, h, a_1, a_2, b_1, and b_2 we obtain finally

$$a_1 = \frac{\partial F}{\partial P_F} = -62.64 + 412.7A_1 \tag{8.13a}$$

$$a_2 = \frac{\partial F}{\partial P_D} = -335.6 - 339.2A_1 \tag{8.13b}$$

$$b_1 = \frac{\partial D}{\partial P_F} = -335.6 - 339.2A_1 \tag{8.13c}$$

$$b_2 = \frac{\partial D}{\partial P_D} = -1,797 + 105.5A_1 \tag{8.13d}$$

Since $A_1 < 0$ and $|A_1| > 1$ in all our estimated equations, $a_1 < 0$, $a_2 > 0$, $b_1 > 0$, and $b_2 < 0$ for the entire range of estimated values of A_1.

Equations (8.13a) through (8.13d) give a set of approximate slopes of domestic and foreign demand curves, expressed as functions of the magnitude of the substitution elasticity estimates from Chapter 3. In the following section, we use these estimated equations and alternative values of the adjustment coefficient estimated in Chapter 3 to compute a range of estimates of the product market welfare loss from a tariff increase equal to 10 percent of the final sales price of imported automobiles.

PRODUCT MARKET WELFARE LOSS: ESTIMATES

In this section, we present estimates of the product market welfare loss from higher import tariffs using alternative approximate values of the substitution elasticity and lagged coefficients from the time series estimates in Chapter 3. We also estimate the product market welfare loss using the substitution elasticity and adjustment coefficients estimated by Cowling and Cubbin for individual manufacturers' autos in the United Kingdom.[3]

Let P_{F0} equal the price of a foreign car before imposition of a tariff, and let P_{F1} equal the price after a tariff change. Then,

$$\Delta W = \tfrac{1}{2} a_1 (P_{F1} - P_{F0})^2 \tag{8.14}$$

where $a_1 = \frac{\partial F}{\partial P_F}$ and ΔW is the change in welfare.

In our example, P_{F0} equals 2,874. A 10 percent increase in the price of foreign cars is equal to an absolute increase of $287.40. Thus, the welfare loss from a tariff that raises the price of imported cars by 10 percent is

$$\Delta W = \tfrac{1}{2} a_1 (287.4)^2 = 41{,}300 a_1$$

The value of a_1, the slope of the foreign-car demand curve, is computed using Equation (8.13a):

$$a_1 = -62.64 + 412.7 A_1$$

where A_1 is the substitution elasticity estimated in Chapter 3.

Table 8.1 shows our computation of the welfare loss combining a typical value of the short-run demand parameters from the time-series equations in Chapter 3 with the long-run substitution elasticity implied by the CRA hedonic market share model. The values of the short-run elasticity from the time series equations center around -1.5, while the value of the long-run elasticity from the hedonic market share is approximately -2.

Thus, the estimated parameters used in Table 8.1 are A_1 equal to -2, and m equal to .250, where A_1 is the implied long-run elasticity and m is the coefficient of the import sales ratio on the lagged import sales ratio.* Column (2) of Table 8.1 gives the cumulative percent of adjustment in each year implied by the lag coefficient. Column (3) gives the cumulative substitution elasticity from the initial point in each year, computed by multiplying the cumulative adjustment percentage in Column (2) by the long-run substitution elasticity. Then, the value of A_1 is used to compute a_1 and ΔW using equations (8.13b) and (8.14). Column (5) gives the undiscounted value of ΔW, while columns (6) and (7) give the present value of the annual product market welfare loss from the tariff in each of the 20 years after the policy change, using discount rates of 5 and 10 percent, respectively. The present discounted value of the sum of future welfare changes at 5 and 10 percent discount rates is given in the last row of the table; this value is to some degree underestimated by the fact that we did not compute losses after 20 years. We find that the present value of the 20 year stream of product market welfare losses from the tariff is $468.7 million at a 5 percent discount rate, and $332.4 million at a 10 percent discount rate.

Similar computations were made for other estimated values of A_1 and m. The results of these computations are shown in Table 8.2. For case 3, the slopes derived from elasticity estimates imply that foreign-car demand becomes zero after a significant portion of the adjustment has occurred; however, we do not believe that foreign-car sales in the United States would totally cease with a 10 percent import price increase. In part, the problem is caused by the use of a

---

*The value of m is computed from the equation $(1-m) = e_1/A_1$, where e_1 is the short-run substitution elasticity (-1.5) and A_1 is the long-run substitution elasticity (-2).

TABLE 8.1

Computation of Product Market Welfare Loss from 10 Percent Import Price Increase, 1974

Case 1: $A_1 = -2 \quad m = .250$

(Col. 1) Year	(Col. 2) Proportion of Adjustment	(Col. 3) A_1	(Col. 4) a_1	(Col. 5) ΔW	(Col. 6) ΔW, 5% Discount	(Col. 7) ΔW, 10% Discount
					In Thousands of Dollars	
1	.7500	-1.500	681.7	28,150	28,150	28,150
2	.9375	-1.875	836.5	34,550	32,910	31,410
3	.9844	-1.969	875.2	36,150	32,790	29,870
4	.9961	-1.992	884.7	36,540	31,560	27,450
5	.9990	-1.998	887.2	36,640	30,140	25,030
6	.9998	-2.000	888.0	36,670	28,730	22,770
7	1.0000	-2.000	888.0	36,670	27,360	20,700
8			888.0	36,670	26,060	18,820
9			888.0	36,670	24,820	17,110
10			888.0	36,670	23,640	15,550
11			888.0	36,670	22,510	14,140
12			888.0	36,670	21,440	12,850
13			888.0	36,670	20,420	11,680
14			888.0	36,670	19,450	10,620
15			888.0	36,670	18,520	9,657
16			888.0	36,670	17,640	8,779
17			888.0	36,670	16,800	7,981
18			888.0	36,670	16,000	7,255
19			888.0	36,670	15,240	6,596
20			888.0	36,670	14,510	5,996
Sum					468,700	332,400

A_t = cumulative elasticity of import-to-domestic sales ratio with respect to import-to-domestic price ratio in year t. a_1 = partial derivative of import sales with respect to import price. ΔW = loss in welfare from import tariff. m = elasticity of import-to-domestic sales ratio with respect to import-to-domestic sales ratio lagged one year.

Source: Charles River Associates.

TABLE 8.2

Summary of Product Market Welfare Loss Estimates from 10 Percent Import Price Increase, 1974

		Present Discounted Value of Welfare Loss	
		At 5% Discount Rate	At 10% Discount Rate
Case 1	$A_1 = -2.00$ $m = .250$	$468,700,000	$332,400,000
Case 2[a]	$A_1 = -7.06$ $m = .7239$	$1,328,000,000	$896,400,000
Case 3[b]	$A_1 = -18.76$ $m = .924$	$1,699,000,000	$1,111,000,000

A_1 = elasticity of import-to-domestic sales ratio with respect to import-to-domestic price ratio.

m = elasticity of import-to-domestic sales ratio with respect to import-to-domestic sales ratio lagged one year.

[a]From Keith Cowling and J. Cubbin, "Price, Quality and Advertising Competition. An Econometric Investigation of the United Kingdom Car Market," *Economica* (November 1971).

[b]From higher range of CRA estimates from time series equations.

Source: Charles River Associates.

linear functional form for demand; while this assumption is reasonable in the neighborhood of current sales, it becomes less sensible as foreign sales approach zero in one direction and total market sales in the other. Even a tariff that would be prohibitive for most popular foreign imports would not eliminate all import sales; some U.S. car buyers presumably would still be interested in Jaguar and Mercedes-Benz. (Note that foreign cars have for decades had some share of the U.S. market, although the share was less than 1 percent until the mid-1950s.) Moreover, our estimated elasticity of -18 is probably too high; it implies that a 7 percent increase in the import price would choke off practically all import sales. We include it to obtain a measure of the product market welfare loss using one of the most extreme, though not necessarily the most reliable, of our estimates of the implied substitution elasticity.

To compute the welfare loss when projected foreign-car sales are zero, we use the implied slope to calculate the price rise necessary to stop all import sales. We then use the formula $\triangle W = \frac{1}{2} \triangle Q \triangle P$ to calculate the welfare loss, where $\triangle P$ is the price rise that would reduce import sales to zero and $\triangle Q$ is 1,369,000, the volume of import sales in 1974. The annual welfare loss is highest for the value of a_1, at which the tariff is just sufficient to reduce import demand to zero.

Table 8.3 presents some sample estimates of the undiscounted annual welfare loss for different short-run values of A_1. The welfare loss is maximized

TABLE 8.3

Annual Product Market Welfare Loss in Final Equilibrium from 10 Percent Import Price Increase with Alternative Substitution Elasticities, 1974

Substitution Elasticity	Undiscounted Annual Product Market Welfare Loss (in dollars)	Loss per Car* (in dollars)
−2.0	36,674,400	4.22
−7.0	121,917,600	14.02
−11.5	198,611,700	22.83
−18.0	125,263,500	14.40

Note: When the substitution elasticity is −18, a 10 percent tariff reduces import sales to zero. The welfare loss is computed by deriving the values a_1 and a_2 in the equation, $F = a_0 + a_1 P_F + a_2 P_D$ from Equation (8.13), and then estimating the value of P_F for which F falls to zero. The welfare loss is then equal to ½ $\Delta F \Delta P_F$, where ΔP_F is the difference between the P_F for which $F = 0$ and the initial P_F, and ΔF is equal to the initial value of F.

*Welfare loss divided by total 1974 new car sales.

Source: Charles River Associates.

at a substitution elasticity of approximately −11.5; for greater elasticities sales remain unchanged (at zero), but the marginal value of foregone sales is lower. It can be seen from Table 8.3 that the product market welfare loss, expressed as a fraction of the total number of all new automobiles sold, is not large, even for extreme, high values of the substitution elasticity.

Conversely, the product market welfare gain from elimination of the current 3 percent tariff is trivial. Since we have shown that the loss is proportional to the square of the price distortion, the loss from a 3 percent tariff is only 9 percent of the loss from a 10 percent tariff. Applying this adjustment to the figures in Table 8.3, we find that the annual net product market loss from the current tariff ranges from $4,074,933 for a substitution elasticity of −2 to $22,067,967 for a substitution elasticity of −11.5. The loss is slightly higher for a substitution elasticity of −18. (For substitution elasticities of over −11, the 3 percent tariff does not reduce sales to zero; thus, the implied loss continues to increase for higher elasticity estimates.)

The computations presented here suggest that the product market welfare loss from a moderate increase in the tariff on foreign cars would not be large; the product market welfare loss from the current tariff is very small relative to total spending on new car purchases. However, as we show below, the present discounted value of the annual stream of product market welfare losses from a tariff still exceeds the value of output gain from reduced unemployment that

would accompany tariff increases for a wide range of demand parameter estimates, using high estimates of social costs of unemployment in the automobile industry.

EFFECTS OF A TARIFF IN AN IMPERFECTLY COMPETITIVE DOMESTIC INDUSTRY

Import competition is an important potential check on domestic prices. If the domestic market structure of an industry is not perfectly competitive, then an increase in a tariff on closely competing foreign substitutes will enable domestic firms to raise prices.

In this section, we discuss briefly how our product market welfare loss estimates would need to be modified if we drop the assumption that the domestic automobile industry is perfectly competitive. While we believe that the assumption of perfect competition is a reasonable working hypothesis for the purposes of this study, it is of some interest to know how our conclusions might be different if this assumption were to be dropped. The most extreme alternative assumption we can make is that prices and output are set to maximize profits for the entire domestic industry. We present estimates in this section of the price change of domestic cars in response to a 10 percent increase in imported auto prices, assuming that domestic automobile demand curves are linear, that increases in the foreign-car price lead to a parallel shift in the demand curve for domestic cars, and that domestic companies act as if they were one profit-maximizing firm. In the absence of more detailed data on the level of cost in relation to price, we cannot compute the exact effect on the net product market welfare loss computation.

Imposition of a tariff on imported cars may not reduce product market welfare as much under imperfect competition as it does in the competitive case; the reason is that in the absence of perfect competition in the domestic industry, the price of domestic automobiles is initially too high, and too few domestic new cars are being purchased. Imposition of a tariff on foreign cars shifts the domestic-car demand curve to the right and leads to increased domestic sales; the marginal value of the increased domestic output exceeds the marginal cost. This gain is somewhat moderated by the probable increase in the price of domestic cars accompanying the demand shift. The product market welfare loss from the tariff is then equal to the difference between the loss from import price changes and the net gain from domestic price changes.

While imposition of a tariff on imported cars does not lead to as large a product market welfare loss under imperfect competition as in the competitive case, it does lead to an income redistribution effect from consumers of new automobiles to factors of production in the domestic automobile industry. The redistribution effect is much greater in magnitude than the net product

WELFARE EFFECTS OF TRADE POLICY CHANGE

market welfare change; thus the cost to citizens other than automobile company stockholders, and possibly employees, of an increase in the import tariff is much larger the further the industry structure is from pure competition.

Figure 8.2 illustrates the effect on domestic output and prices of a change in the import tariff. In Figure 8.2, we assume that the marginal cost of production of domestic automobiles is constant within the relevant range. *ST* is the marginal cost curve. *HRK* is the demand curve for domestic automobiles as a function of domestic car price before the tariff; the tariff, by raising the price of a substitute good (imports) shifts the domestic demand curve to the right to *EABG*. *HM* is the marginal revenue curve before the tariff; *EN* is the marginal revenue curve after the tariff.

Before the tariff, the profit-maximizing output is at the intersection of the marginal cost curve *ST* and the marginal revenue curve *HM* at the point *P*. Domestic production and sales is OD_0; the domestic price is OP_0. The shift in the demand curve from the imposition of the tariff moves the profit maximizing output to point *Q*, raising output and sales to OD_1, and raising price to OP_1. In the absence of the domestic price increase, domestic sales would have increased to OD_1'.

The price of domestic automobiles will rise in response to an increase in demand, if the demand curves are linear and the shift in demand is parallel. More generally, the import tariff will raise the domestic price if the tariff's effect is to reduce the absolute value of the elasticity of domestic demand at the initial domestic price. We would in general except this to occur; a rise in the price of foreign cars makes them less substitutable for domestic cars at any given domestic price and would thus make the domestic demand curve more inelastic.

Figure 8.3 illustrates the welfare effect of the change in domestic auto demand caused by a tariff change. In Figure 8.3 we trace out the price output locus shown in Figure 8.2, eliminating the graphical illustration of the maximizing aspect of price determination. Q_0 and P_0 are the initial output and price of domestic automobiles, respectively; the imposition of a tariff on foreign cars shifts the domestic demand curve from D_0 to D_1, leading to a new equilibrium output and price, Q_1 and P_1. The welfare gain is equal to the area between the demand curve for automobiles and the marginal cost, *C*, of producing the extra units. There is some ambiguity over which demand curve to use; obviously the welfare gain is greater if evaluated at the higher demand schedule. A reasonable approach is to evaluate the demand price at each output as the tariff increases. The curve *EF* traces out the equilibrium locus of price-quantity combinations as the tariff moves from zero to the final level. As the tariff increases, consumers' marginal evaluations of domestic cars increase, because of the increase in the import price. Thus, we can view the area *FEBA* as a measure of the welfare gain—the sum of the differences between consumer's marginal evaluation of one more domestic automobile and the social cost of additional

FIGURE 8.2

Effects on Domestic Industry of Change in Import Tariff Assuming Domestic Industry Profit Maximization

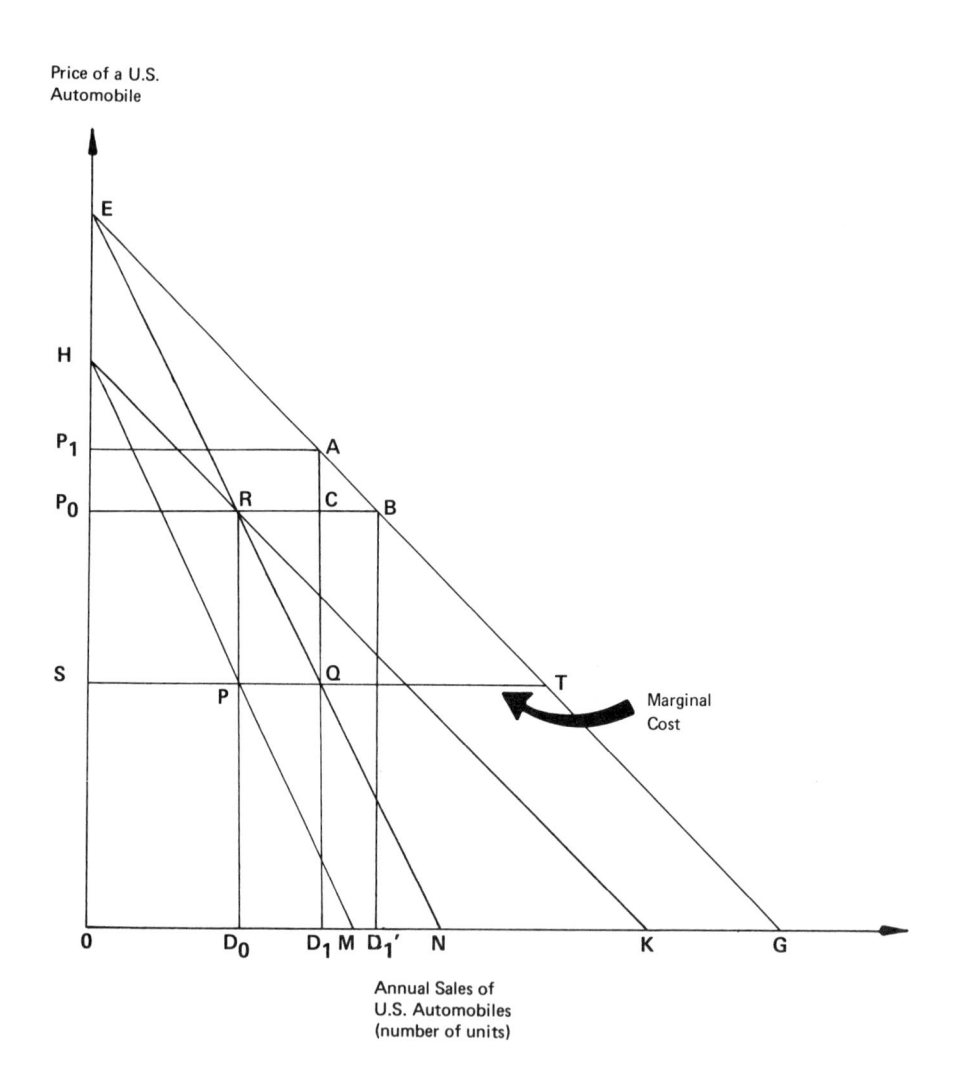

Source: Charles River Associates.

FIGURE 8.3

Partial Welfare Effects of Import Price Change with Industry Profit Maximization in Domestic Market

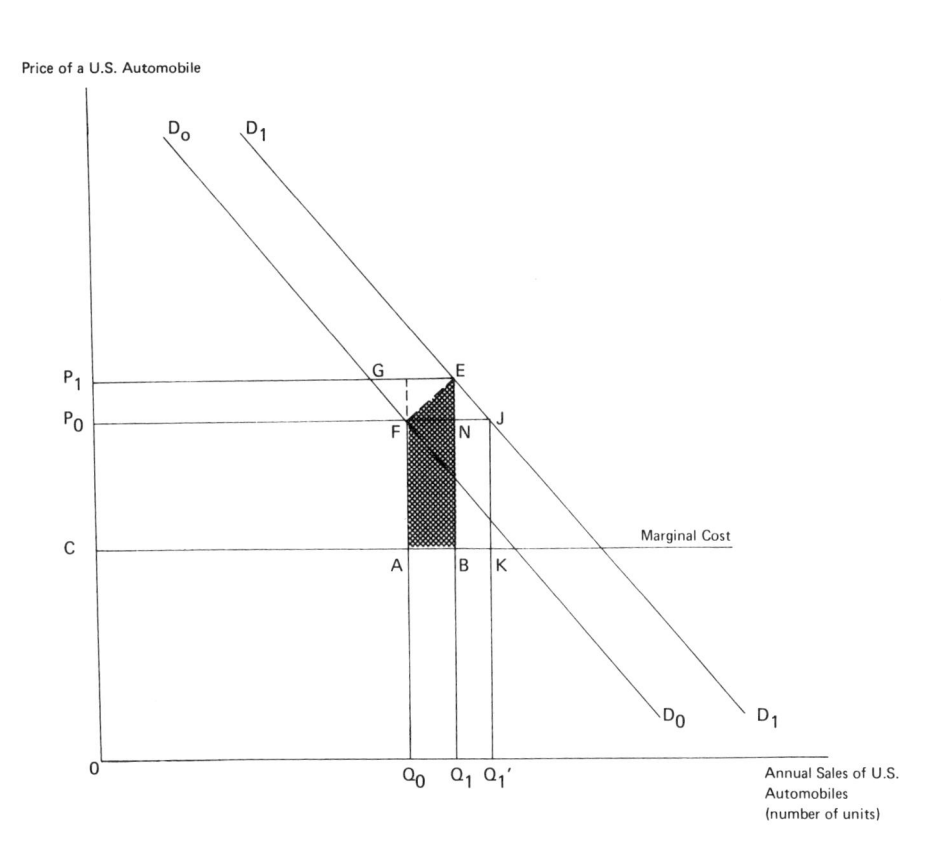

Note: Shaded area is net welfare gain.
Source: Charles River Associates.

production. If the domestic price does not rise in response to the import price change, domestic sales would rise to Q_0Q_1', and the welfare gain would equal the area *AKJF*.

The positive product market welfare gain from increased domestic sales reduces the net product market welfare loss from what it would have been, when we view imports alone. If the distortion in the domestic price is initially great, it is possible that a small import tariff would increase total product market welfare value; however, as tariffs are raised further, the loss in welfare from distortion of the import price will become greater relative to the gain from increased sales of domestic autos.

The gain from increased domestic sales will accrue entirely to factors of production able to share in automobile industry profits. The gain in the industry will equal the sum of the areas P_1P_0GF, the additional revenue received from the price increase on the original Q_0 units sold, and *ABEG*, the excess of revenue received over the additional cost of production for the incremental output Q_0Q_1. Of this gain to producers, *ABEF* represents an efficiency gain; the remainder, P_1P_0GEF, represents a transfer of income from consumers to producers in excess of the additional value of output received by consumers. Thus, the loss to consumers from the domestic-automobile price rise can be approximated by the formula

$$\Delta W_c = (P_D^1 - P_D^0)D^0 + \tfrac{1}{2}(D^1 - D^0)(P_D^1 - P_D^0) \tag{8.15}$$

where ΔW_c equals the change in consumer welfare of U.S. car buyers from an increase in the tariff on imported automobiles, P_D^0 equals the price of a U.S. car before the tariff increase, P_D^1 equals the price of a U.S. car after the tariff increase, D^0 is annual sales of U.S. cars before the tariff increase, and D^1 equals annual sales of U.S. cars after the tariff increase.

To compute the consumer welfare loss from an increased import tariff, recall our system of demand equations for foreign and domestic cars:

$$F = a_0 + a_1P_F + a_2P_D$$

$$D = b_0 + b_1P_F + b_2P_D$$

The domestic equation can be written

$$P_D = \frac{1}{b_2}[D - b_0 - b_1P_F]$$

Total revenue is

$$TR = P_DD = \frac{1}{b_2}[D^2 - b_0D - b_1P_FD]$$

Differentiating total revenue with respect to D, we can write marginal revenue as

$$\frac{d(TR)}{dD} = R = \frac{1}{b_2}[2D - b_0 - b_1 P_F]$$

where R equals marginal revenue.

Then,

$$D = \tfrac{1}{2}[b_0 + b_1 P_F + b_2 R]$$

Let superscripts "0" refer to before-tariff values and let superscripts "1" refer to after-tariff values. If marginal cost is constant, then marginal cost $= R_0 = R_1$, since marginal cost and marginal revenue are set equal for profit maximization. Then,

$$R^0 = \frac{1}{b_2}[2D^0 - b_0 - b_1 P_F^0]$$

and

$$D^1 = \tfrac{1}{2}[b_0 + b_1 P_F^1 + b_2 R^1]$$

Since $R^1 = R^0$,

$$D^1 = \tfrac{1}{2}[b_0 + b_1 P_F^1 + (2D^0 - b_0 - b_1 P_F^0)]$$

or

$$D^1 = D^0 + \tfrac{1}{2} b_1 (P_F^1 - P_F^0) \tag{8.16}$$

From the demand curve equation, we then obtain

$$P_D^1 = \frac{1}{b_2}[D^1 - b_0 - b_1 P_F^1] \tag{8.17}$$

Equations (8.16) and (8.17) express final domestic sales and price as a function of the initial and final import price, and the parameters of the demand equations.

We can solve for the domestic automobile price change by substituting the domestic demand equation, a function of P_F^0 and P_D^0, for D^0 in Equation (8.16). Performing this substitution, and rearranging terms, we obtain

TABLE 8.4

Annual Losses at 1974 Average Prices to Consumers of U.S. Automobiles from Price Increase of 10 Percent ($287.40) of Imported Automobiles: Hypothetical Case of Domestic Industry Profit Maximization

Substitution Elasticity	Change in Domestic Price	Change in Welfare Domestic Auto Buyers
−2	$24.53	$180,400,000
−7	$115.53	$863,700,000
−11.5	$170.20	$1,291,000,000

Source: Computed from Equations (8.18) and (8.19) in text.

TABLE 8.5

Comparison of Annual Losses to Consumers of Domestic and Imported Automobiles from 10 Percent Import Price Increase: Hypothetical Case of Domestic Industry Profit Maximization

Substitution Elasticity	Total Consumer Loss from Domestic Price Change	Total Consumer Loss	Deadweight Loss	Transfer to Taxpayers
−2	$180,400,000	$356,770,000	$36,670,000	$320,100,000
−7	$863,700,000	$271,500,000	$121,900,000	$149,600,000
−11.5	$1,291,000,000	$198,600,000	$198,600,000	0

Source: Table 8.4 and computations from Equation (8.13) of text.

$$P_D^1 = P_D^0 + \tfrac{1}{2}\frac{b_1}{b_2}[P_F^0 - P_F^1] \qquad (8.18)$$

Since $b_1 > 0$ and $b_2 < 0$, $P_D^1 > P_D^0$ if $P_F^1 > P_F^0$—that is, an increase in the import price from a tariff leads to an increase in the domestic price.

Substituting (8.18) and (8.16) into (8.15), the consumer welfare loss can be written

$$\Delta W_c = \frac{1}{2}\frac{b_1}{b_2}[P_F^0 - P_F^1] \cdot D^0 + \frac{1}{8}\frac{b_1^2}{b_2}[P_F^1 - P_F^0][P_F^0 - P_F^1] \tag{8.19}$$

Table 8.4 presents estimates of the effects of a tariff increase on domestic prices and of the resultant annual welfare loss to buyers of domestic automobiles, for several alternative estimates of the elasticity of relative import demand with respect to relative import prices. For high substitution elasticities, imports are much more effective in constraining domestic prices. Thus, tariffs will hurt buyers of domestic automobiles much more when imported and domestic autos are good substitutes.

Table 8.5 compares the losses to consumers from higher domestic prices to the direct losses from higher import prices. The losses from higher import prices are divided into two components: the deadweight loss, which is equal to the total product market welfare loss; and the income transfer from buyers of foreign cars at the new, higher prices to taxpayers. The transfer is zero when the substitution elasticity is sufficiently high (-11.49) that the slope coefficient we use as an approximation implies that the 10 percent tariff would eliminate all import sales.

The distribution cost to domestic consumers exceeds the deadweight loss under pure competition for all values of the substitution elasticity. However, for low values of the substitution elasticity, the income transfer to taxpayers from foreign-car buyers is greater than the income transfer to the industry by domestic-car buyers. For lower substitution elasticities, more consumers buy imports at the higher price and pay the import tariff, and, since fewer shift to domestic purchases, domestic demand price does not rise greatly. As the substitution elasticity increases, the income transfer from domestic-car buyers to domestic companies becomes much greater than the income transfer from foreign-car buyers to taxpayers.

COMPARISON OF PRODUCT MARKET WELFARE COSTS TO LABOR ADJUSTMENT COSTS

In this section, we present estimates of the potential net increase in the value of output from reduction in automobile industry employment resulting from imposition of a higher import tariff. High estimates of the potential output gains from reduced unemployment are then compared to the product market welfare loss from higher tariffs for several estimated values of the demand substitution elasticity.

An increase in the import tariff will increase U.S. sales of domestically produced automobiles. If the automobile industry is initially at full employment, then there is no net social gain from increased automobile employment,

even in the short run. Additional automobile industry employees are acquired by bidding them away from productive jobs in other sectors of the economy. (It is also possible that increased automobile industry employment can come from the pool of unemployed workers previously employed in another industry. While there is undoubtedly a net social gain in providing automobile industry employment for any otherwise unemployed workers, there is no logical reason why it would be easier to employ non-auto-industry workers in the auto industry than anywhere else. Thus, there is no argument for an auto import tariff as a weapon against general unemployment.) Increased demand for automobiles brought about by a higher tariff on auto imports will reduce labor adjustment costs only if there are initially significant numbers of unemployed workers in the automobile industry, and if there are significant costs impeding the shift of these workers to other industries.

High unemployment in the U.S. automobile industry will result if there is a decline in the demand for domestic automobiles. A tariff can counteract the labor adjustment cost caused by employee displacement by preventing domestic demand from declining, or by rapidly reversing a recently past decline. If other economic forces were promoting recovery in the domestic industry, for example, recovery from a recession, or a shift by U.S. producers toward the type of automobiles consumers want, then imposition of a tariff may be unnecessary to increase employment and undesirable on other grounds.

The estimates of the reduction in labor adjustment cost from an import tariff presented below are all high estimates because we assume in the calculations that increases in auto industry employment caused by a tariff on imported cars will be from otherwise unemployed auto industry workers, rather than from workers employed in other industries. In other words, it is assumed that the opportunity cost of employing such workers in automobile production is zero. Using the alternative values of the import substitution elasticity that were used above to estimate the product market welfare loss from a linear demand model, we forecast the change in domestic automobile output that would accompany an increase in the price of imported automobiles. Then, we estimate the change in employment accompanying the output change in the first year from the lag structure implied by the factor demand equation shown in Table 7.5, Chapter 7.

The net increase in the value of output from employing one more worker in the domestic automobile industry is measured by using estimates of earnings losses per displaced automobile worker from a study by the Center for Naval Analysis (CNA). (The CNA study estimated earnings loss per displaced worker from the longitudinal Employee-Employer file of the Social Security Administration, which traces the earnings and industry employment history of individual employees from data on quarterly payments of social security taxes.)[4] The earnings loss per displaced worker is not an exact measure of either the social cost or private cost of unemployment, excluding both some parts of cost and some compensating monetary and nonmonetary benefits to unemployed

workers. The CNA earnings loss measure understates the social and private cost of layoffs because it does not include losses of employers' contributions to pension funds and does not account for the psychic costs, in increased personal insecurity, of unemployment. On the other hand, earnings loss overstates the net social cost of unemployment because it assumes the opportunity cost to employees of time spent at a job is zero* and further overstates the net private cost by excluding both the value of additional time and the unemployment compensation payments received by displaced workers, including payments from the state and supplemental unemployment benefits received from companies under union contracts. (In the automobile industry, supplemental unemployment benefits, when added to unemployment insurance, amount to up to 95 percent of previous take-home pay for an extended time period. While the private losses from unemployment are serious, they are certainly overstated if measured by the total loss in taxable earnings.) On balance, we believe that the earnings loss measure overstates the cost of unemployment, especially the private cost because of the large unemployment compensation payments received by displaced auto workers.

Earnings losses can result both from reduced unemployment and from reduced wages. As wages in the automobile industry are much higher than wages in most manufacturing industries, a permanent decline in automobile industry employment will reduce earnings of displaced workers, on the average, even if these workers find new employment instanteneously. The extent to which this wage loss represents a net social cost depends on the source of the wage differential between automobile workers and workers in other manufacturing industries:

1. The wage differential may result from the fact that work in the automobile industry is relatively more onerous or unpleasant. In that case, the wage differential can be viewed as a compensating differential required to induce workers voluntarily to accept employment in automobile plants. The loss in wages is then neither a private nor a social cost, as the lost income is compensated by a gain in utility from more pleasant working conditions.

2. The wage differential may result from better bargaining power by the automobile workers union. In that case, reduced wages do represent a private cost to displaced workers. They also represent a net social cost because the

---

*In other words, it is assumed that there is no value to increased leisure time or to productive activities for which the individual is not compensated with money wages, such as, for example, time spent fixing his house. In addition, any income a displaced worker might earn from any form of market activity not covered by social security is not captured by the CNA data.

relative social value, at the margin, of an additional unit of employment is greater in the automobile industry than in other industries. However, if union power is causing automobile industry wages, and the cost of producing an automobile, to be above the social opportunity cost, then the net gain to society from increased automobile output and employment is already accounted for in the measure of product market welfare change; including the wage rate change would be double-counting.

(The demand for auto workers is a derived demand resulting from the demand for U.S.-made automobiles. If auto wages, adjusting for disutility of labor and required skills, are set above wages in other industries, then both employment and output will be lower than if wages were competitively determined and the price of U.S. autos would be higher. As we showed in the preceding section, the net deadweight loss from a tariff if there are monopoly restrictions in the domestic industry is lower than in the competitive case because the marginal value of domestic autos exceeds the social opportunity cost of production, leading to a welfare gain from the expansion of domestic output. However, as noted above, the total loss to consumers is greater in the monopoly case; the gains from restriction accrue to factors of production in the monopolized industry.)

3. The wage differential may result from the fact that automobile workers are more skilled than workers in other manufacturing. The data in Chapter 7 on relative experience and education in the automobile industry provide no evidence to support that hypothesis. If falling wages result from the fact that specialized skills used in automobile production are not applicable in other industries, the wage decline may represent a net social (as well as a net private) cost from automobile worker displacement. Though we have seen no evidence that industry-specific skills are of major importance in the automobile industry, some human capital loss may result from a permanent displacement of automobile workers.

The data reported by CNA do not enable us to distinguish between earnings loss due to unemployment, and earnings loss due to a permanent shift of workers to lower wage industries.

Table 8.6 shows the estimates of the earnings loss per displaced worker provided by CNA. The CNA estimates have all been multiplied by 1.79, the growth in nominal motor vehicle industry wages between the sample period (1964) and 1974 to convert the results to 1974 magnitudes. The discounted sum of earnings losses estimated by CNA is $14,092 per displaced worker, if we use a 5 percent discount rate, and $12,451 per displaced worker, if we use a 10 percent discount rate.

Table 8.7 provides a rough estimate of the earnings loss per displaced worker due to unemployment alone, assuming that no workers return to the automobile industry. In 1972, the weekly earnings of automobile workers were

TABLE 8.6

Estimated Earnings Loss per Displaced Automobile Worker

Year	CNA Estimated Earnings Loss	Growth* Adjustment Factor	Adjusted Earnings Loss	Discounted Loss at 5 Percent	Discounted Loss at 10 Percent
0	$2,996	1.79	$5,363	$5,363	$5,363
1	1,944	1.79	3,480	3,314	3,012
2	1,356	1.79	2,427	2,201	1,819
3	1,016	1.79	1,819	1,571	1,180
4	664	1.79	1,119	921	629
5	556	1.79	995	722	448
Sum of losses				14,092	12,451

*Reflects percentage growth in wages between 1964 and 1974. See Table 7.2, Chapter 7.
Source: Louis S. Jacobson, *Earnings Losses of Workers Displaced from Manufacturing Industries*, Public Research Institute, Center for Naval Analyses, Professional Paper 169, Arlington, Va., November 1976.

TABLE 8.7

Estimated Earnings Loss per Displaced Worker Due to Unemployment: Assuming No Displaced Workers Return to Auto Industry

Year	Adjusted Earnings Loss	Earnings Loss Discounted at 5 Percent	Earnings Loss Discounted at 10 Percent
0	$2,365	$2,365	$2,365
1	482	459	438
Sum of losses		2,824	2,803

Source: Computed from data in Tables 8.6 and 7.2.

$164.70, while the weekly earnings in all manufacturing was $116.22, or 29.44 percent below weekly earnings in automobile manufacturing. Thus, if all workers were to be reemployed instantaneously in other industries, we would expect a decline in earnings of 29.44 percent. The remainder of the earnings decline can be attributed to reduced employment; the results of this computation are shown in Table 8.7.

TABLE 8.8

Estimated Earnings Loss per Displaced Worker Due to Unemployment: Assuming 50 Percent of Reemployed Workers Return to Automobile Industry

Year	Adjusted Earnings Loss	Earnings Loss Discounted at 5 Percent	Earnings Loss Discounted at 10 Percent
0	$3,864	$3,680	$3,513
1	1,981	1,797	1,637
2	928	802	697
3	320	263	219
Sum of losses		6,542	6,066

Source: Computed from data in Tables 7.2 and 8.6.

Table 8.7 shows a sum of earnings losses due to unemployment considerably below the total earnings losses shown in Table 8.6. The present discounted value of the sum of losses is $2,824 using a 5 percent discount rate, and $2,803 using a 10 percent discount rate.

Table 8.8 estimates the earnings loss from unemployment if half the reemployed workers return to the automobile industry. In that case, the average decline in annual earnings of fully employed workers is only 14.72 percent, and a much bigger fraction of the total decline in earnings per worker can be attributed to unemployment. In Table 8.8, we estimate the present discounted sum of earnings losses due to unemployment to be $6,542 for a discount rate of 5 percent, and $6,066 for a discount rate of 10 percent.

The duration of unemployment for a displaced worker depends in part on the characteristics of the worker and in part on the labor market conditions in the local economy where the employment decline occurs. We would expect that the duration of unemployment for laid-off automobile workers would be greater, the greater the general unemployment in the nation (or in the region where the industry decline occurs) and the smaller the total labor market in which the plant experiencing an employment decline is located.

CNA has not examined the effect of differential labor market conditions on earnings losses of displaced automobile workers. However, some rough estimates of the effect of local unemployment and labor market size on average earnings losses of employees leaving the steel industry are avaliable in another CNA report.[5]

Table 8.9 shows CNA's estimates of the losses due to high local labor market unemployment and small local labor market size in the steel industry.

TABLE 8.9

Losses Due to High Unemployment and Small Labor Market Size: Steel Industry

(Col. 1) Year	(Col. 2) Average Loss of Leavers	(Col. 3) Loss Due to High Unemployment* (Percent)	(Col. 4) Loss Due to Small Labor Market Size (Percent)
0	$113	$61 (54.0)	$18 (29.5)
1	176	78 (42.7)	32 (41.0)
2	132	120 (90.9)	81 (67.5)
3	89	164 (184.3)	78 (47.6)
Discounted Sum, 5%	477	386 (80.9)	189 (39.6)
Discounted Sum, 10%	449	354 (78.8)	173 (38.5)

*High unemployment is measured by the ratio of a region's current unemployment to its "normal," long-term unemployment level.

Source: Louis Jacobson, "Estimating the Loss in Earnings for Displaced Workers in the Steel Industry," in James Jondrow, et al., *Removing Restrictions on Imports of Steel*, PRI 75-2, Public Research Institute, Center for Naval Analyses, Arlington, Va., chap. 5.

TABLE 8.10

Estimated Losses per Displaced Worker Due to Unemployment: Alternate Scenarios Assuming 50 Percent of Reemployed Workers Return to Automobile Industry

	Present Value of Loss per Worker	
	5 Percent Discount Rate	10 Percent Discount Rate
"Normal" conditions	$6,542	$6,066
High unemployment	11,834	10,846
Small labor market area	9,133	8,401
High unemployment and small labor market area	14,425	13,181

Source: Computed from data in Tables 8.8 and 8.9.

Column (2) of Table 8.9 shows the average losses of employees leaving the industry, while Column (3) and Column (4) show the additional losses in areas with high unemployment, and small labor market size, respectively. (These areas are defined to be areas one standard deviation above the mean, for unemployment, and one standard deviation below the mean, for labor market size.) From Table 8.9, we can see that earnings losses in the steel industry from separations of the work force are considerably higher in labor markets characterized by high unemployment and small labor market size than in "normal" markets.

In Table 8.10, we apply the percentage increase in earnings loss for high unemployment areas and small labor markets in steel shown in Table 8.9 to the estimates of earnings losses from unemployment in the auto industry reported in Table 8.8. These estimates may be regarded as upper-bound estimates of the earnings losses from auto industry unemployment. We estimate the present discount value of the earnings loss from unemployment for displaced workers in areas characterized both by high unemployment and a small labor market area to be $14,425, using a 5 percent discount rate, and $13,181, using a 10 percent discount rate.

TABLE 8.11

Increased Output from Increased Employment Caused by 10 Percent Import Price Increase: Estimated Value for Earnings Loss per Worker of $15,000

(Col. 1) Values of Substitution Elasticity (A_1) and Coefficient of Lagged Share (m)	(Col. 2) Change in Domestic Output (Number of Automobiles)	(Col. 3) One-Year Change in Auto Industry Employment (Number of Employees)	(Col. 4) Dollar Value of Employment Benefit
1) $A_1 = -2$ m = .250	49,780	11,350	170,250,000
2) $A_1 = -7.06$ m = .7239	93,550	21,329	319,935,000
3) $A_1 = -18.76$ m = .924	42,560	9,704	145,560,000

Notes: Change in domestic output computed using implied one-year substitution elasticity, $(1 - m)A_1$, and Equation (8.13c). Change in Employment = .2280 × (Change in Output). (See Chapter 7.) (The change in employment per-unit change in output is the first-year change. It is computed by summing the lag weights for quarters 0 through 4 reported in Table 7.7.) Dollar value of employment benefit = $15,000 × Change in Employment.

Source: Charles River Associates.

TABLE 8.12

Comparison of Upper Limit Employment Benefit and Product Market Welfare Costs from 10 Percent Increase in Price of Automobile Imports

(Col. 1) Values of Substitution Elasticity (A_1) and Coefficient of Lagged Share (m)	(Col. 2) Upper-Bound Estimated Dollar Value of Employment Benefit	(Col. 3) Dollar Value of Product Market Welfare Cost — 5 Percent Discount Rate	(Col. 4) Dollar Value of Product Market Welfare Cost — 10 Percent Discount Rate
1) $A_1 = -2$ m = .250	170,250,000	468,700,000	332,400,000
2) $A_1 = -7.06$ m = .7239	319,935,000	1,328,000,000	896,400,000
3) $A_1 = -18.76$ m = .924	145,560,000	1,699,000,000	1,111,000,000

Note: Employment benefit is measured here as the increased value of output from lower unemployment.
Source: Tables 8.11 and 8.2.

The upper-bound estimate of the increase in the net value of output from increased automobile industry employment resulting from a tariff on imported automobiles is computed by multiplying the estimated earnings loss per displaced worker by the estimated change in employment in the first year after the tariff change.

Table 8.11 presents estimates of the social benefit from increased employment caused by a 10 percent increase in automobile import prices for different values of the demand substitution elasticity; Table 8.12 compares these results with our estimates of the present discounted value of the predicted stream of product market welfare losses.

Column (1) of Table 8.11 gives the range of substitution elasticities and lagged share coefficients for which the employment change was computed. From these coefficients, we compute the implied rate of change of domestic demand with respect to a change in the import price; the total resulting change in domestic output corresponding to a 10 percent import price increase is shown in Column (2). Column (3) gives the implied annual employment change corresponding to the change in domestic automobile output; to compute this, we used the factor demand equation estimated in Chapter 7. The computation of the employment increase assumes that all increased employment in the auto-

mobile industry in the first year after the import price change consists of rehiring of unemployed automobile industry workers, while employment changes in subsequent years are shifts from other industries to automobiles. Finally, Column (4) gives the dollar value of the employment benefit, computed by multiplying the employment change by an assumed value of loss per worker of $15,000, a value slightly higher than the upper range of our estimates.

Column (2) of Table 8.12 lists the employment benefit computation from Table 8.11. The computations are compared to the present discounted value of the future stream of product market welfare losses from the tariff in Column (3) and Column (4) where future costs are discounted at rates of 5 percent and 10 percent, respectively. It can be seen that in all cases the increased value of output from higher employment is less than the product market welfare loss for both the high and low discount rate assumptions.

The total short-run employment loss from a shift in demand away from the automobile industry will be greater than the reduction in auto industry employment in areas where the auto industry is prominent because of a decline in employment in supporting service industries brought about by the decline in income and consumption of automobile workers. On the other hand, the shift in demand to other sectors will tend to increase employment in other industries, some of them in the same regions where the auto industry is located.

The regional multiplier from a decline in employment in any "export-based" industry depends on the ratio between local service activity and export activity; for relatively high values of local service activity the multiplier will be relatively large because changes in income will tend to lead to relatively large changes in demand affecting local firms and employees.[6]

The regional multiplier is likely to be smaller for temporary declines in auto industry employment than for declines in other industries because of the very high supplemental unemployment benefit packages available to laid-off auto workers. SUB enables unemployed auto workers to maintain previous levels of consumption for some time, thereby slowing the decline in demand for supporting local service industries. While SUB may increase the duration of auto industry employment by reducing the incentive of laid-off workers to leave the industry rapidly, it helps to cushion the decline in regional employment by maintaining local levels of consumption.

Inclusion of the multiplier effect on regional employment would raise the estimated gain in output from raising the import tariff. The multiplier would have to be at least 2 in order for the estimated gain in the value of output from increased auto industry employment to exceed the product market welfare loss from the tariff in any of the examples shown in Table 8.12. While some export-base multipliers have been estimated to be on the order of magnitude of 3 or 4, it is unlikely, for the reasons discussed above, that the employment multiplier, in the short run, from a change in auto industry employment would be that high.

In conclusion, the data examined in this chapter indicate that it is likely that the product market welfare loss from a higher tariff on automobiles exceeds the net increased value of output from reduced auto industry unemployment. The conditions under which the social benefit associated with the short-run output gain would exceed the product market welfare loss from a tariff are (1) local areas in which the auto industry is located are experiencing very high unemployment; (2) auto industry layoffs are concentrated in small local labor markets; (3) the earnings losses of displaced auto workers are less than the social cost of unemployment (that is, the value of nonwork time is small, and earnings changes reflect either unemployment or employment changes requiring a diminished use of acquired skills); (4) the induced total employment reduction in affected localities is at least two to three times the decline in auto industry employment; and (5) domestic automobile production and employment is not likely to increase in the absence of imposition of import restrictions. It is unlikely that all of these five conditions would hold simultaneously; if they did however, a case could possibly be made on economic grounds for temporary trade restrictions to increase employment in the domestic automobile industry.

NOTES

1. For a justification of the simple consumer surplus method of evaluation of changes in tax and expenditure policies, see Arnold Harberger, "Three Basic Postulates for Applied Welfare Economics: An Interpretive Essay," *Journal of Economic Literature* 9, 3 (September 1971): 785-97. The method is not strictly accurate in a general equilibrium context if the tariff change causes shifts in supply and demand in other markets where distortions such as monopoly and taxes exist. We take account of one important potential distortion in our discussion below of the additional welfare loss from the tariff if the domestic market is not purely competitive. Also, the demand curve shifts slightly because of real income changes brought about by the tariff change; we ignore these effects, assuming their magnitude is relatively trivial, although they do alter consumers' marginal evaluation of foreign-car purchases foregone.

2. See Chapter 3 for a brief review of econometric studies of demand for automobiles in the United States.

3. See Keith Cowling and J. Cubbin, "Price, Quality and Advertising Competition: An Econometric Investigation of the United Kingdom Car Market," *Econometrica* (November 1971).

4. Louis S. Jacobson, *Earnings Losses of Workers Displaced from Manufacturing Industries*, Public Research Institute, Center for Naval Analysis, Professional Paper 169, Arlington, Va., (November 1976).

5. See Louis Jacobson, "Estimating the Loss in Earnings for Displaced Workers in the Steel Industry," in James Jondrow et al., *Removing Restrictions on Imports of Steel*, PRI 75-21, Public Research Institute, Center for Naval Analysis, Arlington, Va., May, 1975, Chap. 5.

6. For a discussion of the theory of "export-base" analysis, see Charles M. Tiebout, *The Community Economic Base Study*, Supplementary Paper no. 16 (New York: Committee for Economic Development, 1962).

CHAPTER 9
CONCLUSIONS

This book has examined the impact of potential trade policy changes affecting the U.S. automobile industry on domestic economic welfare, focusing especially on the quantitative magnitude of economic benefits and costs from changes in the tariff rate on imported automobiles. The preceding chapters have included separate studies on the demand for domestic and imported automobiles, price formation in the U.S. automobile industry, the shape of automobile industry cost curves, the comparative cost of producing automobiles for sale in the United States in different major producing nations, and the demand for labor in the U.S. automobile industry. We used the parameters estimated in these quantitative analyses of the economics of the automobile industry as input data in evaluating the welfare effects of potential trade policy changes.

The calculations reported in Chapter 8 show that the costs of higher tariffs and/or quotas, measured by the present value of the expected future losses in the efficiency of product market resource allocation, exceed the dollar value of the gain in output that would result from increased domestic auto industry employment under all probable scenarios. The loss from trade barriers in resource allocation in product markets is caused by the artificial diversion of consumer purchases away from imported automobiles; we estimate the quantitative magnitude of this loss using standard methods of consumer surplus analysis applied to a range of estimates from our, and previous, research on the demand for automobiles. Additional losses to consumers may result if higher prices of imported automobiles facilitate price increases by domestic automobile producers. We compare this product market loss with an upper-bound measure of the decline in the value of output associated with adjustment costs caused by a decline in the demand fur U.S.-manufactured automobiles.

(In our analysis, we assume the level of aggregate demand in the economy is determined by macroeconomic policies and is not altered by changes in trade

CONCLUSIONS

barriers affecting automobiles. The social benefit from increased employment caused by policies that shift U.S. demand to domestic automobiles is solely a result of the immobility of unemployed auto workers faced with positive costs of accepting employment in other industries. Our formal analysis does not quantify other potential gains from tariffs, such as improvement in the terms of trade, national security gains, or gains from promoting an "infant industry." We do not believe that any of these potential benefits from tariffs apply to the U.S. automobile industry. On the other hand, the loss from higher auto industry tariffs that might result if our principal trading partners retaliate with higher tariffs on U.S. exports of other goods is also excluded from the calculation.

The annual welfare cost of the current U.S. tariff on imported automobiles is quite small. Our estimates of the annual product market welfare loss resulting from a 3 percent increase in the price of imported automobiles in 1974 range from $4 million per year to $22 million per year, depending on the price elasticity of demand for imported cars; the lower end of the range conforms to a more plausible estimate of the price elasticity. These aggregate figures are equivalent to a loss of between $.50 and $2.50 per car. Because the current tariff applies to a fraction of the retail selling price, the product market welfare loss is somewhat smaller than figures computed from a 3 percent price change indicate.

On more detailed aspects of the automobile industry, the principal findings are as follows:

1. Domestic and imported automobiles are good substitutes. Most of the econometric estimates of the long-run relative price elasticity of substitution are close to −2, suggesting that a 1 percent increase in the ratio of import-to-domestic new-car prices will lead to a 2 percent reduction in the ratio of import-to-domestic new-car sales. However, some evidence points to a considerably higher relative price elasticity in the long run. Consumers' habit formation and the persistence of various automobiles' reputations may be causing a substantial lag in shifts in new-car purchases when relative prices change, and this lag effect proved to be difficult to measure precisely.

2. Domestic automobile prices decline in response to increases in the competitiveness of automobile imports. The effect of import prices on domestic prices lessens to some extent the total shift to domestic car purchases when external events or trade policy changes cause auto import prices to rise.

3. Economies of scale are very important in the production of automobiles. Production below optimal scale leads to substantial per-unit cost penalties, especially for smaller cars. The data show that foreign manufacturers are now approaching a level of U.S. sales at which it may become economical for them to establish production facilities in the United States. VW's decision in early 1976 to establish an assembly plant in the United States and reports that Toyota and Nissan have considered a similar move are consistent with the findings of this analysis.

4. International cost comparisons, derived as the best estimates we could obtain from admittedly incomplete data, indicate that production of automotive industry products was about 17 percent less expensive in Japan, and about 9 percent more expensive in West Germany, than in the United States in 1974. When transport costs are added to production costs, Japan's estimated advantage over domestic producers in supplying autos to the United States is eliminated. The international cost comparisons suggest that, if fuel-price increases or policy changes cause the types of cars purchased in the United States, Japan, and Europe to become increasingly similar, or if either domestic or foreign manufacturers begin producing small cars in the United States in a major way, then international trade in finished automobiles (or major components) between the leading producing nations may decline significantly. Alternatively, competition may become very intense between small cars manufactured in the United States and small cars made in Japan.

5. The employment elasticity with respect to output in the U.S. automobile industry is approximately 1 in the long run. We estimate that about one-third of the adjustment to final equilibrium occurs in the first quarter after the output change, about 80 percent in the first year, and about 99 percent in three years.

6. The average cost of displacement resulting from a decline in auto industry employment depends on the size of the change, the average duration of unemployment, and the opportunity cost of displaced auto workers (that is, their marginal productivity in alternative employment). The monetary cost to the worker depends on the length of unemployment, the amount of unemployment compensation (public and SUB), the cost of mobility, and the difference between wages in the auto industry and the wage at his next best job. Results from research performed by the Center for Naval Anslysis (CNA) under contract to the U.S. Department of Labor, inflated to 1974 magnitudes, suggest an upper-bound estimate of $15,000 for the value of output loss from unemployment per displaced automobile worker.

The effects of proposed trade policy changes can be usefully analyzed within two separate contexts. In the first context, the question posed is: What would the welfare effects have been if the tariff rate (or quota, or other policy) had been changed in a recent year? In the second context, we seek to assess the welfare effects of trade policy changes applied to the world automobile market of the late 1970s and early 1980s. Analysis of the welfare impacts of tariffs within the second context requires a forecast of the changes in trade patterns that are likely to occur in the absence of trade policy changes.

The formal analysis of the quantitative welfare effects of trade policy changes presented in Chapter 8 is performed in the former context; we measure the net welfare gains to the United States from tariff changes applied to the 1974 world automobile industry. As the present value of welfare effects of a tariff change depends on current and future changes in sales of imported autos

caused by the tariff, the analysis required assumptions both about future domestic sales and imports in the absence of a tariff change, and about future demand elasticities. The implicit assumption we used—that conditions would not change from 1974—underestimates the present value of the future product market welfare loss from tariff increases, if the automobile industry is assumed to grow in the two decades following 1974. The social benefit from the employment increase that would have resulted from a 1974 tariff change is not greatly affected by our assumptions about future demand, because the effects on unemployment are largely felt within the first few years after the policy change.

It is reasonable and useful to simulate the welfare effects of policy changes within the first context because such an exercise yields insights into the likely welfare effects of similar trade policy changes in the future. Specifically, even though the level of forecasted sales, domestic output, and prices after the trade policy change is dependent on the base case assumption used, the magnitude of changes in imports, domestic output, prices, and net economic welfare may not be overly sensitive to the base from which the changes are computed. It is worthwhile to know from a formal analysis that tariff changes, if applied to today's world, probably would have caused a loss in the present value of current and future output.

The impact of policy changes within the second context is not as amenable to formal analysis as it is within the first context. The level and composition by size class of future automobile output in major consuming nations and the size and direction of trade flow is heavily dependent on future external political and economic developments outside the automobile industry. For example, the behavior of the Organization of Petroleum Exporting Countries (OPEC) and the response of the Western powers and Japan to it in future years will greatly affect the types of automobiles purchased in the United States. The composition of U.S. demand, in turn, will have a big effect on the magnitude and location of world production of different types of automobiles. U.S. government policy changes not specifically designed for foreign trade reasons, such as legislation affecting fuel economy or the speed and extent to which automobile pollution controls are imposed, may also affect trade patterns.

While we have not performed a long-run statistical forecast of the future of automobile output and sales in different parts of the world, our analysis of the automobile industry in the quantitative chapters of this book, taken as a group, provide some useful insights into the future direction of the world automobile industry and the likely future role of imports in the United States.

To reiterate, we have found the following:

1. Shares of currently produced domestic and imported automobiles sold in the United States are sensitive to relative price changes.

2. The share of imports in the United States is positively affected by increases in fuel prices.

3. Production of the small cars for which European and Japanese manufacturers have found a mass market in the United States is subject to important scale economies.

4. The sum of production costs at minimum efficient scale output in Europe and Japan and transport costs to the United States is not lower, and is possibly higher, than production costs at minimum efficient scale output in the U.S. automobile industry.

These findings suggest the possibility that, if economic growth and sales of passenger cars in Europe, Japan, and the United States continue to increase along the past trend, factors that previously determined the amount and direction of trade in finished automobiles may become less relevant in future years. Specifically, if higher fuel prices or government policy measures cause U.S. buyers to shift dramatically toward smaller cars, the type of automobiles consumed in different world regions will become more uniform. In that event, the reasons for European and Japanese specialization in small car production for the entire world, which have been applicable throughout the 1960s and early 1970s, may diminish, as it will be possible to achieve economies of small car production for several firms selling automobiles in the United States. The findings from Chapter 6, in particular, imply that among the three leading producing nations, the United States, Japan, and West Germany, it is not obvious whether it will be least expensive to source automobiles for the United States produced at minimum efficient scale output levels in Japan or in the United States. Conceivably, other production locations not studied in this book, such as Spain or Brazil, may also become more important in the future.

For that reason, the context in which the welfare effects of trade policy in future years would be analyzed might differ from the type of formal analysis used in Chapter 8 of this book. As will be recalled, imported and domestic automobiles were viewed in Chapter 8 as separate goods, though close substitutes, with a rise in the relative price of one good (the import) leading to a finite change in relative sales of the two goods. In the future, the major long-run impact of a higher import tariff may be to influence where one particular good (that is, a specific model by a given manufacturer) is produced. Similarly, policies designed to increase small car consumption may lead to a big shift to models currently imported, but a much lower import share in the long run as both foreign-owned and domestic companies increase production of small cars in the United States.

If, as our quantitative analysis suggests, the United States has a long-run comparative advantage in automobile production, the U.S. share of small car production for sale in the United States will tend to rise over time. In that event, the rationale for using higher trade barriers to promote short-term employment gains in the U.S. automobile industry would weaken. In an environment of rising domestic output brought about by recovery from the recession and a decline

CONCLUSIONS

in the import share, further increases in domestic output resulting from a tariff would require that extra labor be recruited in increasing proportion from workers outside the automobile industry.

On the other hand, if production in Japan or elsewhere is closely competitive with production in the United States, higher tariffs may lead to large increases in domestic output with a relatively small increase in price. Because the future magnitude of cost differences between production locations in different countries is impossible to forecast with precision, the magnitude of such a price effect, and the resulting product market welfare loss, cannot be assessed with any confidence. However, it should be noted that the employment gain from a tariff change that shifts production location will occur very slowly because of the long lead time in establishing new production facilities. Thus, the value of such a policy for alleviating short term unemployment problems in the automobile industry may be limited.

Even in the event that the domestic share of small car sales rises, automobile imports to the United States will not altogether disappear, and some imports will probably continue to grow in popularity. The demand results reported in Chapter 3 provide evidence that the long-run income elasticity of import demand is positive. While production of high-volume, small economy cars may increasingly shift to the United States, sales of more luxurious imports will probably continue to grow. In addition, new imported models will undoubtedly emerge in future years. The higher-class imports are not in general sold at sufficient volume to justify mass production for North America alone. Further, for more expensive automobiles within a size class, the barrier imposed by shipping costs is relatively less important than for less expensive models. Thus, we foresee that the proportion of imports accounted for by luxury cars is likely to rise in the future.

The findings reported in this book on the welfare impact of trade policies do not contradict a view that unemployment in the automobile industry is an important social problem. Both the design of better macroeconomic policies to lessen fluctuations in national output and employment and the continued, and possibly expanded, use of unemployment compensation and other direct assistance to unemployed workers to ease the private costs of short-term adjustment problems are policy responses consistent with the implications of this book.

The findings do imply that raising trade barriers would probably not have been an appropriate response to the unemployment problems faced by the automobile industry in 1975. In the context of conditions then existing, the gains from such policies did not appear to be worth the cost. Potential future changes in consumption patterns and production location of automobiles produced for sale in the United States suggested by our analysis indicate that the potential benefits from higher trade barriers may be lower than our formal estimates imply.

INDEX

acceleration: as variable in hedonic market share model, 112
adjustment costs, 4, 5, 37, 182 (*see also*, labor adjustment costs)
age: and import shares, 66
algorithm: in hedonic market share model, 109
Audi: sales growth of, 33
Austin, T.C., 96
automatic transmission: adjustments for, in price index, 88; preference for, 75, 77 (*see also*, transmission)
Automotive News Almanac: data from, 47, 49, 72, 77, 85, 86, 87, 88, 89, 112-13
Automotive Products Trade Act and Automotive Products Agreement: Canadian-U.S., 6, 21; presidential reports on, 27, 29 (*see also*, Canada)

Baranson, J., 149, 165
BMW: sales growth of, 33
body type: and construction of price index, 87-88 (*see also*, hardtops, sedans, station wagons)
brake area: and construction of price index, 92
brakes: adjustment for in hedonic price index, 88
Buick: sales in recession, 65
bumping, 180 (*see also*, seniority rules)
Bureau of Economic Analysis, of U.S. Dept. of Commerce, 148
Bureau of Labor Statistics: motor vehicle compensation data from, 148, 149, 150; new car price index, 45

Cadillac: sales in recession, 65
Canada: automobile exports and imports of, 12; automobile industry in, 6; automobile tariffs of, 15; export of new passenger cars by, 15; U.S. automobile trade with, 21-29; U.S. plants in, 192
Canadian-U.S. Automotive Products Trade Act, 6, 21, 26, 28

capacity utilization: and change in output, 188-89; and domestic auto price, 119-22; lag relationship for, 196; output elasticity of, 188
capacity utilization index: construction of, 119-22
capital: as percentage of manufacturing costs, 135
capital cost index: construction of, 125
capital costs: unit, 149
Capri: sales growth of, 33
captive imports, 33, 100
Center for Naval Analyses (CNA), 220, 222, 224, 232
chain indexes: estimation of, 83-85
characteristics, automobile: in hedonic market share model, 74-77; and import competition, 119
Charles River Associates (CRA) (*see*, hedonic market share model)
Chevette, 34
Chevrolet: price indexes for models of, 89
choice models, 109-10 (*see also*, consumers)
CNA (*see*, Center for Naval Analyses)
Cobb-Douglas production function, 146, 147, 162-64, 183
Committee on Motor Vehicle Emissions (CMVE) Report, 129, 131
companies: U.S. automobile foreign investment of, 14 (*see also*, manufacturers)
comparative advantage in auto production of U.S., 234 (*see also*, cost comparisons)
comparative costs (*see*, cost comparisons)
consumer choice theory, 172
Consumer Price Index (CPI): production cost of domestic automobiles deflated by, 119; for ratio of midyear to winter prices, 92
Consumer Reports, 77, 112
consumer surplus analysis, 203, 230 (*see also*, product market welfare loss)
consumers, age of, 66; and finite alternatives, 102-04; and gasoline prices, 76; and relative auto price changes, 36; effects of habit formation, 231; im-

236

plied evaluation of mileage, 75-77; loss from domestic auto price rise, 213-17; loss from import tariffs, 201; modeling of tastes of, 101; potential shift to smaller cars of, 233-34; taste for characteristics of, in hedonic market share model, 103-04; tastes of, 45, 102 (*see also*, welfare loss)

cost comparisons, 146-69; derivation of equations for, 159-64; at different output levels, 152, 154-58; from hedonic price regressions, 166-69; method of computation of, 146-48; of production labor, 165

cost elements, 131-35; cost functions for, 133; for minis, 135-39

cost functions, 129-42; derivation of, 131-40; implications of, 140-42; problems of estimates of, 139-42

cost indexes: capital, 125-27; gasoline, 93; labor, 125-27; materials, 125-27

costs: gasoline, 52, 96; labor, 125-27, 146, 148, 149; manufacturing, 129-42 (*see also*, production costs, transactions costs, transport costs)

Court, L.M., 101

Cowling, K., 44

cross section analysis: of price elasticity of demand, 45, 46, 82-83

cross section demand estimates: for imports, 46, 65-71; for production worker employment, 189-92

Cubbin, J., 44

cylinders, as model classifier in hedonic market share model, 111, 112

Datsun: freight charges within U.S. for, 66; potential U.S. manufacture of, 142, 158; sales growth of, 33; transport costs to U.S., 152-54

deadweight losses: from tariffs, 38-40 (*see also*, product market welfare loss)

dealer preparation charges: as adjustment in hedonic market share model, 113

demand: for auto workers, 169-70, 184-90, 222; for domestic and imported automobiles, 35-37, 43-83; hedonic market share model of, 70-83 (*see also*, time series demand estimates, cross section demand estimates)

devaluation of U.S. dollar: and cost comparisons, 168; and relative import prices, 30

developing countries: automobile sales in, 7; automobile tariffs in, 15; automobile taxes in, 21 (*see also*, nontariff barriers)

dies: durability of, 140, 142; high cost of, 140

disk brakes: adjustments for in hedonic price index, 88

displacement: engine tax based on, 20

distributed lag relationships: factor demand, 195-96

Dodge Colt: sales growth of, 33

domestic auto price formation equations, 118-25

Durbin-Watson statistic, 186

earnings: estimated losses from layoffs, 221, 222-24, 232; relative to U.S. labor force, 171-77 (*see also*, income, unemployment)

Ebner, M., 129

economic profit, 135, 139

economies of scale: in automobile production, 3, 231 (*see also*, scale economies)

economy, U.S.: and domestic car sales, 33 (*see also*, trade policies, United States)

EEC (*see*, European Economic Community)

elasticities: of auto employment, 169-70, 183, 184-86, 188, 191, 195; of auto import demand, 40, 41, 44; of domestic auto prices, 125; of import share demand, 42, 43, 45, 46, 47, 53-64, 66, 68, 80-81 (*see also*, relative price elasticity)

elasticities of substitution: of Cobb-Douglas production function, 146; between domestic and foreign cars, 4, 37-38, 43, 46, 65, 70, 231; in fixed proportions production function, 159; and product market welfare loss, 199

employees: in automobile industry, 170-71 (*see also*, workers)

employment adjustment, 182-86, 188-89

employment, in motor vehicle industry: and automobile output, 181, 184-92; determination of conditions of, 171;

and import price increases, 226-28; location of, 171, 177, 191-92; multiplier effect of, 228
energy conservation: and small car sales, 34
engines, motor vehicle: choice among in construction of price index, 88-89
equipment, standard and optional: and construction of price index, 86-87
estimation problem: in hedonic market share model, 106-10
European Economic Community (EEC): automobile tariffs of, 7, 15
exchange rates: and demand for labor, 199
excise taxes: weight and horsepower, 3 (*see also*, nontariff barriers)
exports, automobile: growth of, 12-15; trade barriers imposed against U.S., 3, 15-22

factor demand equations, 188-92, 193-94; cross-section estimates, 189-92; derivation of, 193-219; time series equations, 183-89
Fiat: foreign automobile production of, 7
fixed proportions function, 145-46, 159-62
foreign cars (*see*, imports)
France: as a leading exporter of automobiles, 12; automobile exports of, 14, 15; nontariff barriers of, 19
freight charges: determination of, 66 (*see also*, transport costs)
fringe benefits: in motor vehicle industry, 171 (*see also*, unemployment)

gasoline cost indexes: computation of, 93-96; and relative total cost indexes, 50-53, 93, 96
gasoline prices: and import shares, 30-33, 65, 66; and total auto ownership costs, 76; trends in, 49-53
gas tank capacity: as variable in hedonic market share model, 113
Germany (*see*, West Germany)
Greece: nontariff barriers of, 20
Griliches, Zvi, 44, 101

hardtops: in hedonic price index, 87
headroom: and construction of price index, 92
hedonic market share model: assumptions in, 101-03; consumer tastes in, 102-03; CRA, 46-47, 70-83, 100-15;

criteria met by, 110-12; data base for, 112-15; derivation of share of sales in, 104-06; discrete alternatives in, 102-04; estimation problem in, 106-10
hedonic regression analysis: for domestic and imported price changes over time, 47-53; for international cost comparisons, 166-68
height, automobile: as variable in hedonic market share model, 112
Hellman, K.H., 96
horsepower: annual road tax based on, 20; and construction of price indexes, 85, 86, 92; as variable in hedonic market share model, 112
hours per worker: lag relationship for, 196-98

import bias: in hedonic market share model, 77
imports, automobile: cross-section demand estimates of, 46, 65-71; demand for, 35-37, 43-83; effect of growth in availability of, 96, 98; effect of price on share of, 4, 35, 36, 44, 46, 53-65, 66, 68, 71, 74, 77-83, 231, 233; freight charges on, 152-54 (*see also*, transport costs); fuel economy of, 53; and gasoline prices, 30, 31, 50-52, 65, 66; history of, in U.S., 29-34; mileage estimates for, in construction of gas cost index, 96; predicted shares for, in hedonic market share model, 77; price index for, 49, 50; prices relative to domestic auto prices, 53; product market loss from tariffs on, 199, 200, 207-11 (*see also*, welfare loss); sales data on, 86; share in new car sales, 29-34; shares of new car sales by states, 66-68; standard and optional equipment, in construction of price index, 87; welfare loss from tariffs on (*see*, product market welfare loss, welfare loss)
income: in motor vehicle industry, 171; and U.S. import share, 30, 31, 64, 68, 83, 98
industry-specific skills, 222
intermediates: prediction of shift to, from

INDEX

hedonic market share model, 82
international comparative advantage: estimates of, 146, 232
International Monetary Fund (IMF): international financial statistics of, 165
International Trade Commission: data of, 27, 28
Italy: automobile exports of, 12-15; automobile imports of, 12; nontariff barriers of, 20

Jaguar, 210
Japan: automobile exports of, 12-15; automobile imports of, 12; automobile production in, 6, 10; automobile tariffs of, 7, 15; factor prices relative to market prices in, 165; growth of automobile industry of, 12, 34; history of U.S. imports from, 30, 33; as a leading exporter of automobiles, 12; nontariff barriers of, 20-21; relative auto supply costs to U.S. from, 145, 154-58; relative labor costs in, 150-52, 165, 166; relative unit production costs in, 145; share of world motor vehicle production, 8 (*see also*, imports)

Kennedy round of tariff negotiations, 15-19
Koyck distributed lag, 188-89
Kravis, I., 166, 168

labor: definition of price of, in cost functions, 155; elasticity of demand for, 169-70, 183, 184-86, 188, 191, 195; international cost comparisons of, 145; productivity data on, 150, 165-66; unit cost indices for, 148-49
labor adjustment costs, 4, 5, 199-200; and demand elasticities, 37-38, 40, 82-83; and product market welfare costs, 219-29
labor cost indexes: for U.S. automobile industry, 125; relative labor cost index, 96, 97
labor force: motor vehicle industry, 170-71 (*see also*, workers)
labor market: in automobile industry, 169-81
labor productivity index: sources for, 165-66

lagged sales ratio: in import demand equations, 61-64
layoffs: duration of unemployment from, 222-26; local concentrations of, 192, 228-29 (*see also*, unemployment)
legroom: as variable in hedonic market share model, 112
length, automobile: as variable in hedonic market share model, 113
linear demand curve parameters: estimation of, 203-07
list prices: compared to transactions prices of imports, 49-50; as poor measure of changes in transactions prices, 47-48; as variable in hedonic market share model, 113
living standards: effects of trade barriers on, 2
location, of automobile plants: among countries, 7-10, 21-22, 29, 34, 129, 130, 131, 132, 142-45, 146, 154, 157, 158, 198-99, 200, 233, 234; within U.S., 171, 177, 180-81, 191-92
luxury cars: imports as, 35-36, 64-65; as rising proportion of imports, 235

McFadden, D., 107, 110, 111
McGee, J., 140
McMenamin, J.S., 44
macroeconomic policies, 2, 231
make, automobile: code for in hedonic market share model, 115
manhours: data on, 166
manufacturers, foreign automobile: establishment of production facilities in U.S. by, 158, 198-99, 232
manufacturing costs (*see*, costs, manufacturing)
marginal costs: in illustrating effect of tariff on domestic price, 213, 217
Market Facts Inc., 46, 74, 82
markup: elasticity of, 125; estimated domestic automobile, 122
Mercedes-Benz, 25, 210
mileage index: estimated, 93-96
miles per gallon: and consumer preference, 74-76; as variable in hedonic market share model, 74-77, 112-13
minis: cost curve for, 135-39; U.S. manufacture of, 131 (*see also*, small cars)
model selection: for construction of price

index, 88-92
models, automobile: codes for in hedonic market share model, 113-15; selection of, in hedonic market share model, 112
monopolies and trade barriers, 2
Monte Carlo technique, 107
Motor Vehicle Emissions, Committee on (CMVE), 129, 131
Motor Vehicle Manufactuers' Association (MVMA): position on trade barriers, 2
multinational corporations: and automobile trade, 15
multiplant economies, 140

Nadiri, M.I., 181, 183
nameplates: choice of for hedonic market share model, 111
National Market Reports Inc.: data of, 45
Netherlands: nontariff barriers of, 20
New England: growth of imports in, 68
nontariff barriers (NTBs), 3, 19-21; of developing countries, 20 (see also, taxes on automobiles)
North America: location of automobile production among countries in, 21-22
NTBs (see, nontariff barriers)

Ohta, M., 101
oil embargo, 68
Opel: sales growth of, 33
output elasticity of employment, 184-86; estimates from cross-section equations, 191-92; estimates from time series equations, 184, 186, 188

Pacific Coast: growth of imports in, 68
parts industry: scale economies in, 132-33
passenger area: computation of, for hedonic market share model, 74-75
patriotism: and consumer preferences, 70-71
percentage markup: for corporate costs, 131-32
perfect competition: assumption of, 212
Peugeot: sales growth of, 33
Pinard, J.P., 44
Pinto: introduction of, 30
plants, automobile: closings, 191-92;
location of (see, location, of automobile plants); wage equality across, 177-80
pollution regulations: and fuel efficiency of U.S. cars, 30; as NTBs, 3-4; potential effects on trade, 233
price, automobile: as characteristic in hedonic market share model, 102; as function of characteristics, 47-48; domestic, [effect of imports on, with imperfect competition, 37, 217-19, 231; estimated effect of imports on, 118-28], international comparison of, 166-68; new list vs. used transaction, as proxy for new transaction, 45, 47-48, 77, 87-89; problems of measuring changes in, 45, 47-49 (see also, price elasticity, price indexes)
price elasticity: relative, of import demand, 42-43, 45, 46-47, 53-64, 65, 66, 68, 80-81; welfare implications of, 37-43, 206-08, 210-11
price formation equations: for domestic automobiles, 118-25
price indexes, for domestic and imported automobiles: construction of, 47-53, 83-93; data sources for, 47-49, 84-89; model selection for, 88-92; relative import to domestic price index, 47, 49-50, 52-53, 92-93; and relative total cost indexes, 50-53, 96
product differentiation: and import sales, 145-46
production, automobile: comparative costs of, 144-69; cost curves for, 129-42; definition of, for intercountry comparisons, 8; joint economies among models in, 130-31; location of (see, location, of automobile plants); minimum efficient scale for, 129, 139-42; multiplant economies in, 140; scale economies in (see, scale economies)
production cost indexes, construction of, 125
production costs (see, costs; costs, manufacturing)
production functions: Cobb-Douglas, 146, 147, 162-64, 183; fixed proportions,

INDEX

145-46, 159-62
product market welfare loss: defined, 198-99; estimates for, 199, 200, 207-11; and labor adjustment costs, 200, 219-29; method of computation, 200-07
profit target: in cost function, 135-37

Quandt, R.E., 109-11
questionnaire: on changes in relative automobile prices, 46, 74, 81
quotas: comparison to tariff, 4, 43; net welfare effects of, 230; opposition by economists to, 2 (see also, tariffs)

recessions: and high income buyers, 64-65; and import growth, 30 (see also, slump)
Red Book: data-base prices from, 49, 77, 87-89, 113
regional multiplier: from decline in auto industry employment, 228
registrations, new car: as weights in construction of price indexes, 86
regulations, safety: as NTBs, 3-4 (see also, pollution regulations)
relative cost of production index, 146-47
relative gas cost index, 50-53
relative price elasticity: estimates from cross section equations, 66, 68, 70-71; estimates from hedonic market share model, 80-83; estimates from time series equations, 53-64, 65; import to domestic sales ratio, 40, 42, 43, 46, 206-08, 210-11, 231
relative price index: comparison to relative total cost index, 50-53; computation of, 92-93; foreign to domestic autos, 50-53
relative total cost indexes: import-to-domestic, 53, 93-96
relocation: relative production costs and, 130-31
Renault Dauphine: failure of, 30
resource allocation cost of tariffs, 198-99, 200-07
retail price: as variable in hedonic market share model, 113
re-tooling: for dies, 140-42
Rolls-Royce, 29
Rosen, S., 181, 183

Russell, R.R., 44

Saab: sales growth of, 33
sales, new car: data used in hedonic market share model, 112, 133; import share of, 1, 29-34, 35, 45, 46-47, 234; small car share of, 33-34 (see also, small cars); trend towards imports, 98-99
scale economies: in automobile industry, 2, 3, 129-42; in body stamping, 140; in distribution, 130; of foreign firms, 131; and optimal firm size, 131; in retailing, 130; and U.S.-Canada trade, 22, 26-28
sedans: in hedonic price index, 87; as variable in hedonic market share model, 113
seniority rules, 169; and fringe benefits, 177; and SUB plan, 180 (see also, unemployment, workers)
shipping costs (see, transport costs)
shutdowns: of auto assembly facilities, 191-92 (see also, layoffs)
simultaneous-equations bias: in price formation equations, 119-22, 124-5; in time series equations, 119
slump: in automobile industry, 4, 10, 192
small cars: competition among different countries for U.S. sales, 231; demand for, 7-10; effect of tariff changes on location of production of, 144, 158; Japanese production of, 152; minimum efficient output for, 137-39, 140-42; and scale economies, 233-34; share of, as variable in import share equation, 98; share of new car sales, 33-34; U.S., sales in, 130-31 (see also, minis, subcompacts)
social opportunity cost: of automobile production, 221-22
sports cars, imported: demand for, 29
stamping, body: minimum efficient output in, 140
Standard Industrial Trade Classification, U.N., 148-49
station wagons: in hedonic price index, 87; as variable in hedonic market share model, 113
steel industry: earnings losses in, 224-26

sticker price: estimated from production costs, 131-32
SUB (see, Supplemental Unemployment Benefits Plan)
subcompacts: prediction of shift to domestic models of from tariff, 81-82
Supplemental Unemployment Benefits Plan (SUB), 2, 171, 180, 221, 228; impact of, 180 (see also, unemployment)
Sweden: automobile imports of, 12; nontariff barriers of, 20

tariffs, automobile: annual welfare cost of, 208-11; and changes in production location, 35, 142, 157-58, 235; deadweight loss from, 38-40, 219 (see also, product market welfare loss); effect on auto industry employment of, 2, 4, 198, 199, 219-20, 226-28, 231, 234, 235; effect on import prices, 35; effect on unemployment of, 2, 198, 219-20, 235; effects if domestic industry not perfectly competitive, 212-20; elimination of, between Canada and U.S., 22, 23; 1974 tariffs, selected countries, 15-19; opposition by economists to, 2; product market welfare loss from, 199, 200, 207-11; variation in, across countries, 15 (see also, nontariff barriers)
tastes, consumers': estimated distribution of, 74-77; in hedonic market share model, 103-04, 106 (see also, consumers)
taxes on automobiles: annual road, 20-21; excise, 3, 19, 20; road use, 19-20; transactions, 20 (see also, nontariff barriers)
taxpayers: income transfer to from auto import tariff, 219-20
Taylor's formula, 101
technology assumptions and production cost estimates, 147, 160-61
time series demand estimates: for domestic and imported automobiles, 46-65, 82-83, 96-100; and product market welfare loss, 207-08; for production worker employment, 181-89
tires, automobile: tariffs on, 22-23; use of in computation of production scale economies, 132-33
total cost indexes (see, relative total cost indexes)
Toyopet, 30
Toyota: effect of tariff on supply price of, 157-58; freight charges within U.S. for, 66; initial introduction in U.S., 30; potential U.S. manufacture of, 142, 158, 231; sales growth of, 33; transport costs to U.S., 152; U.S. sales of, 157
trade in automobiles, 6-34; U.S.-Canada, 21-29; world pattern of, 7, 8-10, 12-15
trade balance: of U.S. with Canada, 21-22, 23-29 (see also, Automotive Products Trade Act; Canada, U.S. automobile trade with)
trade barriers (see, tariffs, quotas, nontariff barriers)
trade policies: effect on unemployment, 192; quantitative welfare effects of changes in, 232-33; quotas and tariffs as, 4; welfare effects of, 230, 234, 235
trailers: tariffs on, 22
transactions costs, 181, 183, 184; and employment adjustment, 184
transmission: automatic, 75, 77, 88; as model classifier in hedonic market share model, 111, 113
transport costs: estimates of, 152-54; in production location decisions, 7, 144, 232, 234
travel mode split problem: Quandt and McFadden models, 109-10; relation to hedonic market share model, 110-11
Triplett, J.E., 44
tubes, tires: tariffs on, 22
turning circle: and construction of price index, 92; and consumer preferences, 74, 77; as variable in hedonic market share model, 113

UAW (see, United Auto Workers)
unemployment: earnings loss due to, 222-28; effect of local labor market conditions, estimated from steel industry data, 224-26; and higher import tariffs,

INDEX

219-20; psychic costs of, 220-21; and seniority rules, 180-81; and shifting demand, 2; social costs of, 211; and trade policies, 192; in U.S. automobile industry, 1, 170, 235; vs. welfare gains to consumers, 3 (*see also*, Supplemental Unemployment Benefits Plan)
unions, 170, 171, 192 (*see also*, United Auto Workers)
unit costs (*see*, cost functions)
United Auto Workers (UAW), 171; and conditions of employment, 180; interest in seniority rules, 180; position on trade barriers, 1
United Kingdom: automobile exports of, 12; automobile production of, 6, 8
United States: automobile exports of, 12, 14-15; automobile imports of, 29-34; automobile tariffs of, 7, 15; cost of manufacturing ratio with West Germany and Japan, 150, 151; import shares by states in, 68; interstate price variation in, 66; as leading importer of automobiles, 12; motor vehicle labor force of, 170-71 (*see also*, labor force); share of world motor vehicle production, 8; trade balance with Canada, 29; unit labor costs in, 150
United States-Canada Automotive Products Agreement, 21-26, 27-28, 29
unit labor cost index, 97
unit labor costs (*see*, labor)
utility: correlation with auto characteristics, 74; functional form in hedonic market share model, 101-03, 106
utility maximizers: consumers as, 101-03, 111

Vega: introduction of, 30
Volkswagen: freight charges within U.S. for, 66; history of U.S. imports of, 30, 33, 34; minimum cost location of, 154, 157; sales growth of, 33; transport costs to U.S., 152-54; U.S. plant location of, 15, 34, 142, 231
Volvo: Canadian plant of, 14, 15; sales growth of, 33

wage differential: between auto industry and other manufacturing, 221-22
Ward's Automotive Yearbook: data from, 88-89, 112-13
weight, automobile: and construction of price indexes, 84, 86; distribution of, as variable in import share equation, 99, 100; tax based on, 20; as variable in hedonic market share model, 74, 113
welfare loss from import tariffs, 37-43, 83, 198-211, 219, 228-29, 230, 233 (*see also*, consumers, product market welfare loss)
West Germany: automobile exports, 14; as a leading exporter of automobiles, 10; relative auto supply costs to U.S. from, 145, 157; relative labor costs in, 150-52, 165; relative unit production costs in, 145
wheelbase, automobile: tax based on, 20
width, automobile: as variable in hedonic market share model, 113
workers, automobile: cross section demand estimates for, 189-92; extended unemployment of, 192; laid-off, 180, 192, 222-26, 228; losses when displaced, 232; time series demand estimates for, 184-89

ABOUT THE AUTHORS

Eric J. Toder is an economist with the Office of Tax Analysis, U.S. Department of the Treasury. Prior to joining the Treasury Department he was a Senior Research Associate at Charles River Associates Incorporated in Cambridge, Massachusetts, and Assistant Professor of Economics at Tufts University. Dr. Toder received his Ph.D. in economics from the University of Rochester. A specialist in public finance and applied microeconomics, he has also published articles on transportation economics and the economics of education.

Ellen Burton is a Senior Research Associate at Charles River Associates. In addition to her work on the automobile industry and labor economics, she has conducted research on technological change in the maritime industry and on the economics of the coal industry. She is a candidate for the Ph.D. in economics at the Massachusetts Institute of Technology.

Nicholas Scott Cardell is a candidate for the Ph.D. in economics at Harvard University and a Senior Research Associate at Charles River Associates. Mr. Cardell specializes in econometric analysis and mathematical model building.

ABOUT CHARLES RIVER ASSOCIATES

Charles River Associates specializes in applied microeconomic analysis for industry, government, and nonprofit organizations. CRA has conducted research in

- Industry Level Forecasting
- Antitrust Policy
- Communications
- Environmental Economics
- Fuel Industries, Electric Power and Energy Economics
- Industry Regulation
- International Trade Economics
- Minerals, Metals, and Durable Goods Industries
- Regional Economics
- Urban and Intercity Transportation Economics

RELATED TITLES
Published by
Praeger Special Studies

CHRYSLER UK: A Corporation in Transition
                                    Stephen Young
                                    Neil Hood

DEPENDENT INDUSTRIALIZATION IN LATIN AMERICA:
  The Automotive Industry in Argentina, Chile, and Mexico
                                    Rhys Owen Jenkins

EXPORT MARKETING MANAGEMENT
                                    C. G. Alexandrides
                                    George P. Moschis

*FOREIGN TRADE AND U.S. POLICY: The Case for Free
  International Trade
                                    Leland B. Yeager
                                    David G. Tuerck

*Also available in paperback as a PSS Student Edition